Topaz Publishing

READING ENTERTAINMENT FOR THE ENTIRE FAMILY

Editor: Kase J. Reed
Line Editor: Topaz Publishing
Genre: Contemporary
WC: Topaz Escape, 95,057
ISBN: TPEB000000016
ISBN-13: 978-0615581590
ISBN-10: 0615581595
Topaz Publishing, LLC
USA

www.topazpublishingllc.com

Topaz Publishing, LLC

Dedication

This book is dedicated to my family and friends, especially those who constantly rendered words of encouragement. A heartfelt thank you to each of you. Love you all.

Blue Blood

Love Hides a Multitude of Sins.

Dr. Lauren Jeffries prepares to accept a new job in Connecticut. The sudden death of close friends threatens to delay her journey. At their behest, Lauren receives the responsibility of raising twin infants. She hires a nanny and continues with her plans.

When Lauren falls for Dr. Thaddeus Bradford, she's thrust into the lifestyle of the nouveau riche. Bradford and his family are highly respected members of society. Unfortunately, Lauren doesn't meet their criteria for a Bradford wife. Attempts are made to thwart her relationship with Thaddeus, but Lauren is determined to stand her ground. Based on her decision, her children, and the man she loves become targets. Now, Lauren is faced with difficult choices. Should she run back to Michigan, or should she stand and fight?

Available in E-Book, and E-Book CD

Blue Blood

By

Beverley Godfrey

CHAPTER ONE

Lauren Jeffries stared across the desk at the lawyer. "That's all Ms. Jeffries. That's the way they had it set up. Instead of their god-mother, you're now the twins' mother. As you know, Stan had no family and Lydia has a brother of whom she said she'd rather see the children go into foster care than to him.

They left everything to you. Care for the children as you see fit. I must say that there will not be a financial burden. Stan and Lydia both carried substantial insurance policies with a double indemnity clause in case of accidental death. In addition, there is a likely settlement from the cruise line."

"Thank you, Ms. O'Hare. This," Lauren took the envelope the lawyer had pushed towards her. "It's just that this, this—this is so final." A sob caught in her throat. It ends a chapter in my life I never wanted to end. It hurts so badly."

"I can only imagine. If it's any consolation, Stan and Lydia came into my office shortly after they learned she was pregnant and amended their wills. They think the world of you and never hesitated about making you guardian of their children. As they said, there's no better choice. If there's anything I can help you with, please don't hesitate to ask." Lillian O'Hare stood and walked toward the door.

"Thank you Ms. O'Hare—for all you did for my friends, and for your compassion and sensitivity in handling this." Lauren patted the envelope. "I will accept your offer of help when the need arises. Thanks, again."

*****

Lauren prayed as she sat in the rocking chair in the nursery. *Dear God. Please watch over these children, and me. And dear God, please give me the strength and courage to do what's right to protect and nurture these precious babies.*

She missed her dearest friends. Tears streamed down her face, and she let her mind wander. *How am I, a single woman, going to raise two babies and work too? Well, I guess I'll manage.*

Women do it every day. Oh, God! Please show me what to do. Do I go, or do I stay? It would be so much easier to stay, but I really want the challenge that new position poses. She pondered taking the position of Dean of Nursing Studies at Eastern Parkdale University, about seven hundred miles away in Connecticut.

How can I manage two new babies, a new job, and a new location all at the same time? I would need to find a babysitter who is willing to relocate or relocate, and then find a babysitter. I would then need to find a place to live, and then pack. Lauren had told the university that she would be ready to assume the position at the beginning of the school year which was only six and a half weeks away. That was before she became an instant *mommy*. Whatever she decided to do, she'd have to do it in a hurry.

*****

Lauren placed an ad to find a nanny/housekeeper who was willing to relocate. After interviewing eleven applicants, she found what seemed to be the perfect candidate. She hired Ms. O'Hare's law firm to do a background check on forty-seven year old Dora Lee Brown, a warm, friendly, divorced mother of two adult children.

She listed her house with a local realtor who could not only sell her house, but could assist her in finding suitable housing in Connecticut. Thanks to the internet, she was able to take a virtual tour of the houses from her home office. She had narrowed the list of more than a dozen houses, to three. Now, she was scheduled for a walk through in two days.

After much self-debating, Lauren concluded that the most logical thing for her to do was to resign her current position at the hospital sooner than she'd planned. She needed more time to prepare for her new venture.

On Wednesday evening, Lauren left the babies with a colleague and took the red-eye to Connecticut to view the houses. The three houses were all beautiful, and each met her specifications. A sprawling three year old, four bedrooms, two-story with a spacious, manicured backyard enclosed in a sturdy, six foot high redwood fence seemed to be beckoning to her.

After the realtor assured she'd be able to lease the house pending purchase, Lauren signed the papers and then flew back to Michigan.

The background check on Mrs. Brown proved she was an up-standing, law abiding Christian woman, with not so much as a parking ticket against her record. *It's almost too good to be true,* Lauren thought as she filed the report away.

Lauren hired Mrs. Brown and two other ladies from her church to help her with the preparation for her move. At the end of the fourth week, she and Mrs. Brown packed up the Frederick's SUV, loaded the twins, and headed east to Connecticut.

Before she left Michigan, Ms. O'Hare had summoned Lauren to her office to inform her that the insurance companies had issued the beneficiary checks, and that the cruise liner had offered a hefty settlement in the death of her friends.

Although Lauren had amassed a sizable nest-egg of her own, she was happy to learn that the payoff on the insurance policies, in addition to the settlement offer, were more than enough to raise the twins, and see them through college. Even at today's rates, it wouldn't put any financial burden on her.

CHAPTER TWO

"Oh, Ms. Jeffries! This is a beautiful house," Mrs. Brown exclaimed. "It's so spacious, and there's lawn on all sides. I love it!"

"I love it too. The lawn space drew me to it. The challenge now is to put some order to the inside."

The movers had arrived a few hours after Lauren had, and in less than three hours had unloaded and set up all the furnishings to her specification.

Four days after their arrival, the house had taken on a homey, lived in feel. The girls were napping, and Lauren was beginning to prepare dinner. Suddenly the doorbell rang. Lauren opened the door to two young women who introduced themselves as Emily Hansen and Lucy Jones.

"We just wanted to welcome you to the neighborhood," Emily stated.

"That's very kind of you. I'm Lauren Jeffries and this is Mrs. Brown. Do you care to come in? I just started dinner."

"Oh just for a minute," Lucy said, as they stepped into the foyer.

Lauren led them into the den. "Won't you have a seat? May I offer you some refreshments?"

"No thank you." Emily scanned the room. "I heard you're one of the new professors at the university." She stroked a diaper bag sitting on a chair. "I see you have a baby."

"As a matter of fact, I have two babies. They're napping now. Do you have children?"

"Yes," Emily stated. "My husband and I have three—two boys and a girl, ages three, five, and seven. They're with their nanny."

Lucy joined the conversation. "And we have a boy and a girl; ages two and six. They, too, are with their nanny. I guess your husband will be along later."

Lauren glanced at her. "I'm not married."

A scowl appeared on Emily's face. "Oh. Are you widowed?"

What's up with all these rude questions? Lauren smiled. "No. I've never been married."

"I see." Lucy glanced meaningfully at Emily.

"It must be pretty hard raising two babies alone," Lucy added derisively.

"It's a challenge," Lauren answered without explanation.

"Well, again, welcome to the neighborhood. We'd best be going." Lucy hurried toward the door. "Good day."

"Thanks for stopping in. I'm sure we'll see each other around the neighborhood." The two women left so fast Lauren had to practically yell to be heard.

Appearing miffed, Mrs. Brown placed her hand on her hip. "Ms. Jeffries, I don't think you'll be seeing them if they can help it. You're an unmarried woman with two babies. Did you see their faces when you said you aren't married?"

"It's all right, Mrs. Brown. I sensed they were on a fact-finding mission. I don't owe anyone any explanations. My life is none of their business. I'd appreciate it if you didn't discuss it with anyone. And please, don't ever feel you have to defend me either." She smiled.

CHAPTER THREE

Lauren attended in-service workshops on each of the three days prior to the beginning of the semester. On the third day, she attended a faculty get-acquainted luncheon as well. The university was the teaching arm of East Parkdale Medical and Research Hospital. Many of the current hospital staff members were graduates of the university.

*****

Six weeks passed. Lauren became acclimated to her new surroundings. There was a mall about six minutes from her house to the north, and a nice park about nine blocks to the south. To the west of her, there was a pre-school, the primary, as well as an elementary school. The area between consisted of residential dwellings on beautiful, clean, tree lined streets.

The Hansens and Jones owned four bedrooms with a pool. Their husbands were executives in the telecommunications field, and neither of the women worked.

Every afternoon before sunset, and on weekends, weather permitting, Lauren walked through the neighborhood, pushing the girls in their stroller.

On one of her walks, she met Jennifer Wallace, a school teacher, and mother of a two year old. Her husband was in the military. They struck up a conversation as they sat on a bench watching the children nap.

Jennifer relaxed on the bench. "I understand the self-imposed welcoming committee paid you a visit. The whole community now knows you're an unwed mother."

"Oh yes, they paid me a visit. I didn't think it would take too long before the word got around. But, since it's nobody's business, I don't let it bother me."

"I understand. I was pregnant with Johnny when we moved here. My husband, John, was deployed a week after we closed on the house, so I had to take care of all the moving. They saw my protruding stomach, and without preamble, asked if I was married.

I guess they didn't believe me because they went so far as to check the post office to see if I was receiving any mail from the military."

"They need a life. It's sad to see them so wrapped up in the lives of others—especially young people. Anyway, it's a federal offense for postal personnel to give out information on its patrons, unless they're bound by law to do so."

"Yeah. I know. I guess I could get them in trouble just for asking, but I let it slide. So? Other than the welcoming committee, how are you finding life here?"

"Truthfully, other than work, I haven't had much interaction with the people here. I have met some friendly people at a couple of churches I've visited, but I have yet to socialize with any of them. Work is another story. I'm in an administrative position, which necessitates making some unpopular decisions. The word has gotten around that I'm an unmarried mother, and that bit of information is fodder for the malcontents."

"You're not bothered by the talk?"

"No. It's true. I am an unmarried mother, but that's not the whole story. Let the tongues wag."

"I guess we're somewhat in the same boat," Jennifer said. "None of the neighbors have met John, nor have they seen him around. Tongues are really going to wag when my pregnancy becomes obvious. This," she pointed to her mid-section, "is a result of our rendezvous in Atlantic City a few months ago." She smiled fondly.

"Congratulations." Lauren smiled as she stood to leave. "I've enjoyed talking with you. Feel free to stop in. Maybe we can have dinner together some evening. I'm going to take the girls in for their dinner."

"Thanks, Lauren. I've enjoyed visiting with you as well, and I will take you up on dinner. I'll walk with you to my turn off."

CHAPTER FOUR

Janet Mosley looked up from the computer when Lauren entered the office. "Good morning, Dr. Jeffries."

Lauren smiled at her secretary. "Good morning, Janet. Did you have a nice weekend?"

"Yes. It was lovely. Dr. Mason asked you to come to the conference room at eleven-thirty this morning. Call him if you're not free."

"Thanks. Will you call and let him know I'm free? That way, there won't be any mix-ups. Are there any other messages?"

"No ma'am, but it's early yet—and it's Monday."

"Come on Janet," Lauren joked. "Where's your optimism?"

"It's lodged somewhere between experience and Murphy's Law."

They both laughed as Lauren entered her office. In the six weeks that she had been at the university, Lauren had learned that Janet Mosley was the dream secretary. She was capable, bright, personable, confident, and loyal, with a warm sense of humor as a bonus.

Shortly before eleven-thirty, Lauren entered Dr. Mason's office. The receptionist glanced at her. "Good morning, Dr. Jeffries. Dr. Mason is waiting for you in the board room. Come with me, please."

Lauren was ushered into a room where there were several men and women sitting around a table. Dr. Mason greeted her, "Ah, Dr. Jeffries. Glad you could make it. I want you to meet some of our other new staff members as well as some seasoned members who were away when you came aboard."

"Everyone, this is Dr. Lauren Jeffries, whom you all know is our new Dean of Nursing Studies. This," Mason said, introducing each of the other members, "is Dr. Lawrence Wilcox-Radiology, Dr. Vivian Reed-Preventive Medicine, Mrs. Linda Abrams-Public Relations, Mr. Paul Hennessy-Community Outreach, Dr. Leland Bland-Nuclear Medicine, and Dr. Thaddeus Bradford-interim Dean of Surgery."

"Welcome aboard, doctor," Dr. Wilcox said. The others chimed in with their greetings.

Vivian peered down the length of the table at Lauren. "I know you've already been here six weeks, but please let us know if there's anything we can do to help make this experience a pleasant one for you. We're one big family here, and most of the time," she quipped, "we're happy."

Lauren engaged the group. "I'm happy to meet all of you, and thank you all for your offers of help. Things have gone so well to this point that I'm almost afraid to exhale."

Leaning back in his chair, Paul Hennessy joked, "Smart lady. Always be on guard for the other shoe to fall."

Dr. Mason pleaded. "If I may, there are a few matters requiring our attention."

After the meeting, Lauren headed back to her office. Linda Abrams called to her. "Dr. Jeffries, may I have a word with you?"

Lauren turned and addressed her. "Sure. How can I help you?"

"Would you have lunch with me? We always do a short bio on new staff members for the campus quarterly. I would like to interview you. The paper comes out in two weeks. The next issue isn't due for three months, but I don't want to wait that long to introduce our new staff members."

"Okay, if you must. I have to stop at my office first. Where can I meet you?"

"There's a nice café called, *Eats* across the street. I'll go and grab a table before it gets too crowded."

"Okay. I'll see you in a few."

*****

"Dr. Jeffries. Over here," Linda called, as she spotted Lauren scanning the area.

Lauren maneuvered through the throng of patrons to where Linda Abrams, Dr. Bradford, and a nurse were sitting.

"I'm sorry," Linda apologized, "but there's not another vacant seat in the house. Dr. Bradford offered us a seat at his table."

"Bless you doctor. Is the food really that good?" Lauren looked around the crowded café.

Dr. Bradford glanced at her. "You mean you've been here six weeks and you haven't had the experience?"

"Seems that I've committed a cardinal sin," Lauren answered with mock contrition. "I usually don't eat lunch."

"Then why are you here?" the nurse asked.

"I invited her," Linda volunteered. "Dr. Jeffries, this is Sandy Yates."

Dr. Bradford offered, "May I treat you ladies to lunch in honor of the new kid on the block?"

Lauren noticed the scowl that appeared on Sandy's face in reaction to his offer. "Thank you doctor, but that's not necessary."

"I know." He smiled. "But I want to." Sandy huffed and rolled her eyes.

Lauren returned the smile. "Well, if you insist. Thank you."

"Dr. Jefferies." Linda got Lauren's attention. "I guess, under the circumstances, I'll have to schedule the interview for another time."

Sandy smirked. "Oh, were you planning to interview her for the *Bio-Feed*? This should be interesting. Why don't you go on with it?" she goaded. "Unless, of course, you have something to hide," she added slyly, looking at Lauren.

Linda favored Sandy with a scathing glare. "Dr. Jeffries, I'll call you for an appointment soon. It would be most insensitive to conduct this interview before an audience."

Lauren cast an appreciative glance Linda's way. "Thank you Ms. Abrams. Call my office later today to reschedule."

Dr. Bradford turned to Lauren. "How are you finding life in this part of the country so far?"

"Do I tell the truth, or do I tell you what you want to hear?"

He leaned closer. "Oh, the truth, by all means."

"Well, the climate is lovely, and the scenery is beautiful. Other than the workplace, I've had very little interaction with the citizens. Therefore, I'll withhold judgment." She glanced at Sandy. "I don't want to paint everyone with the same brush."

Sandy cast her a menacing scowl, then folded her arms.

Linda reached for a napkin, her tone compassionate. "Sounds like you've had a bad experience or two."

"Or two," Lauren quipped, as she pushed her plate aside. She stood. "Thanks for lunch, Dr. Bradford. Since the interview is postponed, I think I need to get back to work."

Linda stood and pushed her chair backwards. "I'll walk with you, doctor. Thanks again Dr. Bradford."

Dr. Bradford nodded. "Ladies."

*****

Lauren and Linda strolled back to the university. "I'm sorry about that, Doctor. I had no idea it would be that crowded. Sandy's remark was uncalled for."

"Not to worry. I think she was posturing for Dr. Bradford."

"That could be. She *is* on a long list of Mrs. Bradford wannabes."

"Going strictly on first impressions, he doesn't appear to be the playboy type."

"He's not. The grapevine has it that he's never dated a staff member in the four years he's been here. Even though, he's had ample opportunity. You witnessed that a few minutes ago. He's very nice— a talented, and smart man."

"It appears he has at least one loyal fan," Lauren teased.

Linda smiled. "Oh. I think he's handsome. He's easy on the eyes, and genuinely a nice person. But, I am an old married woman." She held up her hand to flash her wedding band. "Six years, and very happy." The women reached their destination. "Well, this is where I leave you. Let's do lunch some time; when and where it's not too crowded."

"I'd like that. Call me later to set up the interview."

"Will do. See you later."

CHAPTER FIVE

A week later, Mrs. Brown greeted Lauren as she entered the foyer. "The babies have been fretful all day, Ms. Jeffries. I gave them the medicine you left for them. They seem to have a fever now."

"I'll check them. This isn't an uncommon reaction to immunizations. They should both be better by tomorrow." Lauren made her way to the nursery, stopping on the way to wash her hands. Standing beside their crib, she softened her voice. "Hello, my little angels. Not feeling too well, are you?" She touched each of their foreheads. "They are pretty warm. It's too soon to give them more medicine. Would you run some tepid water into the bathtub for me please? I'll undress them and submerge them a few minutes, then I'll give them something cool to drink. That should reduce the fever."

Lauren shooed Mrs. Brown off to bed just before midnight. She said she'd take care of the girls, and would call her if needed.

She gave the girls another dose of medicine, a sponge bath, and more liquids. They dosed off to sleep, as did she, sitting in the rocker.

Lauren was awakened by Brittany three hours later. Again, she performed the submerging ritual, waiting an hour before administering more medicine. Rocking Brittany, she was careful not to touch the site of the injection. As soon as she laid Brittany back in her crib, Brianna woke up. She again performed the ritual. By the time she laid Brianna back in her crib it was five forty-five a.m.

After checking the girls, she found they were running a low-grade fever. Lauren was thankful they didn't suffer other side effects such as vomiting and diarrhea. By eight o'clock their temperatures were slightly elevated, but they slept peacefully.

Lauren instructed Mrs. Brown to let them sleep undisturbed, and to feed them only the juices and foods she left out for them.

With instructions to call her if their conditions worsened, Lauren showered and went to work.

*****

Lauren greeted her secretary. "Good morning Janet. How are you today?"

Janet stared at Lauren. "Good morning Dr. J. Is everything okay? You look tired."

"The joys of parenthood." Lauren smiled. "The girls had a reaction to their shots. They were fretful throughout the night."

"I'm sorry to hear that. I take it they're okay now?"

"They're doing fine, so far. Is there anything requiring my immediate attention?"

"Just the board meeting at ten. I assembled the packets you asked for."

"Thank you, Janet. I appreciate you."

"That's my job."

"And you do it well, and I appreciate it." Lauren's tone was light. "I'm going to do some research on the computer before the meeting."

"Did you remember that the interview with Mrs. Abrams is scheduled for this afternoon?"

"It's on my calendar, but thanks for reminding me."

*****

As they seated themselves at the table in the boardroom, Dr. Leland Bland whispered to Lauren, "Are you feeling all right?"

Lauren massaged her temple. "I'm fine, just a little sleepy. Thanks for asking."

"I have ulterior motives. Are you too sleepy to have dinner with me this evening?"

"Yes. Even if I wasn't, I have a previous engagement."

"Rain check?"

"We'll see."

After the meeting, Dr. Mason asked Lauren if he could have a word with her.

"Dr. Jeffries." He closed the door, and then walked to stand behind his desk. "There's a delicate matter I must speak to you about."

"Yes, Dr. Mason?"

"Dr. Jefferies, as you know, much of the university's funding comes from endowments and other private sources."

Lauren turned toward the desk. "And how does that concern me?"

"Well, uh, some of our benefactors are calling your character into question."

"Excuse me?" Lauren stared in disbelief.

"The fact that you hold a prominent position in this university carries with it the expectation of your character being beyond reproach. Anything less puts a black eye on the facility."

Lauren took a deep breath and hesitated for a few seconds. "Dr. Mason, did you not do a background check on me before you offered me this position? Did not the FBI, state, and local law enforcement agencies give me a clean bill of health; and did not my family, friends, neighbors, and former colleagues in Michigan entertain hours of questions relative to my character and lifestyle? You hired me. So, what smear has my character sustained in six months that would put a stain on this facility?" Lauren had managed to control her voice, not letting her frustration and anger seep through.

Mason was obviously flustered. "Well, at the time we didn't know you were, ah... are, an unwed mother."

"Dr. Mason. My daughters are four and one half months old. Six months ago, at seven and one-half or eight months, my pregnancy would have been very obvious. You interviewed me eight months ago. Even if you missed it, given all the people you interviewed, don't you think that at least one of them would have mentioned I was an expectant, unwed mother?"

Lauren leaned over the desk. "All of that aside, my being a mother does not interfere with my duties here. Be not deceived, Dr. Mason, I'm very aware of the scuttlebutt that's going around the hospital about me.

Now, if you care more about those who buy a voice in running this facility than you do about those who actually work here; get rid of all the unwed parents, women *and* men, and then see how well you'd be staffed.

In the meantime, if I still have a job here, I would like to get back to it."

"Dr. Jeffries I hope you can see what a precarious position I'm in."

"Oh, I do, Dr. Mason," Lauren said walking toward the door. "And I'm sure you will handle it just fine." As she left the room, she willed herself not to slam the door.

*****

Linda sat in the chair beside Lauren's desk. She couldn't believe what Lauren had just told her. "I'm sorry doctor. If you'd rather postpone the interview, I'll understand. I've heard the rumors too, but I concluded that you're not the first, nor will you be the last employee of Parkdale to have a baby out of wedlock. It's not my business."

"Thanks Mrs. Abrams. They aren't rumors. I am an unwed mother, but that's only half of the story. I'm not ready to publicize the rest of the story yet; especially now. I'm going to see how this mess plays out."

"I'm really sorry, doctor. I hope the powers that be, don't make a stupid mistake and lose you. You've already made a big difference in our nursing program."

"And added fertilizer for the gossip grapevine, no doubt. You can go on with the interview, but other than confirming that I have four and a half month old twin daughters, I won't talk about them or the scuttlebutt surrounding them."

Linda sat her recorder on the desk and smiled. "Deal."

The interview, not unlike any other, consisted of her answering questions about her family roots, schooling, work experience, hobbies, and her reason for accepting her current position, as well as her plans for enhancing the department.

Pushing a button on the recorder, Linda said, "Tell me about yourself."

Lauren leaned back in her chair. "Okay. Well, I grew up with two brothers and two sisters in a small town in Central New Jersey." She cocked her head and bragged.

"I'm the middle child, and a tomboy. ...simply loved climbing trees and sports.

By today's standards; I guess we were pretty good kids, but we were all practical jokesters and did our share of devilment. Anyway, I did well in school—got decent grades." Lauren sighed. "The only grandparent I knew was my father's mother. She died when I was in elementary school. My father died seven years ago and my mother died last year. I became interested in nursing when my parents became ill."

"Got anything else you'd like to add?"

"No. That's about it."

"Fantastic. Thanks for your valuable time." She stood and extended her hand.

When published in the campus quarterly two weeks later, the last line of the bio simply stated that Lauren resided in Dalton with her twin daughters, Brittany and Brianna.

CHAPTER SIX

The first meeting following the interview was a tension-filled affair. Most of the more than a dozen colleagues present had trouble making eye contact with her. But, Lauren held her head high, making eye contact with each board member when she spoke. She noticed that Leland Bland had distanced himself from her after the article appeared in the paper. There was no more jockeying to sit beside her during the meetings. This suited her fine.

Vivian Reed, who had called her after the article appeared in the paper, now sat beside her in today's meeting. "That's right, sister, make them squirm. I got your back."

Lauren laughed. "Am I in a war now?"

"Not really. They're just embarrassed at the way they've treated you."

"They should be. This is worse than junior high drama."

When the meeting was over, Dr. Reed walked out with Lauren. "Dr. Mason was having a hard time facilitating. Don't you think?"

"I guess he was calculating how much money he's losing by keeping me on."

"I heard he's also calculating how much he'll lose if he lets you go, too."

Lauren glanced at her and smiled, but said nothing.

Vivian changed the subject. "Thanksgiving is less than two weeks away. You and the girls are welcome to have dinner with my family and me."

"Please, call me Lauren. Thank you for the invite, but I do have plans."

"I'm sorry you can't make it, but I'm glad you aren't spending the day alone. And, my name is Vivian." She smiled. "Hey want to have lunch?"

"Sure, as long as it's not at Eats."

*****

Lauren looked up from her reading to see Dr. Bradford standing in her doorway. "Dr. Bradford?"

"Hello Dr. Jeffries. May I come in?"

"Of course. Have a seat. What can I do for you?"

"Actually, I came by to ask you the same question."

"Excuse me?"

"I want you to know that I support you. It's no secret that the entire university has heard about your children. Frankly, I don't see the big deal. It's your business."

"I could hug you for that."

"Well?" he teased.

"I might contaminate you."

"I doubt that. By the way, do you have plans for the holiday? I would hate for you to be all alone in this unfriendly place. I would like you to have dinner with me, if you're free."

"How kind of you Dr. Bradford, but I do have plans. You aren't eating alone are you?"

"I guess I will be. I've turned down a couple of invites."

"Dr. Bra..."

"Thad. Please call me Thad, "he interrupted.

"Alright Thad, call me Lauren. Why don't you have dinner with me then? A neighbor and I are planning to have dinner together at my house. Her husband is in Iraq and I don't want her to be alone. The same hens that smeared my name did the same thing to her, and she *is* married."

"I don't want to intrude."

You won't be. You'd be a welcome addition."

"Thanks, I'd love to. What can I bring?"

"A big appetite." Lauren laughed.

Thad laughed. "Now that's the easiest thing anyone has ever asked of me. What time is dinner?"

"How does three o'clock sound?"

"That's perfect for me. Thanks again. I've got another surgery. Remember, I got your back." He stood to leave.

"Thanks, Thad."

* * * * *

Jennifer watched as Lauren put the final touches on dinner. "You're a strong woman, Lauren. I don't know if I could stay around after being treated so badly; by so many."

"The onus is on them. I'm the only one who knows the real story. I learned long ago not to worry about what people say; only what God thinks. Can you believe that a doctor who's been trying to get me to go out with him can barely look me in the eyes now?"

"It's his loss."

"I would like to think so." The doorbell chimed. "That must be Dr. Bradford." Rushing into the foyer, she opened the door. "Good afternoon, Brad."

"Thad."

"I remember that. I know it's presumptuous of me, but Brad is my favorite guy name. Bradford equals Brad, now I get a chance to use it. I'm surprised that no one else calls you that."

Thad chuckled. "It's been done in the past. I'll answer to Brad, but you're the only one who can do that. These are for you." He handed her a beautiful bouquet of flowers. "And these are for Jennifer."

"Thank you, they're lovely." Lauren led Thad into the kitchen. "Jennifer, this is Dr. Thad Bradford. Dr. Bradford, meet Jennifer Wallace. Thad brought you flowers."

"I'm pleased to meet you, Dr. Bradford. Thanks for the flowers."

"Why don't the two of you have a seat in the dining room while I put these in water? Dinner is ready."

Lauren returned to the dining room and sat at the table.

Thad blotted his lips. "Oooh, Ladies. This is scrumptious; it's quite a treat."

"Thank Lauren. She did all the cooking. All I did was baby sit and set the table. She said she's giving me a treat."

Lauren smiled. "And, now I've given you both a treat, and the two of you have given me the pleasure of your company. Thanks for giving."

"She's quite a lady, Dr. Bradford."

"Thad."

"Sorry, Thad. With all she's going through, she still worries about others, and I'm little more than a stranger."

Picking up his glass, Thad added, "As am I. She's right, Lauren, you have, in spite of all you're going through, looked out for others. I heard about the donation you made to the food mission."

Embarrassed, Lauren quickly changed the subject. "So Brad, you have no family to spend the holiday with?"

"To the contrary, I have a large family in Massachusetts. They're all together as we speak. I was planning to be with them, but I had a surgery scheduled for this morning, and another scheduled for seven tomorrow morning. What about the two of you? Do you have any family in the area?"

Jennifer answered, "My family, father and sister, are home in Iowa. My brother is stationed at Camp LeJeune, and I really do have a husband in Iraq."

Lauren tilted her head. "I have two sisters in New Jersey, a brother in Virginia, another in California and several nieces and nephews. I also have two beautiful daughters, but no husband. Excuse me for a moment, please." She stood up, and then left the room.

In a few minutes, Lauren returned with several newspaper clippings in her hand. "The two of you are among the few of my colleagues and friends who have shown me compassion, and without judgment. I'm going to share something very painful with you." She hesitated. "You see, I am an unwed mother, but I've never been pregnant." Jennifer and Thad listened with interest.

"My dearest friends died a few months ago. They stated in their wills that they wanted me to adopt the girls." Lauren eyes began to well-up. "This has been such a traumatic undertaking, and for people to try to taint it is so very painful." She put the clippings on the table for them to read. "I thank the two of you for standing by me even when you didn't know the whole story. Now, that's something to be thankful for." She smiled through the tears.

"Oh, Lauren," Jennifer said, "I'm so sorry for your loss."

Thad scanned the papers. "So am I, Lauren. I admire you for the way you've handled everything.

I don't know if I could have been as genteel as you've been. People can be so cruel, and as you stated, judgmental."

Lauren reached for the papers. "I'm going to take a copy of these to the next board meeting."

"Good for you," Thad declared. "There are going to be a lot of people with egg on their faces. I'm just enough of a sadist to want to see it too."

"Lauren." Jennifer glanced at her watch. "I'm going to help you clean up, and then head home. John usually calls around seven, and I don't want to miss him."

Lauren picked up a plate. "Don't worry about cleaning up. I'll do it. I'll fix you a take-out plate while you wake your son." Lauren smiled at Thad. "I'd appreciate it if you'd take some food with you too, doctor."

Just as she was about to prepare the take-outs for Jennifer. The girls began to fret "Excuse me, please. I'll be back as soon as they let me."

Thad stood in the doorway, watching Lauren and the babies. "What beautiful children."

Lauren turned to see that Thad had followed her into the nursery. "Yes they are. Aren't they? They are replicas of their mother, but with their father's smile. They're good babies." She finished changing the babies, then propped their bottles up for their feedings.

"I wondered how you fed them both at the same time."

"This is the only way. When they wake one at a time, I hold them while I feed them."

Thad smiled and shook his head in wonderment. "Do you do all of this alone?"

"It's not unheard of you know. Women do it all of the time, but I do have a nanny/housekeeper. She's in Michigan for the holiday. Even when she's here, I do most of the care for the girls."

Lauren reached into the crib and removed the empty bottle. "Hey, Brianna. You were hungry weren't you?"

The baby smiled and kicked her chubby legs.

Lauren picked her up and placed her on her shoulder to burp her. After she had performed the same ritual with Brittany, she put them in their walkers and pushed them into the kitchen.

Jennifer turned towards Lauren. "Thank you for a lovely day, Lauren. You have no idea how much I needed this."

"I needed it too. Let's get together again soon. Did you get enough food?"

"Yes, thank you, I did. Thanks again for the flowers, Thad."

"You're welcome. Here, let me help you to the car." Lauren began putting order to the kitchen while she waited for Thad to return.

"Man!" Thad exclaimed as he re-entered the house. "It's turned cold out there. She should have warmed the car before she got into it."

"It would have taken longer to warm the car than it would take her to get home. She only lives seven short blocks away. Are you ready for dessert?"

"I am if you'll join me."

"Okay, I'll join you. What would you like; chocolate or coconut cake?"

"Chocolate. I'll take the other with me if you don't mind."

"I don't mind. Coffee?"

"No thank you. Two conflicting flavors confuse my taste buds."

"Come into the den. We can watch the game if you like." She pushed the girls' walkers ahead of her.

"You are a fan?" Thad looked surprised.

"I know the fundamentals of the game, but it's no fun watching it alone." Lauren put the girls on the blanket she'd spread on the floor.

"Do you like any other sports?"

"I like baseball, basketball, volleyball and horseback riding. What about you?"

"I like the same as well as tennis and swimming."

"No golf?"

"Uh, uh. You don't swim?"

"No sir. That requires too much water."

A few minutes later, Thad tried to stifle a yawn. "Can I help you with the dishes, Lauren? As much as I'm enjoying your company, I must say good night. I'm a little tired, and I want to be rested for surgery in the morning."

"There's nothing to do except to load the dishwasher. Did you get enough food? You are really welcome to it."

"I have plenty, thank you. You're a wonderful cook, and I have truly enjoyed myself. Thank you for a great afternoon." He hugged her tightly. "Goodnight, Lauren."

"Thanks again for the flowers. Drive safely."

CHAPTER SEVEN

The social season in Dalton and the surrounding areas began with Thanksgiving and continued through New Year's Eve. Only a select few received invitations to elite dinners and parties. Two of the largest parties took place between Thanksgiving and the last board meeting of the year. Lauren wasn't invited to either; though a number of her colleagues were.

*****

The following Tuesday, as the board meeting came to a close, Lauren asked Dr. Mason if she could address the board. She stood, looked around the table, and made eye contact with each member. Lauren spoke slowly and deliberately. "I can't begin to tell you how much your callous treatments have hurt me. You've listened to gossip and passed judgment on me. The majority of you would rather I'd just quietly disappear." She stopped and stared at the group, letting her gaze fall on each of them. "What right do any of you have to judge me? How many of you have had premarital sex? Would you have treated an un-wed father the same way you have treated me? What's the difference between what you *think* I did, and what you *know* you have actually done? Is it that you weren't caught? Well, I have news for you; I *am* an un-wed mother, but I have never been pregnant; not that it's any of your business. I want you all to read these articles, and then see if you can undo the damage you've done to my reputation as quickly as you sullied it."

Lauren had made a copy of each of the three newspaper articles for each board member. She winked at Thad as she began placing the articles in front of each member. Vivian and Linda were aware of her intentions before the meeting. After she placed the articles in front of Dr. Mason, she quietly left the room.

*****

Later in the afternoon, Vivian Reed knocked on her door. "May I come in for a minute, Lauren?"

"Sure. Come and have a seat. What's the scuttlebutt now?"

"Oh, you left them cleaning egg off their faces all right. Except for Thad, none of the men could make eye contact with anyone. Larry and Ryan didn't know what this was all about until I told them. Dr. Mason has called on Linda to clean up the mess he's made. There's concern of a possible slander suit. I just stopped by to tell you that I think that you are one classy lady, and that I'm proud of the way you handled this. I would like to think that I would be just as benevolent if I were in your shoes."

"I didn't do this for myself, Vivian. Plenty of women are victims of double standards. There's never a mention of unwed fathers. That right–of–passage thing. These moral do-gooders get on my nerves. In essence, what they are telling me is that it's okay for me to be an unwed mother, if I were a nurse, an orderly, janitor etc., but not the head of a department.

They're so afraid of losing a dollar that they allow these contributors to run the university and the hospital; even telling them who to hire and who to fire. If I hear of this happening to anyone else on this campus again, I'm going to encourage them to sue, and I will testify on their behalf."

Vivian chuckled. "I agree with you. I bet you'll be getting invitations to the season's events now."

"And I bet I won't accept. I'm the same person they've been snubbing for the past three weeks, and they're the same snobs they've been for however long."

"I can't say I blame you. By the way, I'm having a little get together on the sixteenth and I hope you'll come. I'm not sending out invitations and you're one of the first to be invited. Please come, and bring a guest."

"Thanks, Vivian. I'll let you know."

The intercom on Lauren's phone buzzed. "Excuse me, Dr. Jeffries; Ms. Abrams is on line two for you."

"Thank you, Janet. Hello, Linda. What's up?" She held the receiver as she listened to Linda. "Oh, so you're in charge of damage control. Huh? Cowards. Yes, come on over."

"I don't envy her." Vivian stood.

"She has nothing to fear from me. I feel sorry for the perpetrators."

"I guess I'll get back to work. I just wanted you to know that I'm in your corner."

"I appreciate you, Vivian. Thank, you." She opened the door just as Linda was prepared to knock. "Oh, here's Linda now." The three women exchanged pleasantries before Vivian left. Lauren then invited Linda in, and offered her a seat.

"So? You have the awesome task of putting on a coat of paint to hide the dirt. What do they want you to do with me?"

"Offer you anything that will make you happy and stop you from going public."

"They're such bullies. I don't intend to go public. As far as I'm concerned, I've shown them who they are, and I'm through with it. It's up to them whether or not it comes back to haunt them."

"Girl, you're in a position of power right now."

"And if I exploit it, I'm no better than they are." She smiled. "Something good came out of this, though."

Linda raised an eyebrow. "You found something good in this debacle?"

Lauren continued to smile. "I sure did. I found three friends."

"Yes, you did. We like and admire you."

"Ditto."

*****

Lauren couldn't wait to get home to the girls. She needed the peace and joy that being with them brought into her life; especially after a day like today.

After playtime, she put the girls to bed, showered, and then went to bed herself. The fallout from her revelation was more stressful than just letting the rumors fly. Where before, some couldn't look her in the eye because they thought that she was damaged goods; they couldn't do it now out of embarrassment. *In time, this too will pass, but for now, the tension is a lot to maneuver through.*

Lauren was dozing when the phone rang. "Hello," she said groggily into the phone.

"Hello Lauren, this is Thad. Hey, I'm sorry. I didn't mean to wake you."

"Hi Brad. It's okay. I was just dozing."

"So? You called it an early night, did you?"

"Normally I don't. Today was so intense, and I couldn't wait to put it behind me. How are you?"

"Tired. I had intended to call you earlier in the day, but I had a surgery this afternoon, and it took longer than we first anticipated. How are you? I admire the way you handled yourself this morning."

"Thank you. I'm okay. I have no control over how people treat me or what they think of me."

"I think they learned a good lesson today. One, thanks to you, they won't soon forget."

"So did I, Brad. I learned the value of true friends. Thank you for standing by me."

"You're welcome. No one should be treated the way they treated you. Besides that, I think you're a very nice person and an exceptional cook too."

"Thank you. Are you fishing for another invitation?"

"Yes I am, but let me fix dinner for you before I sponge off you again."

"You cook, too? I'm impressed."

"Very basic. Nothing like you. I don't do desserts at all. What do you say; I cook and you bring dessert?"

"I don't know, Brad. I don't usually leave the girls in the evening unless I have a business engagement."

"That's not a problem. Bring them with you."

"Oh, no. I couldn't do that, it's so intrusive." Lauren sat back against the pillow.

"It's not at all. I know you have children, and it won't bother me at all if you were to bring them."

"We'll see. What day do you have in mind?"

"What about six o'clock Friday evening?"

"I'll let you know tomorrow. Okay?"

"That's fine. I'll let you go back to sleep now. Pleasant dreams."

CHAPTER EIGHT

Lauren snickered as she dialed the phone. "Hi, Jennifer. Guess what I got in the mail today."

"It can't be an invitation. It's only been three days."

"I know, right? I received two of them; one from the Masons."

"Are you kidding? Are you going to accept? It's somewhat of a slap in the face if you don't."

"Then they can consider themselves slapped. Their affair is Saturday, the day after tomorrow. Now, tell me who's been slapped. I'm sure they would be happy if I don't show."

"Sounds like a good reason to go. Who is the other one from?"

"It's from someone on the board of directors whom I haven't met. Their affair is the following Saturday and those invitations have been out for a month already. I don't need their charity. By the way, one of the doctors is having a get-together on the sixteenth. She asked me to come and bring a friend. Do you want to go?"

"I'm sure she meant a male friend."

"In that case, she's out of luck. I don't have any here."

"What about Thad?"

Lauren tapped on the phone. "I'm sure he was invited, and he probably has a date. I understand there are a lot of women after him."

"I'll go if I can find a sitter."

"Mrs. Brown said she'd be glad to keep Johnny for you."

"I guess that's settled then. It's been a long time since I've gone to any non-school related functions. Finding something that fits is going to be a challenge."

"Do you want to take the children shopping on Saturday morning; say around ten?"

"Sounds like fun."

* * * * *

Beautiful home. With the girls snuggly secured in their car seats, Lauren parked the car in front of Thad's house on Friday evening. Juggling the babies on each hip, she fumbled for the doorbell.

Thad opened the door. "Welcome to my humble abode. Here, let me help you with the girls." He lifted Brianna out of the stroller. "We can bring them into the den."

"Thanks. I need to get their playpen and diaper bag."

"Let me have your keys, I'll get them for you."

Lauren busied herself with the girls until he returned with the playpen.

Thad locked the legs of the playpen in place, and then placed the toys that Lauren handed him inside it. He then reached for Brianna. "Come on precious, ready to play?" He swung the baby gently into the air before putting her down. The baby gurgled with delight. "Your turn, Angel." He swung Brittany up and around before depositing her in the playpen beside her sister.

Lauren marveled at the ease with which he handled the children. "You act like someone with a lot of experience."

"I used to baby sit my nephews and nieces once in a while. Can I get you something to drink or are you ready to eat?"

"No thanks on the drink, and I can wait to eat. I see we both like R & B," she said thumbing through his CD collection. I like your collection of Christmas music too." Twenty minutes later, they were still thumbing through the music selections and chatting comfortably.

Lauren sat with a stack of CDs in her lap. "I'm partial to the Motown sound, but I enjoy almost all kinds of music."

"So do I. However, I haven't developed a taste for heavy metal or hard rock."

"I haven't either. Jazz and Classical are pretty high on my list."

"Darn. This is scary."

"What's so scary about two people enjoying the same kind of music?" He smiled. "Are you ready to eat?"

"Yes, I am." She stood to follow Thad. "It's not that two people have the same taste in music; it's just that I don't usually come in contact with anyone having the exact same taste as me."

Lauren had fed the girls and they were playing happily on the floor. Now, she and Thad sat at the table enjoying the delicious dinner of braised pork chops, green beans, and rice pilaf with a tossed green salad, rolls and iced tea.

"My compliments to the chef," Lauren praised. "This is delicious."

"Thank you. I had to learn to cook or go broke eating out."

Lauren glanced at him and smiled.

"What? Do I hear a comment or question?"

Lauren smiled. "No sir. I'm stuffed. This is a wonderful treat. Thank you."

"Do you do your own cooking too, Lauren?"

"Most of it. Mrs. Brown is both nanny and housekeeper or vice versa. She's a wonderful cook, but I enjoy cooking. She does the majority of the housework. I never thought I'd see the day that I would employ domestic help so I have a hard time letting someone else take over. Come on; let me help with the dishes."

"Can we have dessert first?" Thad pointed to the cake. "That looks so tempting."

"There's no wonder," Lauren giggled. "It has a devil's food cake base."

"Being tempted by the devil? Now that's a novel observation," Thad kidded. "How old are the girls now, Lauren?" Thad asked, as she washed, and he dried the dishes.

"Six months. You know, it's hard to believe that it's been four and a half months since I came here, and a little more than five months since my friends died. It's not easy being alone with the memories." She cleared her throat. "Up to this point, I've been so busy becoming acclimated to my new surroundings and taking care of the girls that I haven't had time to grieve." A tear escaped from her eyes.

Thad put the dishtowel down, and then draped his arms around her shoulders. "On top of all of that, you've had to put up with that mess from the university. I'm so sorry for all you've had to endure. You have done an exceptional job with the girls."

"They are precious. I couldn't love them more if they were my own."

"They *are* yours, Lauren. You are their mother—all that they have."

"I think I need to get them home." Lauren sniffed as she slid out of Thad's arms. "It's past their bedtime. Thank you for a lovely evening and the shoulder."

"Any time my friend. Here let me help you."

CHAPTER NINE

Since the university closed for the holidays, Lauren decided that she would visit her family in New Jersey for a few days if the weather stayed favorable. She invited Jennifer to accompany them. In the meantime, she and Jennifer went on a mini shopping spree. Included in their purchases were several outfits suitable for holiday entertaining.

Jennifer's eyes sparkled with anticipation as she prepared to spend an unencumbered evening with adults. The soft green velvet and lace pantsuit hid the subtle bulging of her stomach, and complimented her blonde hair and green eyes.

She looks more beautiful and less stressed than at any time since I've known her, Lauren commented to herself.

Lauren wore a mauve cashmere sweater with a burgundy, floor length, velvet skirt. Her shoulder length hair was swept into a flattering up-do, and she wore diamond and garnet chandelier earrings.

Lauren teased. "We look pretty good for two branded women of the evening, don't we?"

"Not bad if I do say so myself," Jennifer agreed.

Mrs. Brown ushered them out the door. "The two of you look great. Now go and enjoy yourselves. You both need this. Don't hurry back on my account. The children and I will be fine."

*****

At the party, Vivian answered the door. "Lauren! You made it. Come in. Let me take your coat."

Lauren introduced Jennifer. "This is for you." Lauren gave Vivian a gift-wrapped box.

"Thank you. Come in and mingle."

Vivian and her husband, Blake, lived in an up-scale neighborhood. The house was beautifully decorated for the season.

There was an intimate group of about seventy guests, which included several of the university's staff. Jennifer had blended in and appeared to be enjoying herself.

After the buffet dinner, there was dancing in the great room. Later, when Lauren was making her way toward the powder room, her path crossed that of Thad and Sandy Yates. Sandy glanced at her with a sneer on her face. "Congratulations on being vindicated, doctor."

Lauren narrowed her eyes. "Excuse me?"

"Oh. I read that the babies aren't really yours?"

Thad turned on her quickly. "Don't start that tonight, Sandy. It's over." Turning to Lauren, he offered his hand. "Will you dance with me, Lauren?" He led her to the dance floor, and pulled her close. "I'm truly sorry about that."

Lauren sighed deeply. "It's not your fault."

"What's the matter, Lauren? Did that comment bother you?"

"I know that I shouldn't let it, but it did."

They finished the dance, and after thanking Lauren, Thad went in search of Sandy.

Although the weather was a little chilly, it was still unseasonably warm. Lauren stepped onto the terrace for some fresh air. She leaned against a column, watching the moon rise above the horizon. A chill shook her body just before she felt the warmth of a jacket drape over her shoulders.

"Better?" Thad pulled her against his chest.

"Better."

"Lauren, I'm sorry. It seems that some people are not happy unless they are making others unhappy. That remark about your children was uncalled for and I let her know it."

"You don't have to defend me, Brad. I feel sorry for people who have to put others down to make themselves look good. I would have let her have it if it hadn't been for you."

"You shouldn't have let me stop you. Whatever you might have said, she had it coming."

"Ooh! Did you see that?"

"What?"

"A shooting star. It looked like it had a long, fiery tail."

Thad pulled her a little closer. "I'm sorry I missed it, but I was concentrating on the moon and the effects it's having on me. Lauren, may I ask you a personal question?"

"You can, but I don't promise to answer."

He chuckled. "Pretty and cautious, too. After a moment's hesitation, he asked, "Is there a special man in your life; as in love interest?"

"Not anymore. Why do you ask?"

"I'm being cautious, too. What are your plans for Christmas? I hate to think of you being here alone."

"If the weather holds out, Jennifer and I are going to New Jersey for a few days. When are you leaving for Massachusetts?"

"Thursday morning. I'll be gone until the first of January."

"Well, you have a Merry Christmas, and a blessed New Year."

"Have you received any more invitations?" Thad caressed her arm.

"Yes, several. It seems that the more I refuse, the more I get. By now, they've figured that I'm not going to accept so they can take the chance of inviting me."

"I'm so sorry, Lauren."

"Stop apologizing for them, Brad. I'm not a socialite, and being snubbed doesn't bother me. I feel that most of them are phonies anyway, and I'd rather not be bothered."

"You're like a breath of fresh air. No one has to guess at what you're thinking. No hidden agenda. I like that."

"We'd better go back inside before Vivian sends a search party for us. I'm surprised that Sandy hasn't come looking for you."

I'm not. She's not my date, Lauren."

"Thanks for the jacket." She faced him as she attempted to slip the jacket from her shoulders, but he held it in place and used it to pull her closer to him. A smile touched her lips when he lowered his head to kiss her. *I wonder if I'm supposed to resist this first kiss,* she thought, as his lips touched hers.

After a while, the kiss ended, and he pulled her to him and held her for a little while longer. Shortly he spoke, his voice husky. "Let's go inside."

*****

The next day, Jennifer and Lauren sat at her kitchen table, drinking coffee when she declared, "I owe you, Lauren. That was the best time I've had since John left, other than dinner at your house, of course."

"I'm happy for you, Jennifer. I had a wonderful time, too. Not only is Vivian a good hostess, she is a good person. I like her husband too. So? Are you ready for our trip to Newark?"

"All packed. I've had a lot of fun since I met you. You've opened Pandora's Box and I'm beginning to feel alive again. I've let those busy bodies control my life long enough. Maybe when they find that we are going on with our lives, they'll start minding their own business."

"There's always hope." Lauren laughed. "I'm going to take my leave now, my friend, I've had a long busy day and I'm missing my girls." Lauren grabbed her coat and opened the door. "Wow! It's brutal out here. I'll talk to you tomorrow."

*****

Lauren fed and bathed the girls, then played with them for a while before she put them to bed. *They are growing so fast.* She gazed into the crib. Although they seemed happy and well adjusted, she wondered if there were any memories of their parents left.

She had noticed that Mrs. Brown referred to her as *mommy* when she talked to the girls, but she had yet to refer to herself that way when she talked to them. She thought that in doing so, she was being disloyal to her friends.

Lauren climbed into bed, planning to do some reading before she turned the lights out. Christmas music was playing softly on the disc player. For the first time since her arrival in Connecticut, she felt an overwhelming sense of loneliness and grief. Just as the tears began to roll down her face, the phone rang.

She quickly dried her eyes on the sheets, and doing her best to control the tremor in her voice; she picked up the receiver on the third ring. "Hello."

Thad detected the tremor in her voice. "Lauren? Lauren? Are you okay?"

"Hi, Brad. I'm okay."

"Are you sure? You sound as if you've been crying. Do you need me to come over?"

"No. I'm fine." She sniffed. I'm just a little homesick."

"I understand. Do you feel like talking?"

"Yes. Give me a few minutes and I'll call you back. Say in about fifteen-twenty minutes?"

"All right, Lauren."

After she hung up the phone, Lauren went into the adjoining bathroom and washed her face in cold water. She checked on the girls, and after changing their diapers, she went back to the bedroom to return Thad's call. The doorbell rang. *Who could that be at nine o'clock in the evening?* Lauren reached for her robe just as the bell chimed again. Peeping through the peephole, she was more than a little surprise to see Thad standing on the steps. Lauren jerked the door open. "Brad! What are you doing here? I was just about to call you back."

"I didn't like the way you sounded so I came to see about you."

For a few moments, she stared at him. "I told you that I was okay."

"I know you did, but I needed to see for myself," he said softly.

"You are a great friend, Brad."

He cast a quick glance in her direction then, averted his eyes. "Yes, Lauren, I'm your friend."

"Why were you calling?"

"Just to say hello. I hadn't spoken to you since Saturday. That was a nice get together, wasn't it?"

She led him to the den, and then sat on the sofa with her leg beneath her. "It was a nice party. I enjoyed it."

Lauren picked up her empty teacup and stood. "I'm going to have some more tea, will you join me?"

"Sure, I'd like some tea, thank you."

"Excuse me for a moment."

Leaving Brad alone, Lauren went out to the kitchen to make tea. When she returned, Thad was standing near the fireplace listening to a Christmas CD he had put on. Her hand shook slightly as she passed him the cup; some of the tea splashed into the saucer. Thad took the tea and placed it on the mantle, then he caught both her hands in his. "What is it Lauren?"

She averted her eyes and answered, "Nothing." Her voice caught on a sob.

Thad led her to the sofa and pulled her to him. "Talk to me, my friend."

Once again, tears flowed down her face. Thad gave her a handful of tissues from the box on the coffee table, and then draped an arm around her shoulder. She leaned into his chest as the sobs racked her body.

He held her tighter, but remained quiet, letting her decide when she was ready to talk.

After several moments of crying, Lauren attempted to extract herself from his arms, but Thad held her in place, still not speaking.

"Brad, I'm sorry." She sniffed against his chest. "I miss her so much. She was my best friend and like a sister to me. We had so much fun together last Christmas. Her babies need her." Lauren cried anew. "She gave me the CD that's playing."

"This is the first time you've allowed yourself to really cry for them isn't it?"

Lauren nodded.

"That's the best Christmas present you could have given yourself. You've had all of this bottled up inside of you for more than six months. Listen to me, Lauren."

He stared at her. "I sense that you're feeling some guilt relative to your role in the girls' lives.

You feel guilty that Lydia was taken away from them, and now the only mother they'll ever know is you—that you're taking her place. You must remember that this is not a choice you made, and I believe it's not a choice Lydia would have made if she'd had a say in it. The girls need you. You *are* their mother. This is what Lydia and Stan wanted. If they couldn't be here for them, they wanted the next best person. I think they made an excellent choice. I know that you miss them. Grieve for them, but remember the girls are dependent on you. They have no one else."

They sat in silence, listening to the final cuts on the CD. When it ended, Lauren offered Thad a fresh cup of tea. She excused herself to splash some cold water on her puffy eyes. When she returned, she offered an embarrassed, "Sorry."

"Don't apologize, Lauren. I'm glad I was here with you when it happened, and I'm glad it finally happened. That's healthy. When are you leaving for Newark?"

"I'm leaving Thursday morning. Mrs. Brown has a sister in New York, and I'm going to drop her off there to meet her children. Jennifer and I will go on to Newark."

"Please be careful on the highway. I pray that the weather holds up."

"What! No white Christmas?"

"Not if you're going to be driving in it," he stated with a serious scowl.

"You're going to be driving, too."

"I know, but you'll be transporting precious cargo–yourself included."

"No more precious than you, my friend."

Thad smiled and changed the subject. "By the way, I was calling for something else, too."

"Oh?"

"Will you have dinner with me tomorrow evening–a dress-up dinner at a restaurant?"

"Another invitation?" She giggled.

"Funny." He chuckled. "Are you accepting?"

"Dr. Thaddeus Bradford, Ms. Lauren Jeffries accepts your invitation with thanks, sir."

"I like you, Lauren Jeffries."

"And, I like you Thaddeus Bradford."

"Are you feeling better?"

"Much. Thank you."

"Anytime." He playfully cuffed her chin with his fist. "Good night."

"Good night, Brad. Thanks for being a great friend."

*****

Lauren's sixth sense told her that when Brad asked her to a dress-up dinner at a restaurant, it would not be your average everyday restaurant; and she was right.

Because she had chosen to wear an elegant, deep plum, velvet, floor length dress with a subtle beaded bodice, she was pleased with herself. She added simple diamond studded earrings with a matching bracelet. Her hair was styled into a soft pageboy with one side tucked behind her ear.

They both laughed when she answered the door. Thad was standing there in a dark brown tuxedo that appeared, in the night light, to be the same color as her dress.

"This is scary." She laughed. "You look great."

"And you, my friend, are beautiful. This is not scary, it's confirmation."

"Confirming what?"

"You'll get it, later. Are you ready?"

Lauren wasn't at all surprised when Thad drove to the most fashionable restaurant in the surrounding area. Everyone from the valets, to the maître d', to the waiters knew him by name. He was greeted by several elegantly clad, important looking patrons as they were escorted to their table.

They were seated in the upper tier of the four-tiered restaurant that boasted a panoramic view of the city and the harbor. The sky was star studded, and on the horizon, one could see the first hint of the not yet visible moon. *What ambiance.*

Thad perused the menu. "May I order you a drink?"

"Thank you, no. I don't drink alcoholic beverages."

"Really? Not even a glass of wine once in a while?"

"No. I never acquired a taste for alcohol. I've tried different brands and flavors, but I just don't like it. The funny thing though is that I like the bouquet of many wines."

"Is there anything that I can order for you in lieu of?"

"I would like a lemon wedge for my water, thank you."

"May I order for you? I have something in mind that I think you would like."

"Please do." Lauren closed her menu. "I was going to ask you to do it anyway."

They engaged in small talk while they waited to be served.

"Lauren, you said you don't have a love interest anymore. Is there a sad ending to that story?"

"Not really. It's just that he couldn't find what he was looking for in me —or shall I say, what his mother was looking for."

For a millisecond, it appeared that the light went out in Thad's eyes. Before she could investigate further their orders arrived.

Lauren pulled her fork between her lips. "Brad! This is delicious. What is it called?"

"My French is pretty rusty. I'll ask the waiter to pronounce it for you when he returns. It means three sea animals in sauce."

She laughed. "I'm sorry I asked. The visual I got was not very appetizing."

"Actually, it's crab, lobster, and scallops in a special sauce." He smiled. "Given your love for seafood, especially crab, I thought you might enjoy it."

"You thought right. This is very tasty and very frightening." She smiled.

"How is it frightening?"

"There's nothing frightening about the food. It's just disarming that you know me this well after such a short period of time."

"Oh, that. That's my little secret.

Now, back to your previous relationship, how long has it been since you ended it? Or, did he end it?"

"It was a mutual decision. Given the fact that he was already seeing someone it was best. That was over a year ago."

"You mean to tell me that you didn't mind sharing?"

"I didn't know that I was sharing until we had called it quits."

"How long had you been dating?"

"Almost two years."

Thad's brows knitted in surprise. "No one since then?"

"No. I'm not particularly interested. Now, I'm here, and I don't really know anyone. What about you, anyone special?"

The light in Thad's eyes dimmed again before he spoke. "That's an easy question that requires a complicated answer." He hesitated for several moments, and then sighed. "There's what amounts to a family arrangement. Abigail and I grew up together, and as was expected, we dated through high school and college. When I went off to med school, she went to work in her uncle's Public Relations firm as an assistant manager to wait for me. Now, she, her family, and mine are waiting for me to propose."

"What about Sandy Yates?"

"Sandy isn't a part of my life, although she has made it very clear that she wants to be." They continued talking through desert, after which they relaxed in the lounge. The candles on the walls and tables, the fire crackling in the fireplace, and the artfully placed flower arrangements created a very cozy and relaxing atmosphere. A seven-piece combo and two vocalists provided the music.

"May I have this dance, mademoiselle?"

"Oui, monsieur."

"Are you enjoying yourself, Lauren?"

She gazed at him and smiled. "I'm having a wonderful time, Brad. Thank you."

Thad gave her hand a gentle squeeze. "The pleasure is mine."

Just as they returned to their seats, a couple approached them. "Thad?"

Thad stood and extended his hand to the gentleman. "Mrs. Bickers, Mr. Bickers, it's good to see you. This is my friend, Lauren Jeffries. Lauren this is Mr. and Mrs. Stanley Bickers, friends of my parents."

"I'm pleased to meet you ma'am, sir." Lauren extended her hand, which Mrs. Bickers barely touched, and Mr. Bickers touched as if he was afraid something would rub off on him.

"We're also your friend, Thad—Abigail's, too," she added. "Well, we'll be going now. We just came down to have lunch with the mayor, and we decided to take in a show since we were here. We stopped in here to have a late dinner. I'll let your parents and Abigail know that we ran into you. Goodnight."

Thad and Lauren watched the couple as they headed for the exit. "My parents will know about this before they get to the state line…actually before the valet brings the car around."

"Are you concerned about that, Brad?"

"No, I'm not. I'm having a wonderful evening, and I'm not letting anyone's veiled threats ruin it for me. I'm hoping you won't either."

"Have no fear. This has been a wonderful adventure."

"It's getting late. Are you ready to go?"

"I am whenever you are."

* * * * *

After dinner they returned to Lauren's house. "Would you like to come in for a while, Brad?"

"Just for a little while. I have to be at the hospital early. Or shall I say, later this morning."

"Another surgery?"

"No. I have a family consult. I also want to check on a couple of my patients before I leave." Thad helped her out of her coat. "It feels good in here. I hope we don't get any precipitation. If we do the roads are going to be treacherous, and I worry about you all being out there."

"Come and sit down, worrywart. I lived in Michigan for the past five years and in New Jersey before that. I'm used to driving in snow and ice."

"I still worry. Come here." After a quick hug he handed her a gift-wrapped box. "This is for you."

Laruen opened the box and fingered the gold pendant of a woman and two identical girls. "Oh Brad," she whispered. "This is— this is absolutely—oh, Brad it's beautiful. Thank you." She glanced at him through moistened eyes. "You're so thoughtful. I love it."

"You're welcome."

"This, my friend, is for you." Lauren gave him a box containing a sweatshirt.

Thad read the inscription: *He who finds a friend has found a gold mine. I hit the mother lode.* "This is precious, Lauren. It's an original saying. Isn't it?"

"It is. For an original man." Lauren embraced him.

Thad returned the hug, and then kissed her gently on the lips. She returned the kiss, and soon they were in an embrace, kissing each other hungrily.

"It's best that I leave now." Thad's hoarse whisper brushed her ear. He hugged her tightly again, then released her. "Merry Christmas. Please be careful on the highway."

"You too, Brad. Merry Christmas."

*****

Lauren crawled into bed after he left. The last thing she remembered before she fell off to sleep was the kiss she and Thad had shared. The babies' wailing awakened her at four in the morning. She and Mrs. Brown reached the nursery door at the same time. Brittany was fine, but Brianna's cries had awakened her.

Brianna was very hot to the touch, and she was flailing her little arms and kicking her legs as if she was in pain. Lauren placed her on the changing table to examine her. Her temperature was 104.2. There were no other outward signs of illness, but the examination of her ears and throat, found them both to be red and inflamed.

She deduced that a trip to the ER was in order.

Although Mrs. Brown insisted that she accompany Lauren to the emergency room, Lauren told her that she would be of more help if she stayed home with Brittany.

After four hours in the ER, and a diagnosis of strep throat and an ear infection, she brought Brianna home.

Since Jennifer had planned to meet her family in Newark, Lauren insisted that she and Mrs. Brown go on the trip as planned. They exchanged Christmas gifts and bade each other a Merry Christmas. Lauren wished them a safe trip, and then turned her full attention to the girls.

Lauren sanitized the nursery, gave Brianna her meds and a drink, and then returned her to the crib as the medicine began to take effect. She pushed Brittany's crib into her room to avoid a possible contamination.

At noon, she administered the prescribed doses of antibiotics and a fever reducer to Brianna, and after getting her settled, she fed Brittany and put her down for a nap. She then put a load of clothes in the washer, and decided that she too, needed a nap.

She heard her cell phone ringing as she exited the laundry room. Expecting it to be a family member, she didn't bother to check the caller ID. "Hello?"

"Lauren, its Thad. Are you all right? Where are you? I've been calling you since early this morning.

"Hello Brad. I'm at home. I'm…"

"At home! What happened? Are you okay?"

"Hold on worrywart. I'm going to tell you," she teased. "Brianna has strep throat and an ear infection. I was at the emergency from four-thirty to about seven-thirty this morning. I guess when I turned the phone off in the hospital I forgot to turn it back on until about an hour ago. I haven't had time to check to see if I have any messages.

"You scared me. I'm better, now. How is Brianna doing?"

"She's resting. I'm keeping her throat sprayed so that she can swallow without pain. Her temp is down to 101.3 now.

"How high was it?"

"A little over 104 by the time we reached the hospital."

"Listen Lauren, I'm going to call Richard McKnight. He's a pediatrician, and a friend. I want him to check on Brianna."

"I'm sure that's not necessary, Brad."

"Please. Do it for me, Lauren. I wish I were there to check on her myself. How's Brittany?"

"So far, so good. I moved her into my room."

"Good move. Is Mrs. Brown okay?"

"I hope so. She's in New Jersey. Since she and Jennifer were planning to meet family I told them to go on with their plans."

"That means that you and the girls are going to be alone for Christmas."

"We're okay, Brad. It's probably best that no one is around us, right now."

"You could be right. I'm willing to bet that you haven't had any rest since four o'clock this morning."

Lauren chuckled. "I was getting ready to take a nap when the phone rang."

"In that case, I'm going to let you go. I'm going to call Rich right now, and then call you later this evening, okay?"

"Thanks Brad."

* * * * *

Dr. Richard McKnight stopped by to check on Brianna, and declared that she would be fine with the medicine she had been prescribed. Lauren was able to rest for an hour or two after the doctor left. She had just awakened when the phone rang.

"How'd it go with Rich?"

"He's satisfied, worrywart. He said he'll stop in again tomorrow to check on her. Brad, I'm sorry. I never asked you how your trip was."

"Uneventful. I spent most of the drive worrying about my friend. By the way, take my cell phone number. I thought I had given it to you, but I realize now that I gave you the cell number that I use for the hospital. This is my personal cell. Promise me you'll call me if you need me. No matter the hour."

"Doesn't sound like I have much of a choice," she kidded

"You don't. Did you get any sleep today?"

"I was able to get a couple of hours in after Dr. McKnight left. I think the girls will sleep through the night. Therefore I'll be able to rest. How has your visit been so far?"

"It's been okay. What's that I hear playing in the background?"

"Brahms' lullaby." She giggled. "You like?"

"You're a funny lady. It's bedtime for you, too. Sleep well."

"And you, my friend. Thanks again for being you. Goodnight, Brad."

Lauren was thankful that since Brianna got sick, it happened while she was off from school. She was able to spend lots of time with both girls, one on one and together. By Christmas Eve, Brianna was crawling around and playing on the floor with her sister.

Dr. Rich had stopped in to check on her on Friday, as he had promised, and said that she was recovering very well, but to keep her indoors for at least two more days. That advice suited Lauren well because she had no plans to go out anyway. The few friends she usually socialized with were either away for the holiday, or they thought she was away.

Mrs. Brown and Jennifer called every day to check on Brianna, and again tonight to say Merry Christmas.

As she lay in bed, watching television, she felt the loneliness creeping inside. Lauren refused to let the tears come. She hadn't realized how much she had looked forward to Brad's daily call until it didn't come. What a way to spend Christmas Eve.

*****

Lauren spent most of Christmas day talking to family friends, and playing with the girls. The other part of the day, she spent hoping Brad would call.

On Monday afternoon, she noticed she had a text message from him: *Haven't been able to call. How was Christmas?*

Although the week's span between Christmas and New Year's Eve was bitterly cold, every day Lauren dressed the girls snuggly, and took them for a stroll.

On her daily treks, she encountered several neighborhood children who were braving the weather to try a new toy as well as other parents who were pushing carriages.

Several nodded or waved in response to her greeting, not one person spoke to her. Some even found it necessary to cross the street as she approached them.

I guess it's hard to remove ground-in dirt, Lauren thought as she returned from her walk on Saturday. New Year's Eve. Lauren was looking forward to Jennifer and Mrs. Brown's return. Although, she had talked with a family member or a friend each day, she still experienced profound loneliness.

Thad called while she was feeding the girls their dinner. This would be the first time she'd spoken to him in ten days. As much as she had looked forward to hearing from him, she was peeved at not having heard from him sooner.

"Hello, Thad."

Thad seemed to cringe at the cool tone of her voice. "Lauren, you only call me Thad when you're upset with me. Did I do something wrong? Are you all right?"

"I'm fine," she answered, her voice still frosty.

"And the girls? How is Brianna?"

"We're all well, thank you."

"Lauren, what's the matter? You sound distracted."

"I'm feeding the girls."

"I see. I can call you back if you like. I've missed you, Lauren.

Suddenly she heard a voice in the background. "Thad? There you are, darling. Everyone is waiting. Tell whoever you're talking to that you'll call him back, later."

"Excuse me, Lauren. Abigail, I'm having a conversation, and I'll be out as soon as I'm finished."

"But Thad," the female voice pleaded, "We have reservations for six o'clock. We're going to be late."

"Then go without me."

Abigail's voice sounded sulky. "Our parents are going to be upset."

"I'm sorry about that, Lauren. As I was saying, I've missed you. We were at a ski lodge and I couldn't get any service to call you. How was your Christmas?"

"Brad, maybe you should go. I'm going to finish feeding the girls. Happy New Year." She heard Brad calling her name as she hung up the phone.

At midnight, Lauren kissed her daughters, got into her bed, and then slid deep under the covers to attend her pity party.

CHAPTER TEN

"Happy New Year, Dr. Jeffries," Mrs. Brown called, as she came through the door laden with bags.

"Happy New Year, Mrs. Brown. You look prosperous." Lauren embraced her housekeeper. "Where's Jennifer?"

"I dropped her off at her house. She said she's tired, and that she'll call you later. I think she might have over done the celebrating. She looked a little peaked, as do you ma'am. Are you feeling okay?"

"I'm fine, Mrs. Brown. I'm glad that you're back. I was beginning to talk to myself just to hear an adult voice," she kidded.

"Is Brianna all better?"

"Yes ma'am, she's as fit as a fiddle."

"Do you mind if I rest for an hour or two? I partied until early this morning then fought traffic coming home. I'm bushed."

"Partied, huh? A secret gentleman friend?"

"How I wish. The family, and lots of friends, ate, danced, lied, and some drank the New Year in. I haven't had that much fun in years."

"Good for you. Now off to bed." Lauren started towards the nursery. "Oh, I cooked a surprise for you."

"I can guess what it is. I might not be as sleepy as I thought I was." The doorbell chimed. "Oops. I'll get that."

Mrs. Brown opened the door. "Happy New Year, Dr. Bradford."

"Thank you and Happy New Year to you, Mrs. Brown. Is Ms. Jeffries in? Oh, there she is." Thad spotted Lauren heading to the den.

Lauren entered the room. "Happy New Year, Thad. This is a surprise."

"Happy New Year, Lauren. I hope it's a pleasant surprise." He kept his eyes fixed on her face.

Lauren sat in a nearby chair and offered Thad a seat.

Instead of sitting, Thad stood with his back to the fireplace, continuing to gaze at her. "What is it Lauren? I sense you're upset with me."

Lauren sighed deeply and sat back in her chair. "I'm not upset with you. I've had a lot of time for reflection during the past week, and I've come to the realization that I've become too dependent on you. I've set unreasonable expectations, and allowed myself to get used to certain behaviors. You're a wonderful friend, and I have to remember that. You're my friend, not my protector, doctor, advisor, or anything else."

"It's not like you to be vague, Lauren. What exactly are you saying?"

"I'm saying that maybe we shouldn't spend so much time together."

"Is that really what you want, Lauren?"

"I think it is best," she answered quietly.

"Best for whom, Lauren?"

"For both of us. I don't want..." His cell phone rang, interrupting her. "Excuse me. Hello, Mother. Mother, I can't discuss that right now. No. I'm not at home." He paused. "Yes mother, I'm at my friend's house. Goodbye, Mother."

Lauren attempted to leave the room to give Thad some privacy, but he had taken her arm to arrest her steps, he held on as he talked. Though, she couldn't understand the words, she could hear the tone of Mrs. Bradford's voice. It wasn't a happy one.

"Lauren?" Thad continued to hold onto her arm.

She turned to face him, but didn't speak.

He pulled her against his chest. "Please. I'm in need of a friend now."

"I'm sorry. What is it? What has happened?" Lauren's displeasure was forgotten.

"Will you trust me if I said that I need to wait to talk about it? I need a little time."

"You know that I trust you. I'll be here when you're ready to talk."

"Can we sit together on the sofa for a while?"

"Don't you need to call your mother back?"

"Right now, I need to be with my friend."

*****

A few days later Lauren answered the phone to hear Jennifer scream. "Lauren! John is home. He's home, Lauren."

"Jennifer, I'm so very happy for the two of you. I would tell you to calm down, but you deserve to be overjoyed. When did he get in, and how long is he going to be home." Lauren smiled as she listened to the joy in Jennifer's voice.

"He came early this morning, and he will be home for thirty whole days. He's not going back to Iraq. He's going to Germany from here."

"Good for you, Jennifer, and thanks for letting me know. I'll wait until later in the week to meet him. I want to give you all some time alone."

CHAPTER ELEVEN

School had resumed for the second semester and everything seemed status quo at the university.

Lauren and Thad had begun to have dinner out together at least once a week during the month of January. The last weekend of the month, he informed Lauren that he needed to take a trip to Massachusetts.

Usually, when he was away overnight he'd call her, but she had not heard from him since Friday morning before he left. She had left a message on his cell phone that morning, but he had not returned her call, and she was becoming very concerned. A call to his office revealed that he had been to work, but he would be out for the next two days.

Mrs. Brown touched Lauren's shoulder. "Ms. J.! Ms. J.!"

Lauren jumped. "What is it?"

"The phone. It's for you. Didn't you hear it ring?

"I guess not. Thank you. Hello?"

"Hello, Lauren, it's Thad."

"Brad, where are you? I've been calling you all day. Do you realize I haven't heard from you since Friday? Are you all right?"

"A little tired, but I'm okay. I'm in Annapolis at a medical seminar. I'll be back on Thursday. I miss you."

"I miss you too. I'm worried about you."

"Don't be. I'm okay."

"Listen, I feel much better now that I've heard your voice. Why don't you get some rest?

"Thanks, baby. I'll do that, and I'll talk to you tomorrow."

"Goodnight, Brad."

* * * * *

Lauren and Jennifer sat on the park bench, watching the children sleeping. "So? Are you going to Germany, too?"

"I am. Not in the near future though. The baby will be here by the time my contract is up." She rested her hand on her abdomen. "I'll probably leave in July."

"If I had any sense I'd leave, too. This is a cold place, and I'm not referring to the weather. Outsiders aren't welcome here unless, of course, they're blue blood."

"You'd consider leaving Thad?"

Lauren gazed out into the park. "Thad is spoken for."

Jennifer retorted sarcastically, "I know. That's why he spends so much time with you."

"We're good friends who enjoy each other's company."

"Uh, huh. Tell me anything."

"I guess we had better get the children inside. They've had enough fresh air for today."

"I noticed you're dodging the subject, my friend. Anyway, I'll see you next week. John is taking us to New York for the weekend."

"Sounds like fun. Enjoy."

*****

Thad approached Lauren's office. "Knock, knock."

"Brad, hi. What are you doing slumming in these parts?"

"I want you to meet my brother and sister-in-law." Thad turned to the couple who had followed him into her office.

Lauren stood, and then stepped from behind her desk.

"Lauren this is my brother, Gene, and his wife, Joan. This is Lauren Jeffries."

"Pleased to make your acquaintance, Gene, Joan." Lauren extended her hand.

"I'm pleased to meet you as well, Lauren. I've heard a lot about you." Gene smiled.

She glanced at Thad. "Are you here on business?"

"Actually, we are passing through on our way home from New York. We decided to stop by to check on little brother."

Lauren smiled. "That's what big brothers do. Isn't it? I've been a victim of that myself."

Gene glanced at Lauren. "We've invited Thad to dinner this evening. I'd be delighted to have you join us."

She glanced at Thad again and received a subtle nod.

"Thank you, Gene. I'd love to."

"We'll pick you up at seven if that's okay."

"Seven is fine."

* * * * *

Thad and Gene arrived at Lauren's house promptly at seven o'clock. "Wow, lady!" Thad exclaimed. "You look great. Hey, can't we just ditch them and..."

"Don't even think about it, brother." Gene scolded, and then turned to Lauren. "You do look great, Lauren. Are you ready? We have reservations for seven-thirty."

They were eating at an up-scale restaurant on the West side of the city. Not quite as posh as the *Jarden de la Fleur Francaise,* but full of atmosphere.

Lauren learned Thad was well known by staff and patrons here as well. She felt a sense of power, position, and money surrounding him. It didn't feel like new money, either. They chatted amicably as they ate.

Gene glanced at Lauren. "So, Lauren, you're a doctor, too. What is your specialty?"

"I'm not a medical doctor. I have a doctorate in nursing."

"Do you really? You seem so young to have accomplished so much, and to be holding such a powerful position."

Thad, buttering his bread volunteered, "She's just a smart lady. We all thought the same thing when she came aboard, but it didn't take her long to put us in our places."

Lauren cast Thad a painful glance. "Now, I never heard that one before. Did I step on someone's toes by accepting that position? I can't win for losing in this town, can I?"

"It sounds as if you've had a rough time of it, Lauren. How long have you lived here?" Joan asked.

"Almost six excruciating months," Lauren answered, with intensity in her voice that surprised her. "I can only imagine how the grapevine flourished with that bit of fertilizer. Please, excuse me." She stood to leave the table.

Joan followed Lauren into the lady's lounge. "Are you all right, Lauren?"

"Yes. I'm fine. I'm sorry for letting that comment get to me. Nothing I hear should come as a surprise to me anymore.

I've been tarred and feathered. All that's left is to be run out of town. I don't know what's behind the obsession with my life. Women have babies out of wedlock every day." Lauren repaired her make-up. "Thanks for caring enough to check on me. Are you ready to go back?"

Thad and Gene stood as the two women approached the table. "I'm sorry, sweetheart." Thad whispered in Lauren's ear as he held her chair for her.

"Gene, please forgive my behavior. I should have grown a thicker skin by now.

Gene looked at Thad and raised an eyebrow.

Thad gazed into her eyes. "Do I have your permission, Lauren?"

Lauren shrugged her shoulders.

"Well, thanks to a couple of her loosely connected neighbors, Lauren has been the subject of some very ugly gossip, and she's been treated badly because of it." Thad proceeded to tell his brother and sister-in-law the story. He then leaned towards Lauren and whispered, "I'm so very sorry for that comment. I trust you know I'd never, deliberately, say, or do anything to hurt you."

She favored him with a faint smile.

Gene turned to her. "Lauren, I'm an attorney. Is there anything you want me to do about this? You may have a good case for slander."

"Thank you. No. The damage has already been done. For the girls' sake, I just want it to go away."

"I'm very familiar with that incident. I represented three families who brought suit against the liner, and I have a list of all the passengers."

"Lauren, I can't tell you how sorry I am about this." Joan touched her hand. "No one deserves to be treated so mean. I wish you would let Gene exact some revenge."

"Thanks Joan, but it's not worth it."

Thad asked Lauren to dance with him. While they were dancing Thad apologized again as he tightened his hold on her.

"Please don't apologize anymore. I know that you didn't mean any harm."

"Will you have dinner with me Saturday evening?"

"Saturday? That's Valentine's Day. Aren't you going to Boston?"

"No. I'm hoping to be here, having dinner with you. Will you have dinner with me?"

Lauren smiled. "I would love to."

Thad gave her a quick kiss. "Thank you, my friend."

When they returned to the table from their dance, Gene announced that it was time for them to leave.

"Lauren, I'm happy we had a chance to meet you." Instead of shaking her hand, Gene hugged her, as did Joan. "If you need me just call. I don't like what they've done to you."

"Thank you both for dinner and your compassion. Drive safely."

"Brother, take care of her. You two be very careful."

CHAPTER TWELVE

After a lovely Valentine's dinner, Thad led Lauren to the dance floor. "Did I tell you how beautiful you look tonight?"

"Yes you did. Just before I told you how handsome you are. Thank you."

"You are very welcome. Are you enjoying yourself?"

She gazed at him. "Oh yes. Very much. Good food, good music, and great company. What more could anybody ask for?"

Thad pulled her closer. "I can think of something more."

"Oh? And what could that be?"

Thad tightened his grip on her hand as they continued to dance slowly across the floor. Lauren tilted her head back and gazed up at him. His eyes held hers, and for several moments, they didn't speak. Without breaking their gaze, he said, "I'm in love with you, Lauren. Will you be my valentine?"

Lauren gasped. Until this very moment, she had not admitted to herself that she was in love with Thaddeus Bradford. Still gazing at her, he asked again, "Will you, Lauren?"

She nodded her head. "I love you, too."

Intending to seal the revelation with a light kiss, they found themselves locked in a gentle embrace, which stopped the dance traffic; a fact that they weren't aware of until they heard the applause. Blushing brightly with embarrassment, Lauren buried her head against Thad's chest. Smiling, he took her hand and bowed to the crowd, which caused more applause. Lauren's face reddened. "Please, let's sit down," she whispered.

*****

Given all that Lauren had endured at the hands of gossipers, she and Thad decided that it was best that they keep their personal relationship a secret from the work place for the time being.

As time permitted, they spent at least two days a week as well as most weekends together, making sure that the girls were a part of most of the activities, even if it was just for a stroll in the park.

They reveled in getting to know the little things that made the other who he or she was.

Easter fell in March this year, and Thad had invited Lauren to dinner in Boston with his family. She declined, saying that she wanted to be with the girls. He begged her to come and to bring the girls with her, but she insisted that she was not ready to subject the girls to more scrutiny, yet.

Although, she didn't tell Thad, she still experienced a sense of uneasiness that she couldn't quite put her finger on when it came to his family. Even Thad had an aura of sophistication about him. Blue Blood came to mind. And with Gene, though he had been very friendly, and had offered a helping hand, she sensed the 'I'm used to taking charge, I know best', almost condescending attitude; not affected, but expected.

Lauren learned that Thad's parents held positions of esteem. Mr. Bradford, a graduate of Princeton, was now CEO of a large bank chain and Mrs. Bradford, a Brown graduate, had in essence, given up her lucrative position of city manager to become a member of the non-working social elite.

The two of them had raised their perfect children, two boys and two girls, to one day take their rightful places in society.

The girls had both, as expected, graduated from their mother's alma mater. Both boys were expected to follow in their father's footsteps, which Gene did, but Thad had earned an academic scholarship to Harvard.

All of the siblings were employed in jobs that commanded annual salaries in the six figures. Except for Thad, each of the siblings was married, and had at least one child. They all lived within a ten-mile radius of their parents and their in-laws.

* * * * *

Thad had returned to Boston for the Easter holiday. Lauren had expected him to stop by when he returned to Dalton, but he had called at about nine o'clock to say that he was exhausted, and that he would see her the next day. She noted that he did sound tired, weary, and a little sad.

* * * * *

Thad invited her to accompany him to his parents for dinner the second Sunday after Easter. This time she accepted, but insisted that the girls stay home with Mrs. Brown.

Sunday dinner at the Bradford's was at three p.m., sharp. In order to be there on time and have a few minutes to visit beforehand, they had to leave Dalton at twelve-thirty.

"Wow!" Lauren thought to herself as they entered the gates. *Are we in Boston or Atlanta? Tara revisited! There goes that feeling again. Money, power, and prestige.*

The family was sitting in the Bradford living room when Thad arrived with Lauren. "Hello everyone, this is my friend, Lauren Jeffries. Lauren these are my parents, L.C. and Velma, my sisters Elaine Varner and Anna Poston and their husbands, Alex and Jerry. You've met Gene and Joan."

Lauren smiled and extended her hand. "Mr. and Mrs. Bradford, it's nice to meet you." She received a barely there response from Mrs. Bradford and a limp, you're not important handshake from Mr. Bradford. Thad's sisters and their spouses greeted her with a nod. Gene and Joan smiled as they spoke and greeted her with an embrace. Thad ushered her to one of the two vacant chairs near the unlit fireplace. She noted that other than having them scan her from head to toe, no one paid any attention to her.

After a few minutes of the family engaging in subjects of conversations that Lauren couldn't possibly join in, an attractive young woman joined them. She kissed the elder Bradfords, who smiled and returned the affection warmly.

When the young woman attempted to embrace Thad, he arrested her arms and spoke, "Hello Abigail. This is my friend, Lauren Jeffries. Lauren, this is Abigail Higgins, a family friend."

"Hello Abigail," Lauren greeted.

Abigail ignored her greeting. *What has Thad gotten me into? An igloo would seem stifling by comparison right about now.* She was relieved when the cook announced that dinner was served—until she learned that Abigail was seated beside Thad. Lauren was seated across from them, where she had an unobtrusive view of Abigail fawning over him.

It was obvious Thad was very uncomfortable and quite peeved. He glanced at her. His body language said he was about to protest their seating arrangements, but Lauren smiled and gave him a subtle shake of the head.

"So? Ms. Jeffries how did you meet my son? Are you a doctor, too?" Mr. Bradford questioned.

Here it comes, she thought. *It only took forty-five minutes. I guess they had to wait until everyone was in place and attentive.*

Lauren laced her fingers. "I met Thaddeus at the university, sir," she answered with mock piety.

"Are you a student?" Elaine asked.

Everyone beat up on her. Maybe she'll go away. "No. I'm not a student." *If you want information out of me, you'll have to drag it out of me.*

Elaine seemed frustrated. "Then how did you happen to be at the university? Do you work there?"

"Lauren is Dean of Nursing Studies at the university. She and I are colleagues." Thad smiled and cast *a naughty girl* look her way.

Mrs. Bradford asked, "Where did you attend medical school?"

Lauren sighed. "I didn't. I'm not a medical doctor." She glanced at Thad and added, "I have a doctorate in nursing."

"Is Connecticut your home?" Elaine asked.

"No. I'm a Virginian by birth."

Abigail quipped with a derisive snort, "A southern hillbilly."

"And, I am proud of it. I'm in great company."

Elaine continued with a barrage of questions. "Do you have sisters and brothers?"

Lauren sipped her water. "I have two of each." *Dang! What's with all these questions?*

"What do your parents do?"

"My father was a building contractor and my mother was a school teacher."

"Do you attend church?"

"Of course I do. Doesn't everyone?" Lauren answered casting an innocent air. Thad smiled her way.

"What religion are you?" Velma asked.

"I'm of the Baptist faith."

"Oh. I see. Well, we're all Catholic," she said with relief. As if to say there's nothing to worry about, Catholics marry Catholics, at least in her family they did.

*****

After the dinner, Thad and Lauren headed back to Connecticut. "I apologize for my family's behavior. I never dreamed they could be so rude to a guest." Lauren laid her head on the back of the seat. "Do you mind if we don't discuss this right now? I have a terrible headache." They continued the trip in silence.

Thad parked the car in front of her house. "How are you feeling, now? Do you still have the headache?"

Lauren had taken some ibuprofen before they left Massachusetts, and there was barely a trace of the headache now. "I'm better. Do you want to come in for a while?" He unlocked the door and stepped aside to allow her to enter. "I noticed you didn't have dessert either. I have some chocolate cake and some whipped topping."

"It must be devil's food because you have tempted me, but first things first. Do you realize I've been in your company for over nine hours, and haven't gotten so much as a peck on the cheek?" He reached for her and received a kiss. "That's much better. Now, I'll help you with the other dessert," he teased. "I'm going to be forced to start a vigorous exercise routine if I'm going to be staying around you. Do you make desserts every week?"

"I do. Half of this I gave to Jennifer. I usually make something to take to the workers at the senior citizen center every week. Now, what is this, if I'm going to be staying around you?"

"I think I should amend that too, since I am."

"That's better, mister." She laughed.

"I like you, Lauren. Let me have that." He reached for her plate and fork. After he had rinsed them, he placed them on the rack. Catching Lauren's hand, he then led her into the den. "Come here, sweetheart." He sat on the sofa and pulled her to him so that her head rested on his chest. "I'm ready to talk now, love. I don't know how much of what I'm going to tell you, will have an effect on our relationship."

He stroked her hair. "First, I'm going to apologize, again for my family's behavior. It was rude and crass. Second, this should have been first. I'm deeply in love with you. I know what I'm going to tell you might drive you away." He sighed deeply. "But, it's a chance I must take."

Brad went on to say, "You see, my family is fourth generation Bostonians, third generation money, and second generation snobs. They've fought to attain the highest degree of acceptability, and they're on first name basis with all of the muck-a-muck senators, governors, former presidents, etc. They run with the Martha's Vineyard, Cape Cod country club set. Having switched from the Baptist faith, they raised us as Catholic because that's the faith of most people they want to impress."

Lauren snuggled closer to him.

"Gene and I were expected to attend Princeton, but not on financial aid— that was considered beneath the Bradfords. My parents paid Gene's tuition, but I earned a four-year academic scholarship to Harvard. Both of us joined fraternities, lettered in sports, and joined all the elite academic and social clubs. In other words, we made our parents proud. It didn't matter whether or not we were happy.

Our sisters did the same at Brown. After school, they married the men our parents had selected for them. They've made their contributions to family and society by having at least one child each. At any time, they could quit work and claim their rightful positions as society ladies. Their husbands earn enough to keep them in the lifestyle they are used to. But I think they continue to work because they are bored and unhappy.

Abigail's parents and my parents are best friends. She was born a year after I was. Our parents decided we were meant for each other. All the way through college, she and I went along with it." Again, he stroked Lauren's arm.

While I was in med school, Abigail was involved with several guys, and became pregnant. She had an abortion. Neither she, nor my parents know that I'm aware of this. Even without that bit of knowledge, I wasn't going to marry her. I'm not going to let my parents push me into a loveless marriage.

I've been fighting with them continually since Thanksgiving, about what they deem as my lack of commitment. When I learned all the families were planning a ski trip together, during Christmas, I would have come back here had I not let Gene talk me into going. Things didn't go well. Abigail did a lot of crying, and both sets of parents treated me as if I was some kind of ogre.

My parents, as usual, hosted a large New Year's Eve party for about two hundred of their closest friends. During that time, I was summoned to my father's office where he and Mr. Higgins were. He told me that he and my mother, as well as Mr. and Mrs. Higgins, were expecting me to propose to Abigail at mid-night. They had even purchased the engagement ring." Lauren glanced at him. "I told them I was sorry for their trouble, but I wasn't in love with Abigail, and I had no intention of marrying her. My father read me the riot act, and among other things, said that for thirty-three years the two families had been planning this marriage, and they were not going to let me spoil it now. If I wanted to sow my wild oats with that little tart I'd been running around with, then so be it, but I was going to marry Abigail Higgins.

A few minutes before midnight, I wished my sisters and my mother Happy New Year, and then I left. That's the reason my mother called on New Year's Day. My father had relayed the entire encounter to her, and she was furious with me.

At the end of January, I went back to Boston, thinking everyone had had time to calm down, but my parents were still angry with me, telling me how much I'd hurt and embarrassed them. They said, poor Abigail had been ordered to bed. She was on the verge of a nervous breakdown, as was her mother.

I had gone to see Abigail to tell her how sorry I was if I'd hurt her. She was only concerned about being embarrassed. Now, she'd have to go away, she couldn't hold her head up in this town, any more.

As you know, after Thanksgiving, I stopped going to Boston every weekend. I hated what they did to you at the university. In the world I grew up in, if it had been one of ours with children born out of wedlock, the subject would never have been brought up. Your neighbors are socialite wannabes. They're loosely connected to someone on the board of directors who was pushing his own candidate for the DON position. They were seeking brownie points.

As I told you before, I admired the way you handled the entire situation. You could have made a public stink, and embarrassed the hospital and university, but you put the concern of your daughters before your own needs. Only a handful of people knew, or even cared about what you were going through. You held your head high and continued your pursuit of helping others. I was then, as I am now, so very proud to be your friend." Thad caressed her hand.

I was very surprised when I woke up Christmas Eve and realized I'm in love with you. I tried the love on to see how it fits, and I love the free, unencumbered feel of it. When you told me the story surrounding your friends' death, my heart ached for you and the girls. I should have known you were becoming more than just a friend.

Gene and I talked several times since New Year's Eve. During our last conversation before you met them, I told him about you. He and Joan liked you right away.

Gene is his own man, but he lets our parents think they rule him, to a certain extent. Anyway, they really were on their way home when they stopped by, but they detoured on purpose hoping to meet you. I'm glad they did."

A blush reddened Lauren's cheeks. "Thanks."

"Unless there's a drastic change, my sisters will always go along with whatever our parents say. Their husbands will never go against our father. I should have known better than to think my parents would accept you, or any woman other than Abigail. I believe my parents asked me to bring you to dinner, just to prove you wouldn't fit in, and that Abigail is their choice for me. They were rude, bullying, and selfish.

Again, Lauren. You exhibited what a lady you are, and probably saved all of us some embarrassment. However, I'll let my mother know how I feel about what she did. She can't force me to change my mind. You were wise not to let your daughters become subjected to this. Even you couldn't have kept me quiet, if they were attacked.

I love my family, and I'm proud of their accomplishments, but I don't like the way they wield authority or the way they look down on anyone they think is beneath or inferior to them. I don't like the fact that they're snobs or the fact that I have exhibited some of the same tendencies in the past."

Thad turned to face Lauren. "I'm telling you this because I love you. It would hurt me so much if you feel that my family's snobbishness is more than you want to put up with, but I'll understand. If you decide to stay with me, my parents are not going to make your life easy. They're used to people complying with their wishes. Please know that whichever way you decide. If it's at all in my power, I won't let anyone harm you or your daughters. You are my love."

They sat in silence for several minutes without changing positions.

"Brad, would you care for something to drink?"

"Yes, some tea, please if it's not too much trouble."

Lauren brought the tea back to the den. They sat sipping. Only their breathing penetrated the quietness.

"Lauren?"

Lauren placed her cup on the coffee table, and turned so she once again faced him. "What do you want me to say?"

"I can tell you what I want you to say, but I really want you to tell me what you're feeling."

Lauren took a deep breath and let it out before speaking further. "During the past few months, after I admitted to myself that I have deep feelings for you, I've grown to like and love you even more. You've become a very big part of our lives, and I don't want to lose that. You've told me enough that would make the average woman run for her life. Your family has treated me shamefully. There's a lot more that I could say about that, but it profits me nothing. You say you love me. Well, that love is about to be put to the test. How much are you willing to sacrifice for this love? From all you've told me, and from all I've seen—you stand to lose a lot. It boils down to you having to choose me over your family.

You said you will let no harm come to my daughters or to me. I'm holding you to your word. I love you dearly, and I can endure almost anything as long as I know you are supporting and protecting me. Please know that I'll go against even you to protect my children. Is that what you want to hear?"

"That's what I needed to hear, my love." Thad reached for her hand. "Remember on New Year's Day I told you I needed a friend, and I asked you to trust me. To give me some time? This is what it was all about. My love for you, and you loving me in return, far out- weighs anything tangible that I could lose. I'm committed to our love."

After a moment of quiet reflection, Thad stood and announced it was late, he should be leaving. Lauren stood and he embraced her. "I love you, Lauren. Thank you for not running away."

"Why would I run away from the man I love? I think we should continue to keep our relationship out of the workplace. The less drama, the better."

"I agree. Good night, darling."

"Good night. Drive safely."

CHAPTER THIRTEEN

At the end of April, Thad hosted a small surprise party at his house to celebrate Lauren's birthday. As a ruse, Thad's nurse had called her at about five-thirty to tell her Thad was about ten minutes from wrapping up an emergency surgery. He'd asked if instead of him driving to her house to get her, that she'd meet him at his house at six-thirty.

Thad answered the door, appearing to be rushed as he paused in buttoning his shirt cuff to kiss her. "Come in, love. I'm about ready." He led her to the den.

"Surprise!" Everyone yelled, when Lauren entered with Thad on her heels.

"Thaddeus Bradford, you're in big trouble," she whispered, as happy birthday was sung. "Thank you, guys." She smiled with her hand over her heart, and teased the heart surgeon. "Ryan, now you see why you were invited? You guys are wonderful. Thank you for being here." She mingled with the celebrants.

Lauren approached Gene." Thanks for coming. You don't know how much this means to me, and to Thad. I'm indebted to you."

"You've made him very happy. He's happier than I have ever seen him. It is I, who am indebted to you." He hugged her and wished her happy birthday, again.

At ten o'clock, everyone gathered around the table for cake cutting, toasts, and gifts. Thad was the last one to make his presentation and toast. "Lauren, you are the embodiment of integrity, beauty, intelligence, warmth, compassion, diplomacy, and love." He dropped on one knee and opened a box containing a beautiful diamond engagement ring. Taking her left hand in his he asked, "Will you marry me?"

With tears of joy brimming in her eyes, she embraced him. "Yes."

The guests recovered well enough to applaud her decision. Now, there were the inevitable questions to answer.

Vivian was the first to speak. “You mean to tell me that the two of you have been dating? And, you never told anyone? Why the secrecy?”

“Wow!’ Linda interjected. “Hidden in plain sight. Right under our noses.”

Thad draped an arm around Lauren’s shoulder and pulled her close. He smiled and called out, "May I have your attention please?” Everyone stopped talking and turned their attention to him. "Those of you here, are among our dearest friends. You all know what Lauren has endured these past months. We didn’t want her subjected to more gossip, so we kept it quiet. We’ve been seeing each other since Thanksgiving. We’ve discussed telling you all several times, but we had other hurdles to jump first. This was my way of killing two birds with one stone.” He glanced at Lauren and gave her a loving squeeze.

Troy spoke up, “Congratulations to you both. Lauren, we haven’t known you as long as we’ve known Thad, but we love and support you.”

“Hear, hear,” the others chimed in.

*****

Lauren and Gene sat at the table talking after the other guests left. "Lauren, as much as it pains me to have to own up to this, you need to know that you and Thad are in for a rough time from our parents. I know you’ve already been subjected to their rudeness, but it’s going to get much worse once they hear that Thad has asked you to marry him. I love my family, but I don’t always agree with them.”

Lauren brushed a strand of hair out of face. “I appreciate your support, Gene. I told Thad that I can put up with a lot as long as he stands by me. I'll never intentionally disrespect your parents, but I will protect myself.”

Joan had sat quietly listening to the exchange between Gene and Lauren. "Since you didn’t know Thad was going to propose, I'm sure you don’t have an idea when you'll get married.”

“No. I haven’t had time to give it any thought.

This," she held her hand up to show the ring, "is a complete surprise. We aren't in a hurry are we, Brad?"

Joan raised an eyebrow. "Brad?"

"She's the only one who can get away with calling me that," answered Thad. "And yes my love, I am in a hurry."

"Is September too long to wait?"

"It is, but I'll give it some consideration."

* * * * *

Thad asked Lauren to accompany him to Boston for Mothers' Day. She refused, saying she was the last person his mother wanted to see on Mothers' Day, or any day for that matter. Instead, she attended church services with Mrs. Brown, Jennifer, and the girls. Afterwards, she treated Mrs. Brown and Jennifer to a Mother's Day dinner.

When Lauren returned home, she noted a Boston area phone number on the caller ID. She assumed Thad had left his cell phone at home and was calling from a family member's phone. Instead of returning the call, she decided to wait until he called again. When Thad called later that night, he didn't mention an earlier call, and she forgot to ask him about it.

CHAPTER FOURTEEN

For the girls' first birthday, Lauren took them to a studio to have their portraits taken. As she was preparing to leave, she saw an unfamiliar car parked across the street from her house. It appeared unoccupied. Thad met her at the studio so they could take the girls to the zoo.

While Lauren strapped Brianna into her car seat, she glanced up to see what looked like the same car. She closed the door, and turned so her back was to the street. "Kiss me, Brad."

"Huh?" He seemed surprised.

"Kiss me, sweetheart." After a gentle kiss, she held him to her and gazed into his eyes. "Do you see that black sedan over my left shoulder? I think I saw that same car parked across the street from my house before I left."

"Let's continue as if we haven't seen it. I don't see anyone in it. I'm going back inside. You head home. I'll follow you in a minute."

"Brad." She could hear the alarm in her own voice.

"It's all right, baby. I'm going inside so I can take a picture of the vehicle with my phone. I don't want to be seen doing it. I'll be right behind you. Drive normally." He kissed her again and whispered, "It'll be all right."

With nerves on fire, Lauren drove the five miles to her house. She noted that the vehicle followed her, but continued on when she turned into her driveway. She parked the car in the garage, and sat there trembling until Thad drove up. He closed the garage door, and then helped her out of the car. She immediately went to her daughters. Neither she, nor Thad spoke until they had taken the children inside.

Lauren stayed near the girls. "Do you think I need to call the police? This can't be just a coincidence."

"Come here, sweetheart." He held her shaky body close to his. "It doesn't seem like a coincidence to me, either. I was able to get a couple of good pictures of the car, but not of the plate number.

Lawrence's brother, Alan, is a captain on the police force. I promised you that I would take care of you and the girls. Do you trust me to take care of this for you?"

"I trust you, but I'm afraid for my children. I have no idea what this could be about."

"Neither do I, baby. Let me call Alan and see what he says. We aren't going to let this incident dictate our lives. Okay?"

"I really don't feel up to going to the zoo, now. I'm going to change the girls, then give them lunch. Are you hungry? I have cold cuts, chicken salad, and cold fried chicken"

"Chicken salad would be fine, thanks. I'm going to call Alan. You do what you have to do."

The twins were taking a nap, and Mrs. Brown was out for the afternoon. Lauren and Thad had eaten lunch, and sat in the living room talking when the doorbell rang. Lauren glanced quickly at him.

"I'll get it." Thad went to the door and opened it. "Hello, Alan. Come in. Thanks for coming by. Lauren, this is Alan Wilcox, Larry's brother."

"Please to meet you, Captain. Have a seat," Lauren invited.

"Call me Alan, and it's nice to meet you too. Thad tells me you might have a problem. Tell me about it."

Lauren related the details of the day's events, including all that Thad had witnessed. When asked if there were any other unexplained happenings, she answered no except for the call on Mother's Day.

Thad assured her that he had not tried to call her, and that he did have his cell phone with him.

Alan asked if the number was still on the caller ID. Lauren located the number, and the captain copied it. "Lauren, no matter how insignificant, please write down anything that occurs out of the ordinary. I'm not ready to say that today's activities are significant, nor am I ready to dismiss them. However, I'll investigate them. Thad, I'll need a copy of those photos if you can download them for me. It would be best if you don't speak to anyone else about this. If there's something to this, we don't want to tip our hand."

Thad closed the door behind Alan, and then draped an arm around Lauren. "Feel better?"

"Not really. For this to have happened at all is very unsettling."

"Do you want me to spend the night?"

"Wouldn't that be tipping our hand? If indeed someone is following me, they already know that you don't live here."

"You have a point, but since we planned to spend the day together anyway, I'll just stay the rest of the day with you."

"Thank you. You'll not get an argument from me on that. Let's sit in the den."

Later in the day, after dinner, the phone rang. Since the ID showed unknown caller, Lauren decided to let it go to voice mail.

Mrs. Brown returned home at about eight-thirty. "Hello Ms. Jeffries, Dr. Bradford." She looked around. "Oh. I saw a car parked across the street in front of the house. I thought you had company."

Thad jumped up. "Is it still there?" He crossed the room to the window.

Mrs. Brown glanced from Lauren to Thad. "It was, when I came in. What's going on?"

"It's gone now. Did you see anyone in the car, Mrs. Brown?"

"I couldn't see anyone, that's why I thought someone was visiting."

"Mrs. Brown, come and sit with us for a bit. We need to discuss something with you." Lauren patted a spot on the sofa.

Thad concluded the story of the day's events. "So, we need you to be very observant as you go about your daily activities. Until further notice, don't take the girls for their daily walk, and keep an eye out for any strange vehicles or people in the vicinity."

Just as he was ending the warning, the phone rang. This time, the words no data appeared on the screen. Again they opted not to answer it. Lauren stared at the phone.

"That's odd. It's been months since we've gotten so much as a wrong number, and suddenly there are three suspicious calls-two in the same day."

Thad looked thoughtful. "It is strange. Are you sure you don't want me to spend the night?"

"I'm sure about tonight. I can't be sure about any other night if this keeps up."

"Lauren, I have to be going." Thad reached for her. "Promise me you'll call me if anything else happens. No matter what time it is."

"I will. Are you going to call Captain Wilcox, or shall I?"

"I will, since I witnessed all that you did. You take care, darling." He pulled her into a tight embrace. "Call me just before you turn in for the night."

The phone rang at ten o'clock. Recognizing the Wilcox name, Lauren picked up.

"Ms. Jeffries?"

"Please, call me Lauren."

"Okay, Lauren. Thad stopped by to tell me the latest. I don't believe these incidents are coincidental. A patrol car has been assigned to make several passes on your block during the night. You be careful, and call the number I gave you at any time. I'll check in with you after business hours tomorrow."

Lauren had spent most of the night peeking out the window, trying to see if she could spot the strange vehicle. She took a little comfort in seeing the police cruiser go by. She'd had very little sleep by the time she had to get ready for work.

The phone was ringing when Lauren stepped into her office the next morning. She picked it up and answered. "Lauren Jefferies."

"Good morning, sweetheart. How are you?"

Lauren plopped into a chair. "I was awake all night, and I'm exhausted. How are you?"

"Concerned. Nothing new, I hope?"

"No. Nothing. Thank God. I did spot the police car last night. I'm so sleepy that I can barely function. After the board meeting I'm going home."

"That's a good idea. I'll see you at the meeting."

*****

Later, in the boardroom, Dr. Mason nodded toward Lauren's finger. "Dr. Jeffries I see congratulations are in order."

Oh, darn! In all the excitement of the past twenty-four hours, she'd forgotten to take the ring off. This was the first time she'd worn it to work.

"Thanks." She replied, her tone dry.

"Lauren!" Vivian cried. "How beautiful! Congratulations." Vivian acted as if she wasn't aware of the engagement.

Several others added their congratulations.

The cat is out of the bag now, Lauren thought as she neared her office after the meeting. *How careless of me. I need to call Thad and apologize.* The phone was ringing when she stepped into her office. She rushed to answer it. "Hello."

"Congratulations, Dr. Jeffries." She heard Thad laugh into the phone. "Anyone I know?"

"You are a funny man, Thaddeus Bradford. Are you watching me? You always manage to call just as I'm walking in the door."

Thad laughed. "Yes I am. So you'd better be careful lady."

"Oh Brad, I'm so sorry. I guess I was too weary to take the ring off last night and too exhausted to think to do it this morning."

"Don't worry, sweetheart. If it wasn't for the trouble it would cause you, I would shout it from the roof top. I love you, woman."

"Thank you, darling. I'm about to leave, now. I'll see you later. Won't I?"

"Of course, you will."

*****

Nothing suspicious happened on Monday or Tuesday. However, on Wednesday morning, Janet told Lauren that two calls had come in for her, but the caller didn't leave a message. She couldn't identify the caller as male or female. Since the calls had come through the university's switchboard, there was no way of determining their origin.

When she left work later in the afternoon, Lauren admired a yellow Mustang convertible parked two spaces down from where she parked. Later, when she turned into her driveway, she noticed a yellow Mustang convertible passed her driveway just as she drove into her garage. The driver wore a baseball cap and sunshades; making an identification almost impossible.

CHAPTER FIFTEEN

Gene and Joan invited Lauren to a cookout at their home to celebrate Memorial Day. Gene added the disclaimer that the entire family would be there, and as much as they wanted her to come, they would understand if she decided not to. Thad also understood her reluctance to attend, but begged her to go anyway. He told her not to let his family intimidate her. In addition, he didn't want to leave her in lieu of the strange activities of the past weeks.

At one year old, the girls were wobbling around, testing their footing, and like most toddlers, were very curious. They got into everything, therefore had to be watched every second. They were pretty little girls who were the mirror image of each other. In order to distinguish one from the other, Lauren always added an article of clothing with their name on it. Today, they wore little baubles in their hair that spelled out their names.

Joan greeted them as they entered the spacious back yard where the family was gathered. "I finally get to meet the twins." She cried. "Lauren, they are beautiful. How do you tell one from the other?" She reached for Brianna who was in Lauren's arms while Brittany looked on from the security of Thad's arms.

"I branded them," Lauren joked, as she pointed to the names on the baubles.

Lauren noted that the Bradford clan, sans Gene and Joan, all sat together, and they all wore scowls of disapproval at the sight of Lauren and the twins.

Elaine scowled. "They are beautiful, Lauren. I didn't know you had children. I thought you said that you had never been married."

Lauren glanced over her shoulder at Elaine. "That's right. I haven't."

Joan handed Brianna back to Lauren. "Here it comes. Hang in there," she whispered.

"Where is their father?" Elaine continued.

Dang! Again with the questions. "He's dead."

Elaine's lips turned up into a sneer. "Too bad you couldn't get him to marry you before he died."

Thad turned sharply. "That's enough, Elaine," he warned.

"Your sister is right," Mrs. Bradford chimed in nastily. "That's the chance you take when you sleep around."

"At least she didn't have an abortion," Thad shot back.

Lauren decided that this was a good time to take the girls inside to feed them. Mrs. Bradford paled. She sputtered, and then practically ran into the house.

Mr. Bradford turned on Thad. "How dare you upset your mother behind some low life tart? You bring her and her bastards around decent people, and expect us to accept them. Well, if that's what you think, you can think again."

Thad was happy that Lauren had taken the girls inside, so as not to witness his father's tirade. Not so for his siblings and the other guests, many who hung their heads in embarrassment.

Gene approached his father and calmly told him that Lauren and her children were his invited guests, and that he expected them to be treated with the same respect afforded the other guests.

Mr. Bradford continued his loud rant. "Well, you can have them at your house, but I'm telling you, Thad, they are not welcome in my house."

"If that's the case Father, I guess I'm not welcome either." Thad replied with quiet fury.

"What! What did you say?" Mr. Bradford shouted in disbelief. "You would turn your back on your family for some…"

"What, Father? What do any of you know about Lauren? Absolutely nothing. You're a bunch of judgmental snobs." He turned and stomped into the house.

Thad headed for the kitchen. "Joan, I'm sorry, but it appears that inviting Lauren was a bad idea. I'm taking her away from here before I say or do something that I'll later regret. Thanks for everything. Let's go, sweetheart." He picked up one of the girls and headed for the front door.

Gene rushed into the kitchen. "Hey, Thad wait up. I'm sorry about that, man. You don't have to leave. This is my house. You, Lauren, and the girls are my guests. You're always welcome here, and you can stay for as long as you like."

"I know that, Gene, and I appreciate it, but I'm not going to subject Lauren and the girls to anymore of this. I can't believe that he and mother can be so shameful; so hypocritical."

"Thaddeus!" Mr. Bradford bellowed, as he entered the kitchen. "I want to talk to you. Right, now. In private."

"Not today, Father. I think you've already said enough. Let's go, Lauren."

"You walk out of that door and you'll…"

"Father!" exclaimed Gene. "I think enough has been said today. Leave him alone."

"Who do you think you're talking to? Stay out of this."

"This is my house, Father. Thad and Lauren are my guests, and they've been hurt enough. They're leaving, now."

Lauren and Thad settled the girls in their car seats. Lauren glanced at Thad. "Do you want me to drive, love?"

Thad squeezed her shoulder and held the door open for her. "No. I'm okay."

Lauren could see the muscles tensing in Thad's jaw. He clenched and unclenched his teeth. She slid closer to him, caught his hand in hers, and gave it a gentle squeeze, which he returned.

Once home Lauren put the girls down for a late nap and returned to the den where she spied Thad standing on the porch with his hands in his pockets staring out into the yard. Her heart ached for him. *No man should have to choose between the woman he loves and his family. If I had any doubts as to whether or not he loves me, he erased them today.*

Thad turned toward her when she stepped onto the porch. He leaned against one of the columns and stretched out his hand to pull her to him. "I'm so sorry, baby. I don't know what I've gotten you into. I can't believe that those people are the same parents I've known all my life. They are like strangers. I wouldn't blame you if you walked away from this mess."

Lauren slipped out of his arms to look up at him. She placed one hand on either side of his face and stared intently into his eyes. "Darling, I love you. I promised you that if you protected my daughters and me, I would stay with you. You've done that. I have no reason to turn away from you. I just don't like what it's costing you."

"I really need you, now."

"I'll always be here."

* * * * *

The ringing of the telephone roused Lauren out of a deep sleep. She groaned and glanced at the clock on the nightstand. *Three a.m.! Who would be calling at this ungodly hour?* "Hello? Hello?" All she could hear was heavy breathing, so she hung up and went to check on the girls and Mrs. Brown. All three were sleeping soundly. She peeked out the window but all she saw was the patrol car as it went by.

The next afternoon Lauren and Captain Wilcox sat in her kitchen talking. "Lauren, I told you to call me if anything else happened as soon as it happened."

"I know, but I just couldn't bring myself to call you at three in the morning."

"You should have told me about the other calls, too." He shook his head. "So? There have been two vehicle sightings and three phone calls since Sunday? I suggest we put a trace on your phone. I don't believe that anyone is out to do you physical harm. Someone is trying to frighten you. We're going to need a list, detailing every incident or run-in you've had since you came here. I'll need it as soon as you can compile it.

At this point, I think you're the only target. Remain vigilant and don't talk about this with anyone except Thad and Mrs. Brown. Don't mention any of this to anyone. We're still trying to protect our edge. Right now we don't know who or what we are dealing with. And Lauren, anytime, okay? Any time."

"Okay, Captain."

The phone rang just as Alan stepped out of the door. He hesitated until Lauren answered it. "Hello? Hello?" Again, she could only hear heavy breathing before the caller hung up.

"What is it, Lauren?"

"Another heavy breather, but this number has an out of state area code."

"Here, let me record the details." Alan pulled a pad from his breast pocket. I'm going to schedule the set-up for the phone trace, and I'll call you to give you the particulars. Wait a minute. He pulled a cell phone from his hip and dialed a number. After a short conversation, he turned back to her. "They should be here within the next hour. Give me a call when they've finished."

Lauren placed a call to Thad's office to ask what time he would be finished for the day. His secretary said that he was still in surgery and expected to be out in thirty to forty minutes. She left a message for him to call her as soon as he finished.

While she waited for Thad's call, she began to compile the list that Captain Wilcox had asked for. Unless the welcoming committee was up to their old tricks again, she couldn't see anything to be concerned about in what she had written.

At six-thirty, she called the hospital again. Dr. Bradford had already left the hospital. She reached him at home. "Hello, sweetheart, why didn't you return my call?"

"I'm sorry, Lauren. I didn't know that you called. I hurried home to shower and change before I came to see you. Is everything okay?"

"I need you."

"What is it?"

"Just come. I'll tell you when you get here."

"All right. I just stepped out of the shower. I'll be there in fifteen or twenty minutes."

The technicians from the police department arrived at the same time as Thad. A male and female agent shook his hand and embraced him, "Just in case we're being watched." The female whispered in Thad's ear to follow their lead.

"What's going on?" Thad asked as they entered the house and closed the door behind them.

"You're Thaddeus Bradford?"

“Yes I am. Who are you? What’s going on?” He asked for the third time as he stood near Lauren.

“We're FBI. I’m Agent Dan Coles, and this is Agent Rona Peters. The technicians are going to install surveillance equipment and put a trace on Ms. Jeffries’ telephone. Right now, we're treating this as harassment and we want to stop it before it escalates.

Thad draped an arm over her shoulder. "Are you all right, Lauren?”

“As all right as I can be. I’ll be so happy to get my life back to normal. Who could be doing this? And why?”

“That’s what we are trying to find out, Ms. Jeffries,” said Agent Coles.

*****

On Tuesday morning, Janet buzzed Lauren’s phone. "There's a Mrs. Bradford on line two for you, Dr. Jeffries.”

Lauren picked up the receiver. “Hi Joan, what’s up?”

“This is Mrs. L.C. Bradford.” Velma Bradford spoke with an air of superiority.

“How are you, Mrs. Bradford?”

“I’m well. I will be in Elmwood today and I want you to meet me for lunch.”

“Thank you, no. I don’t want to have lunch with you, unless you're planning to apologize.”

"Apologize? To You? Never!”

“Goodbye, Mrs. Bradford.”

At five o’clock, Lauren returned to her office to see Velma Bradford sitting in her outer office. "Mrs. Bradford.” She greeted and continued into her office.

Janet Mosley stood in open mouthed astonishment as Mrs. Bradford followed Lauren into the office and closed the door in her face when she attempted to follow them.

Lauren pressed the intercom button. "Ms. Mosley, hold all of my calls, please. This shouldn’t take long. I left your steno pad near the phone.”

This was a signal that Lauren and Janet had devised to let Janet know that the intercom should be left on, and that any conversation she heard needed to be transcribed. "Now, Mrs. Bradford, what can I do for you?"

"You can leave my son alone. If you think that his father and I are going to sit by and let you sully our family name, you are sadly mistaken. You will never marry my son you little, low life harlot. The nerve of you! Do you think that you and those sniveling brats of yours will ever get your hands on any of the Bradford fortune?"

At the reference to her daughters, Lauren moved from behind her desk and headed for the door. She opened it and lashed out, "You can take your bigoted, selfish, society rear end out of my office."

"Why you—" Mrs. Bradford raised her hand to slap Lauren, but Lauren caught it before it landed a blow.

"Be careful." Lauren clenched her teeth. "If you slap me, I will slap back. The choice is yours." She released Mrs. Bradford's wrist.

Velma Bradford stormed out of the office. "You will pay for this, you slut. Just you wait. You will pay!" Lauren turned and walked slowly back to her desk.

Janet stood at the door, her mouth opened in disbelief. "Dr. Jeffries, are you all right? Was that Dr. Bradford's mother?"

"Come in Janet and close the door. None of what you just witnessed is to leave this room. None of it. Do you understand?"

"Yes. Of, course. I taped the whole conversation, but I can't believe she attacked you like that."

"I guess she was trying to protect her own the best way she could. Through intimidation."

"Dr. Jeffries, I hate to tell you this, but I was really afraid for you. She was so angry. Her face was so distorted, she looked like a demon. Was she really going to hit you? What did she mean leave her son alone?"

Lauren glanced at Janet and smiled.

"What? Am I missing something?"

Lauren opened a folder and continued to smile. "Dr. Bradford and I are engaged to be married."

Janet fell into a chair. "You're what! Are you kidding me? How did the two of you manage to keep it off of the hospital grapevine?"

"By not telling a single soul."

"How long have you been engaged?"

"Five months."

"You are kidding! No one knows?"

"Except for a few members on the board, no one knows. At least they didn't. I think that after that little demonstration a few minutes ago it won't be a secret for long."

" Are you going to tell Dr. Bradford about this?"

"Not unless I'm forced to. Now, may I have that tape, please?"

Janet brought the tape back to Lauren. "Congratulations, doctor. I hope you know that you can trust me. You're a spunky lady, and I'm learning a lot from you."

"Thanks, Janet. I do trust you, but it doesn't hurt to reiterate ever so often. I think things are about to get really ugly."

*****

The calls came at least twice a day at the office as well as at home at no particular time. Without explanation Lauren had asked her family to call her on her cell phone or at the office when they needed to talk to her. She purchased a cell phone for Mrs. Brown to use as well.

On Thursday evening, Lauren strolled with the girls to Jennifer's house for a visit. On her return trip home, she spotted the infamous black sedan following at a snail's pace behind her. She steeled herself not to run or look back. She took out her cell phone and pushed a number on the speed dial. "Alan, this is Lauren Jeffries. I'm walking four blocks from my house with my daughters, and there is a black sedan following me."

She was within two blocks of her house when she saw the patrol car turn the corner. She hadn't heard the black sedan stop, but now she heard a vehicle speeding along an adjacent street.

Again she picked up the phone. "Alan, the vehicle sped away before the patrol car arrived."

"We checked the camera after you called and did catch a dark colored sedan passing your house at five-thirty. Be careful, Lauren."

The next day, as Lauren was backing out of her garage, she spotted a package on her front doorstep. As she neared the steps, she could see what appeared to be blood seeping from the box. She turned toward the street just in time to see the black sedan speed away. On shaky legs, Lauren approached the box. Instead of opening it, she rang the doorbell. Surprise registered on Mrs. Brown's face when she opened the door to see Lauren standing there. "Ms. J., I thought you left minutes ago. Did you forget something?"

"No. I didn't forget anything." Lauren pointed to the box. "I need you to be here when I open this box."

"Oh my! Oh my!" Mrs. Brown exclaimed at the sight of the blood. "Maybe you shouldn't open it. Let's call the police."

"Let me take a peek first, and then we'll call them." Lauren broke a twig from a nearby tree, and then with caution, used it to open the flap on the box. The two women hesitated, leaned forward and peered into the box. Their faces paled as they eyed the carcass of a cat. "Go back inside, Mrs. Brown. I will call Agent Coles."

* * * * *

Lauren had called Agent Coles to report the incident, but told him that because of work commitments, she couldn't meet with him until after work hours.

Later in the day, they sat discussing the incident. "Mrs. Jeffries, I no longer feel that this is simple harassment. A dead cat is a not so veiled threat of violence. We're going to assign an agent to you and your family. Now, I need you to go over everything that has happened since we last talked."

After Lauren finished relating the latest incidents to Agent Coles, Thad asked her if he could have a private talk with her. She escorted Dan to the door, and then led Thad into the study.

He closed the door and stared intently at Lauren for a few seconds before he spoke. "I thought you trusted me."

Lauren frowned. "I do trust you. How can you doubt that?"

Thad stared into her eyes for a long moment. "Why didn't you tell me that my mother paid you a visit?" Lauren gasped. "If you trusted me, you would have told me, Lauren."

"I didn't tell you because I love you, and I didn't want to hurt you. It had nothing to do with trust. It was very ugly, Brad."

"Together, Lauren. You and I are in this together, against the whole world if necessary. I heard her side of the story. Do you want to tell me yours?"

"Don't put yourself through this. I'm not concerned about it, anymore. She had her say, let it go at that."

Thad sighed and massaged his moustache. "I need to know the truth, Lauren."

" Are you sure you want to hear it?"

"I'm sure."

Lauren unlocked a desk drawer, removed the tape, and placed it in the player. She watched as the pain of what he was hearing ravished Thad's face. The muscles jumped in his face as he clenched his jaws and pounded his fist into the palm of his hand.

"I'm sorry. I didn't want you to hear this."

"You're sorry?" Thad exploded. "I should be apologizing to you. She lied and told me that you had attacked her, and that she had to defend herself. How could she!"

Lauren touched his arm. "Let it go, darling. Janet witnessed the entire episode. As a matter of fact, she's the one who secretly taped it. I warned her not to mention it to anyone."

"This, on top of all of the other mess. I'm going to spend the night tonight."

"That's not necessary. An agent is going to be stationed here around the clock." She hesitated for a second. "There's something else." Thad glanced at her.

"Agent Coles told me to write down everything that's happened in the past two weeks. I didn't mention the incident with your mother."

"You should have told them. It would give them a chance to exonerate her."

"I didn't want to hurt you. So, do I amend the list?"

"For the sake of credibility I think you should. And Lauren, thanks for wanting to protect me, but don't keep anything from me again, no matter how much you think it would hurt me. Promise?"

"I promise." They shared a warm embrace before going back to the den.

The phone rang just as Lauren was saying good night to Agent Wendy Green. "Go ahead answer it, Ms. Jeffries."

"Hello?"

"You've been warned." A raspy voice uttered before the phone went dead.

There were several heavy breathers over the weekend, but no more dead animals. Lauren was encouraged to go about her normal activities as much as she could.

Early Saturday morning, she and Thad took the girls on a drive two towns away where they perused antique shops for several hours, ate lunch, then returned home without incident.

On Sunday morning, Agent Green accompanied Lauren, Mrs. Brown, and the twins to church. Lauren was pleasantly surprised when Thad slid into the pew beside her and took her hand in his.

Normally, she would let the girls go to the nursery, but today she decided to let them stay with her. She held Brittany, and Mrs. Brown, who sat between her and Agent Green, held Brianna.

Just before the benediction, Lauren called Agent Green's attention to a tall brunette, wearing a wide brimmed hat that all but covered her face, hurrying out of the church. Agent Green hurried after her, but the woman was nowhere to be seen.

After lunch, Lauren sat on the lawn in the back yard, watching the girls play while Agent Green kept a watchful eye on them all.

Thad joined them for dinner, and afterwards, he and Lauren walked to Jennifer's house to see one week old, Megan Renee. Jennifer was to join her husband in Germany in five weeks. Due to all of the drama in her own life, Lauren had not been able to spend as much time with Jennifer as she would have liked.

On the way home from the visit, Thad and Lauren decided to take an indirect route back to her house. As they crossed one of the streets that ran parallel to hers, they saw two cars parked in the middle of the street. The two drivers appeared to be carrying on a conversation. Lauren became anxious when she noted that one of the vehicles was a black sedan. Thad linked her arm in his. "Easy, baby. Let's just keep walking. I'm sure that they can't recognize you from this distance."

CHAPTER SIXTEEN

"Ms. Jeffries, since you're going to be starting summer vacation in a week or so, why don't you plan a trip out of town for a few weeks?" Agent Coles suggested. "We can get you out of town without being detected."

Thad's brows flattened. "That's a great idea, sweetheart. You'll be able to relax for a change."

"No!" Lauren's voice was laced with irritation as she began pacing the floor. "We don't know who is doing this or why. We do know that they are operating in two different states. Where can I go? Remember, I was featured in 'Bio-Feed'. Everyone knows where I came from, where I went to school, and where I was born. So where can I go? I just want my life back. I want to be left alone. I'm so tired. I can't function in unfamiliar surroundings. I need to be able to keep my daughters safe." Tears of frustration and fear rolled down her face.

"Sweetheart." Thad wrapped both of his arms around her.

"Ms. Jeffries…"

"My name is Lauren." She sniffed.

"Lauren. You have a point. Quite honestly, you have weathered this better than any of us have a right to expect of you. If you want to go away, where ever you go, you'll have an agent with you at all times. If you decide to go, let us know so that we can make the arrangements."

Lauren spent the final week of the semester on paperwork and readying materials for the assistant dean of the department, who would be taking over for the summer.

When she neared her car at the end of the day on Tuesday, she noted she had a flat. Upon closer inspection, she noticed that the tire had been slashed.

Lauren summoned the law enforcement personnel to her house. After recounting the tale of the slashed tires, she announced, "I'll be ready to leave any time after church services on Sunday." Thad and Alan Wilcox breathed a sigh of relief.

"I thought you didn't want to go back to Michigan," Alan said.

"I'm not going back to the same town. My house sold three months ago, but my daughters have a house in Bayington. It's about twenty-five minutes from where I used to live. I can hide out there for a couple of weeks."

"Perfect," the captain agreed.

"I'll plan to go with you," Thad announced.

"No, Thad. We need you to continue your normal routine for a while."

"I hate this."

"I know, baby," Thad added, "but for your safety, we've got to do it."

*****

Two days later, Lauren was sitting at her desk when Janet knocked on her door. "Flowers for you, doctor. Looks like long stemmed."

Lauren lifted the lid off the box, and then let out a blood-curdling scream.

"Oh, My God!" She gaped at the contents of the opened box.

"Dr. Jeffries, what is it?"

Lauren stood with one hand covering her mouth, and the other pointing at the box.

"Oh, God!" exclaimed Janet as she eyed the lone, perfectly formed, black rose and one very dead rat.

*****

The FBI deemed the delivery of the black rose and a dead rat a serious threat to Lauren's life. After much coaxing, the bureau convinced Lauren that for her safety she should leave town right away. As a distraction, they would use the cover of a birthday party for her to sneak out without notice.

On Sunday afternoon, Thad and Lauren drove to Jennifer's house for a farewell visit. Lauren had told Jennifer that the welcoming committee was up to their antics again so she wanted to get away for a while.

She wouldn't be back before Jennifer left to meet her husband in Germany. In the meantime, if anyone asked any questions as to her where about, just to say as far as she knew, she was home.

After the visit with Jennifer, Lauren hurried home to prepare for her *birthday party.*

At dusk, cars began to arrive at the house, and the guests, all law enforcement personnel, carried gift-wrapped packages.

The music played loud, the food and drink flowed freely. When the party was in full swing, Lauren and the girls, accompanied by Agent Pamela Thatcher, were on a plane half way to Bayington.

CHAPTER SEVENTEEN

Because Lauren had hired a woman to do general cleaning of the Fredrick's house on a regular basis, it was ready for occupation when they arrived.

So intent was she in putting order to the personal effects of Lydia and Stan that a week had slipped by before Lauren had time to reflect on the reason that she was there.

She didn't have the phone disconnected before she had left for Connecticut, and since no one knew that they were there; they were startled when it rang. Anyone needing to call her still called her on her cell phone. Agent Thatcher checked the caller ID and lifted the receiver. "It was a telemarketer," she announced.

*****

Most of the houses in the neighborhood were occupied by families with small children. Each house had a six-foot high security fence surrounding the backyard. This made it easier for Lauren to relax there with the girls in relative obscurity.

Everyone had agreed that it would be best if Agent Thatcher made all necessary contacts with the public i.e. grocery shopping, gassing the vehicles etc.

Lauren opted not to attend church services while she was hiding out. To the neighbors who had come to call, Pam had reported that Mrs. Davis was recovering from an illness, and was not yet receiving visitors.

Instead of returning to Michigan, Mrs. Brown had decided to spend the time until Lauren returned in New York with her daughter.

*****

On their tenth day in Michigan, Agent Thatcher answered the door to find a thin, unkempt man who appeared to be in his mid-thirties, standing on the other side of the security door.

"May I help you?" she inquired.

The man was obviously nervous and unsure of himself. "Are you Lori Jeffrey?"

"Who wants to know?" Thatcher asked.

"I do. I'm Walter, Walter Burke, Lydia's brother."

"How can I help you, Mr. Burke? Why are you here?"

Burked shuffled his feet. "I want to see the children. My sister's children."

"I'm afraid it's not possible at this time."

"What do you mean not possible? I'm their uncle. I have a right to see them."

"As I said, Mr. Burke, you cannot see the children. Good day."

"I have a right to see them. They're my family. One way or the other," he threatened, "I will see them." Abruptly, he stormed away.

Thatcher watched the man as he skittered down the street. "It's obvious that he doesn't know who you are. I doubt if he's the one behind all those incidents in Connecticut."

"I wonder where he's been all this time. Why is he just showing up? He doesn't know how to pronounce my name either. He referred to me as, Lori Jeffery.

"I noticed that, too." Thatcher reached for her cell phone. "I need to inform my boss of this."

*****

That evening Lauren's cell phone rang. "Hello, Brad. How are you today?"

"I'm well. How are you? I trust that everything is still nice and peaceful."

"I guess all good things must come to an end. Lydia's brother showed up today wanting to see the girls."

"You didn't allow that did you?"

"He didn't see them. Agent Thatcher handled it. I guess he assumed that she was me, and neither of us corrected him. He made a veiled threat that he would see the girls."

"Are you frightened by his sudden appearance?"

"Given the fact that he wasn't able to identify me, I'm not overly concerned. I believe that this is a separate situation."

"Even so, be very careful. I'm going to take a few days off and fly out as soon as I can."

"I'd love that. I miss you so much."

"I miss you like crazy, too. I've got to run. I'll call you later. I love you."

"Love you back."

*****

Lauren learned that she and Agent Thatcher, Pam, were the same age and had a lot in common. They had the same taste in music and fashion; they both enjoyed sewing, but neither had time to devote to it, and they both loved to read and to play board games.

They were enjoying a game of scrabble when the doorbell rang early Wednesday afternoon. "I'll get it." Pam opened the door. She returned with a beautiful arrangement of flowers. "Oh, how I envy you."

"Don't be too quick to do that. You know what happened the last time I received flowers."

"This looks different. Here's the card."

Lauren read, *"By the time you read this I will be there. Thad."*

"What is it Lauren?" Pam asked in response to the furrow on Lauren's brow.

"This is a strange message."

"Is it, darling?" Thad stood smiling from the doorway.

Lauren turned and ran into his outstretched arms. "Brad! Oh, Brad."

Pam took the flowers from her and headed to the kitchen. "I'll put these in water. No one seems to know I'm here, anyway." She mumbled sarcastically.

"Lauren, I've missed you so much. How are you? How are the girls?"

"We are all fine. I just put them down for a nap about fifteen minutes ago. They're going to be so happy to see you."

"You don't think they've forgotten me?"

"No." She laughed. "They're females, and we don't easily forget men like you. Anyway, there's a picture of you in their room."

"Really? How sweet of you. Is there one of me in your room, too?"

Lauren pointed to her chest. "Uh, huh. One in here, too."

"Thanks, Lauren. I love you."

"Are you hungry?"

"A little. I didn't take time to eat before I left this morning."

"Come into the kitchen. Where are your bags?"

"They're in the rental car. I need to make hotel reservations. Any suggestions?"

"Yes. Up the stairs and down the hall to your left."

"Are you sure, Lauren? I don't want to compromise..."

"You're not," Lauren interrupted. "You have your own room and Pam is here to chaperone."

"She's right Dr. Bradford..."

"Thad."

"Okay, Thad it is. She's right. I make a mean chaperone." She patted her gun holster. "Seriously, it would do her good to have you here."

"Thanks, ladies. That's what I really want, but I don't want to cause any trouble."

After dinner, the three adults sat on the porch chatting amicably while they kept a watchful eye on the girls.

Thad brought Lauren up to date on the latest goings on in and around the university. The only gossip about her was that she was engaged to be married, but no one knew to whom.

"I guess you'd better put the cardio-pulmonary unit on alert for when they do find out," Lauren warned.

"You guys have just as much drama going as we do at the agency; envy, jealousy and backbiting," Pam added.

"It's the nature of the beast. Anywhere you have a group of people, no matter the size; you're going to have drama."

"Especially women," she said.

"Not necessarily so, Pam," Thad interjected. "Men can be vicious too. Don't let one think that he's been over looked or by-passed for a position. He'll plot for years to get even."

"Women will too. After they've bad-mouthed you to anyone who would listen." chimed Pam.

"Sounds like a lot of experience talking here." Lauren laughed.

"Been there, seen that," Pam confirmed.

"Ditto." Lauren stood. "You two enjoy the evening. I'm going to take the girls in for their baths and tuck them in."

Pam stood and stretched. "I'm going inside in a bit myself. I have to report in at eight o'clock, and then I have some cases that I have to study."

Brianna spotted Thad standing in the doorway. "Fen," she bubbled as Lauren laid her in the bed.

"Fen," repeated Brittany.

Lauren looked over her shoulder to see Thad standing in the doorway. She smiled and beckoned him to join her. "They were calling you. Fen is friend."

"You taught them that? Thank you. I'm happy that you know that I'm their friend as well as yours."

"Like you and me friends first." She smiled.

"Goodnight." She kissed each of the girls.

Lauren closed the door to the nursery and she and Thad went into the den. "Dessert?" She put an oldies CD in the player.

"Not now, darling, come and sit with me for a while."

"I've been waiting for that invitation ever since you arrived." Lauren snuggled close to him, and they sat quietly listening to the music. Thad gently caressed her shoulder as she continued to snuggle.

"How are you holding up?"

Lauren didn't answer right away. Thad continued stroking her shoulder. She sighed. "It's tough," The added pressure on her shoulder gave her comfort.

"Do you want to talk about it?"

"There's not much to say. It's a little easier now that I've put away most of Lydia and Stan's personal items. She and I decorated this house, and I'm using her furnishings, linens and her pots and pans. The reminders are all around me."

"I wanted to ask you not to come just because I knew it would be hard on you. On the other hand, I figured that the distraction would be good for you. Have you been sleeping well?"

"Because I spend a lot of time outside in the air with the girls, I slept very well last week. I worked until late in the evening, sorting and packing, and when I finally went to bed, I was exhausted."

Thad kissed the top of her head. "You know, Lauren, you never talked much about your friends. How did you and Lydia meet?"

"We met as freshmen at Michigan State. It was strange to us that we both had the same major and minor, and that we liked the same music and movies. As much as we liked sports, we didn't have much time for them. We asked if we could exchange roommates. That's how we ended up rooming together for four years."

"Did the two of you look alike, too?"

Lauren chuckled. "Oh no. Not at all. Wait a minute." Lauren stood and walked across the room to one of the boxes she had packed. "Here is a picture of us together."

Thad scanned the photo. "You are right. There's no resemblance. She is very attractive too. You are so much taller than she. Is she bi-racial?"

"She is. Was." Lauren resumed her place in Thad's arms.

"With so much in common, I'm surprised that she got married so young, and you are still not married."

"She told me that she and Stan fell in love at first sight. They married less than a year after they met. It appeared that they were the happiest couple. As for me," she smiled at Thad, "Mr. Right didn't come along until now. He was worth waiting for."

Thad gave her a gentle squeeze. "I'm happy to hear that."

"Anyway, I wanted to get my doctorate behind me before I considered marriage. And, since I had no prospects, it was easier to do it."

"This house? Had they lived here long?"

"Well, four years. They moved in a year after they got married. We had so much fun here. We argued over decorating ideas, but in the end we agreed on the same thing. I love her kitchen."

"Speaking of which, you're not eating well, are you? You've lost a few pounds."

"I haven't had much of an appetite of late, but the weight-loss started before I left Connecticut."

"I understand, but you can't afford to get sick. There are too many people depending on you." He laid his chin on her head. "I hope my being here will help you relax enough to sleep and eat better, and we can start by having desert. Banana pudding is one of my favorites."

"I didn't know that. I thought chocolate cake and lemon meringue were."

Thad laughed. "Baby, dessert is my favorite dessert."

Lauren kissed him on the cheek. "Thanks for letting me talk about her, Brad. I miss her so much." She went to serve up dessert.

"I sense that you do. I'm here any time you need to talk."

"By the way, how long are you planning to be here?" Lauren asked as she served the dessert.

"I have reservations to leave Wednesday afternoon."

"I see. I'm planning to leave the Monday after that. I'm going stir crazy here. At least back in Connecticut I could leave the house, even if I did have to look over my shoulders all the time."

" Are you sure you're ready to go back?"

"I'm sure. Agent Coles said there haven't been any vehicle sightings or dead animals since I left."

Thad frowned "I didn't know you'd been in touch with Coles since you left."

"Oh, we talked several times during the week. We're still going over every incident, trying to see what we've missed. Hasn't he spoken to you?"

"Once or twice. Anyway, speaking selfishly, I'm happy you're planning to go back. I've never missed anyone the way I've missed you."

"I've missed you, too. I need some stability in my life. I feel so disconnected."

"I can only imagine how you feel. I'm praying that things will settle down and get back to normal when you return." Thad stifled a yawn. "Please, forgive me. I'm exhausted. I need to turn in." They both stood.

"Of course you do. You've been up since five this morning, that's a total of seventeen hours." They headed up the stairs. "There's no clock or phone in the room to disturb you. Why don't you plan to sleep in tomorrow? I'm sure you could benefit from a good night's sleep, too."

"I might just do that. Now, do I get tucked in?" He teased as they reached the top of the steps.

"No, you don't. We have a pistol packing chaperone downstairs, but I will give you a good night kiss."

The kiss ended. "That'll last me until morning. Goodnight, my love."

"Goodnight, sweetheart." She turned to walk down the hall to her room.

"Hey," Thad called. "Do you realize that this is the first time we've said goodnight to each other, but never left the building?"

"I do." Lauren smiled and threw him a kiss.

* * * * *

The next morning, Lauren received an official letter in the mail from an attorney stating that he was representing Walter Burke in the matter of the children of his late sister, Lydia Burke Fredricks. "Calm down, sweetheart." Thad held her close. "Let's call your attorney and let her handle this."

"Gosh, Brad! What am I being tested for? It's been one thing after the other."

"I know, baby. You've been so brave. I can't imagine how hard this must be for you. If I have to, I'm going to take some more time off to be with you. In the meantime, call your attorney."

* * * * *

Lauren opened the door to Lillian, the attorney. "Thanks for coming, Lillian." Lauren led the attorney into the study. "This is my fiancé, Thaddeus Bradford. Thad this is Lillian O'Hare."

"Wait a minute, Lauren." Lillian smiled, looking Thad over. "Are you telling me that you have been gone just shy of one year, and you have met a man and become engaged already? What am I doing wrong?"

"I can't answer that, but it seems I was in the right place at the right time. I'm blessed." Lauren reached for Thad's hand.

"And how." Lillian eyed Thad, again. "Now, what can I do for you?"

Lauren handed her the letter. "Here, read this for yourself."

Lillian perused the letter. "There's nothing to worry about, Lauren. Lydia and Stan made their wishes very clear, and there's no legal ground for contesting. Your adoption of the girls was consummated six months ago." The attorney stuffed the letter back into the envelope and handed it to Lauren. "How long are you planning to be here?"

"Nine more days. Why?"

"I'll speak to Judge Evans on Monday. He's the one who signed off on the adoption."

"Thanks, Lillian. I appreciate it."

"Good. Now, when is the wedding?"

"We're looking at September, but I have a few things to work out before then. I'll let you know."

"Well, congratulations to you both. Dr. Bradford, except for what Lydia and Stan told me, I don't know much about Lauren, but from what I do know, your fiancé is quite a lady."

"She is from what I know too, Ms. O'Hare." He smiled at Lauren.

"I'll give you a call on Monday. You all have a wonderful weekend."

Lauren escorted the lawyer to the door. "Thanks for everything, Lillian."

*****

Lauren was relaxing in the swing on the patio watching the girls at play, when Thad asked if he could have a word with her. "Sure. Have a seat." She patted the space beside her. "What's up?"

Thad sighed as he sat beside her. "Lauren, you told Ms. O'Hare that we were looking at September to get married. I thought that that was a definite. As a matter of fact, I was hoping that I could persuade you to get married even earlier."

"Brad." Lauren hesitated. "I'm not going to marry you until all of this mess is cleaned up. We don't know what's waiting for me when I return to Connecticut."

"It would have been nice if you had discussed it with me before you made your decision. After all, this is our life you're deciding." Thad's eyes held a pained light. "I thought that we'd agreed that we're in this together. That means in everything."

"I know, darling, I know. But, there's a possibility that my life is in danger, and it could spill over onto you. I can't let that happen."

"I'm willing to take that chance."

"I'm not my love. Let's wait until I'm back in Connecticut and see what happens. Please?"

"I guess I don't have much say in the matter." Thad sounded irritated.

"That's not fair, Brad."

"And you think you're being fair? If this mess, as you call it, is not cleared up within the next six weeks, does it mean that we still won't get married?"

"I can't answer that."

"When will you be able to answer it, Lauren?"

"I can't answer that either."

Thad turned to enter the house. "I guess you'll let me know when you think things are in order for us to get married."

"Brad, please don't do this…"

He turned to look at her. "Don't do what, Lauren? Don't love you enough to want to marry you and take care of you and your daughters?"

"Brad, can't you see that for the past year, my life has been turned upside down? I have to get my life together before I can invite anyone else into it. Until that mess in Connecticut, I thought I was ready.

Now added to that, is the threat of my daughters being taken away from me." She turned to face him again. "You have no idea how badly I would like to have someone deal with all of these problems for me.

I would love to bury myself in oblivion, and not come up until it's all gone away. I know, too, that you will gladly do this for me, but I can't allow you to. If I'm going to be any kind of role model for my daughters in the future, I have to take charge now."

Lauren stepped to Thad. "I love you too much to let you get tied up in this. As I said before, we don't know what this is all about. Right now, the thing I want most is peace of mind. The peace that comes with knowing my daughters are safe, and that I stand a reasonable chance of being here to take care of them. The peace of knowing that no matter what, I will have the support of the man that I love. Am I asking for too much?"

"No, not when you put it like that. I do have some idea of what you are going through, Lauren. I see the toll that it is taking on you physically and emotionally, and, yes, I do want to take care of you. One of the reasons I want to get married now is that I don't want to compromise your reputation by spending nights in your house without the benefit of marriage. I want to take care of you and the girls. I'm becoming more attached to them every day, just as I am to their mother." He smiled. "I guess in my desire to take care of you all, I overlooked the enormity of how this is affecting you. Honestly speaking, it only makes me want to get married that much sooner. Having said that, I understand where you're coming from. I won't pester you about getting married anymore."

"Pester? That's a strange thing to say. Do you think I feel that you're pestering me?"

"Poor choice of words," he answered with an edge in his voice. "Do you want to go for a drive? It will do all of us good to get out."

"You might be right. We're all suffering from cabin fever. I'll get the girls ready."

They all piled into the car in search of a restaurant. Thad steered the car toward the interstate. "Are you known in Ann Arbor, Lauren?"

"Not really. I went to grad school with several people from there, but we didn't socialize, and I don't know if they still live there. Why do you ask?"

"I thought we could go there for dinner."

"That's an hour and a half away."

"It's either that or take a chance of you being recognized here."

"We don't have to go that far. Unless someone recognizes me from the hospital, there's little chance anyone within a ten or fifteen mile radius of Bayington will know me."

"Can you recommend a place to have dinner?"

Lauren rattled off several choices. They chose a restaurant, *The Farmhouse,* about twenty-five miles southwest of Bayington. The Farmhouse boasted the best seafood, steak, and chicken platters east of the Mississippi. The restaurant's decor reminded Lauren of an old world farm, with seating for one hundred patrons.

Lauren sat Brittany and Brianna in their highchairs and sat between them. Thad sat on Brittany's right and Pam to the left of Brianna. Pam had excused herself just before the waiter arrived to take their orders. Lauren had ordered for the girls and herself when the waitress asked, "Will you be ordering for your wife, sir?"

Lauren stared at Thad intently. As innocent as the question was, it did not sit well with her. It was bad enough that Pam thought it safer that she rode up front with Thad, but her being mistaken for his wife was a little much.

Holding Lauren's gaze Thad answered, "No, the lady will be ordering for herself."

I can't believe he didn't correct her.

Brittany and Brianna seemed to be enjoying the meal she had ordered. Lauren ordered the platter for herself, but having lost her appetite, pushed it aside and concentrated on assisting the girls.

Pam returned to the table. "Are you okay, Lauren? You've barely touched your food."

"I lost my appetite."

Thad gazed steadily at her for a few seconds before beginning a conversation with Pam.

When they left the restaurant a short time later the girls were buckled in their car seats with Lauren sitting between them, and once again, Pam was riding shotgun in front with Thad.

As they prepared to leave the parking lot, Lauren glanced up to see Thad staring at her in the rearview mirror. With arms folded over her breast, and her head cocked to one side, she stared back. *It's best you don't say anything to me now, mister.* The girls had begun to get a little fussy so Lauren concentrated on comforting them on the ride home.

Once home, she set out to bathe the girls. Afterwards, she read and played with them until they began to doze. She could hear Thad and Pam laughing as she stepped out of the room. Instead of joining them, she went to her room, took a shower and got into bed. She refused to answer the knock on her door, or Thad, when he called out to her.

"Lauren?" he called softly as he opened the door. She continued to lay in the semi-darkness without answering.

Thad approached the bed. "We need to talk, Lauren."

Instead of answering, she turned her back to him.

"Okay. Maybe this is not a good time, but we *will* talk in the morning." Lauren sensed that he had stood at the door a few minutes before he slipped out the room.

*****

One of the babies whimpered and awakened Lauren at one a.m. She found Brianna was wet, and after changing her, she laid her back in the bed, and then checked on Brittany who she found to be sleeping soundly.

"Wadda, Mommy, "Brianna said.

"Thirsty, sweetheart? How would you like some juice?"

"Deuce." Brianna grinned.

"Okay, sweetie. Mommy will be right back."

Lauren was surprised to see the sliver of light beneath the door as she neared the kitchen. *I guess someone forgot to turn off the light.* She pushed the door open. To her amazement, there sat Thad and Pam in their pajamas, having coffee, and enjoying what appeared to be a good joke. Her heart thudded to the pit of her stomach. They both stopped talking when she entered the kitchen. "Don't let me interrupt you." Without another word, she went to the refrigerator, poured the juice into the cup for her daughter, and in a voice laced with sarcasm, she said good morning, and then left the kitchen.

Thad was waiting for her as she exited the nursery. "Lauren." He reached for her.

"Don't." She pushed away from him as she headed back to her room.

*****

A few hours later, Lauren stood watching Thad and Pam sitting on the patio steps drinking coffee and talking like old friends, or something more. She wondered how long they'd been out there. He hadn't been in his room when she'd taken a glass of orange juice to him earlier. His bed didn't look as if it had been slept in, and now this.

Lauren retraced her steps back to the kitchen where her daughters were. She took the girls out to her car and strapped them in their car seats. Back in the kitchen, she grabbed her purse and keys and headed back to the garage. She drove away from the house not knowing where she was going. After an hour's drive, it dawned on her that the girls must be hungry and wet too.

Once she fed them, Lauren drove to a park that she located several blocks from the restaurant. The girls played with other children in the toddler play area, as the parents looked on. Her cell phone rang again for the sixth or seventh time within the past two hours. The ID showed that the calls were alternately coming from her home phone, Thad's cell phone or Pam's cell phone.

"Deuce, Mommy," Brittany said.

"Deuce," echoed Brianna.

"Okay, girls," Lauren answered as she filled their cups. "Here you are. How would you like a snack too? I guess we should head home after you finish eating."

Two hours later, Lauren arrived home to see two strange cars parked in her driveway. She maneuvered around the vehicles to get into the garage. Lauren unbuckled the girls' seatbelts and opened the connecting door to the kitchen. There she encountered a very frightened Thad, and an angry Agent Thatcher. Beyond them, she saw two uniformed officers, and one plain clothed, but obvious, law enforcement officer.

"Where have you been?" Pam shouted.

"Out."

Thad approached her. "Are you all right? You could have told us you wanted to go out, and you could have answered your phone."

"Excuse me. I have to take care of my daughters." Lauren left the kitchen. Thad followed her up the stairs.

"Lauren, what's going on?"

"Please, leave me to take care of my children. I don't want to talk to you, now."

"You need to talk to the agents. Everyone was worried about you. Are you coming down?" The sound of pain and relief ravished his voice.

"I will, once I've taken care of my daughters."

After she put the girls down for a nap, she splashed water on her face then returned to the kitchen. All eyes turned to her as she entered the room and stood near the refrigerator with her arms folded across her chest.

"Now, if any of you have any questions I might feel like answering, you may ask them now. If there aren't any questions, you can all leave."

A fortyish looking man extended his hand to Lauren. "Ms. Jeffries, I'm Agent Bob Carson with the FBI. Agent Thatcher called to report that you were missing. You hadn't been seen or heard from for more than two hours. Do you care to fill us in? You're under our protection, you know."

"If you must know, I felt stifled and needed some fresh air. I took my daughters and went for a drive. I drove to Lindale, and stopped at Mickey D's to get my children something to eat and drink. That was at about ten thirty. After that, we went to a park; I didn't get the name of the park where the girls played T-Town. I chatted with two mothers as we watched the children. One's name was Irene and the other was named Carla. We stayed there for approximately one and one half hours. On the way home, I stopped at Petrol Plus and purchased forty-one dollars and thirty-three cents worth of gas. I didn't stop again until I got here."

"Why didn't you answer your phone?" Carson asked.

"No one called that I wanted to talk to."

"Ms. Jeffries, we can't protect you if you're going to leave without your escort. We also need to know where you are at all times."

"You're right, Agent Carson. Anytime you're ready to pull your people is all right with me."

"Lauren!" Thad cried. "What's gotten into you? You're not behaving rationally. That's so unlike you."

She cast him a scathing look that caused him to flinch. "I've had a very revealing past twenty-four hours, and it's taken a lot out of me. So, if you have no more questions for me, I'm going to rest for a while."

Pam turned to Lauren. "I think we need to set some ground rules, Lauren."

"It's a little late for that. Don't you think?" Lauren shot at her.

"Well, now that we know you're safe, I'll go back to the office and file my report. Ms. Jeffries, would you please let us know the next time you plan to go for a drive alone?"

"I just might do that, sir. If you're finished with me, I'm going to bed."

*****

A short time later, Lauren saw Thad standing in the doorway. "May I come in?" he pleaded.

"I'd rather you didn't."

"Lauren, please. We've got to talk."

"No, you do. I've said all I have to say."

"All right, I need to talk." Thad walked into the room and sat on the side of the bed. "Lauren, what happened today? What made you run away?"

Lauren sat up and glared angrily at him. "You have the audacity to sit here on my bed and ask me that! You know exactly what happened!"

A frown creased Thad's forehead. "What are you talking about, Lauren? You told Agent Carson that you have had a very revealing twenty-four hours. What did you mean by that?" He reached for her hand, but she pulled away from him.

"You know what, Thad? I've come to the conclusion that we are not ready for marriage— not now, and probably not ever."

"Lauren you can't mean that! For God's sake, please tell me what happened. Talk to me, please!" He stared at her as she lay back against the pillow. "Darling, I love you. Please talk to me."

Lauren sat up. "Okay, you want to know what happened. You and Pam happened."

Thad continued to frown. "What! Lauren, what do you mean by that? I don't understand."

"What? What?" She paused for a few seconds. "Okay, first we go for a drive. You are already not too happy with me because I made the decision about us not getting married soon without consulting you.

You then suggest that we all go for a drive where Pam decides, and you agree, that it is safer for me to sit in the back seat while she sits up front with you. Then in the restaurant, she excuses herself, and leaves the table, but not before she gave you a nice little squeeze on the shoulder, and even in that she wasn't in a hurry to remove her hand. If that wasn't enough, you didn't bother to correct the waitress when she referred to her as your wife."

"Lauren, I..."

"Wait." Lauren interrupted holding up a hand. "There's more. I go downstairs at one thirty in the morning to find the man to whom I'm engaged to marry, sitting in his pajamas, sharing a cup of coffee with a woman who is also in her pajamas. Then, at seven thirty in the morning, I take my fiancé a glass of orange juice; thinking I'll wake him so that we could talk. Instead, I find his bed made and him nowhere to be seen. Then I hear the laughter. My fiancé, still in pajamas, and Pam still in her pajamas, are sitting on my patio steps together. Not one on one step; and one on another, but on the same step as cozy as cozy can be. Now, you tell me, what in blazes is going on? It looks like the fox guarding the hen house to me."

For several minutes, Thad stared at her in silence. Then he ran a hand over his face and sighed deeply. "Lauren, I am sorry, so very sorry. Listening to you string everything together like that makes everything seem suspect. I can understand why my actions appear to be suspicious, but I promise you, nothing untoward happened between Pam and me." Lauren stared at him, but said nothing.

"You don't believe me do you?"

"It doesn't matter."

"It does matter, Lauren." Thad caught her hand in his, rubbing a finger over where the engagement ring should be. She attempted to remove her hand from his grip, but he held tight. "Where is it, Lauren?"

"It's on the dresser."

Thad dropped her hand and walked to the dresser, picked up the ring, examined it for a moment, and then put it back. Lauren saw the muscle twitch in his jaw as he turned to face her again. "I listened to you; now, I want you to listen to me. When I'm finished, you decide whether or not you want to wear that ring again. If you do, you'll have to put it back on yourself.

If I had wanted it off, I would have removed it." He hesitated. "I *was* upset with you for not consulting me about planning a date for our wedding.

As for Pam riding shotgun; taking into consideration all that's happened of late, I thought it was safer, nothing more. Yes, she did squeeze my shoulder, but I don't know why nor do I care." He sighed.

"I didn't think correcting the waitress would have an effect on our relationship one way or the other. You and I know that Pam is not my wife.

Thad sighed and stuck his hand in his pocket. "I didn't want you to know, but recently I have begun to have nightmares, something that hasn't happened to me since I was a child. Most of the nightmares are about you and the girls. I woke up from a very bad one last night. I checked on you and the girls, and then went down stairs. Pam was already there, having coffee. She offered me a cup, and I accepted. I would have preferred something much stronger at that point. I did not want to go back to sleep. The dream was just that unsettling. After you went back to bed, I went back to my room and lay across the bed. I must have dozed off for a couple of hours, but at six a.m. I was wide-awake, again. I made the bed, went down for another cup of coffee and took it to the patio. Pam joined me at about seven-fifteen. She may have sat there for twenty or thirty minutes. At eight-thirty I went to check on you and the girls. You know the rest of that story. What you don't know is that I thought my world had come to an end when we couldn't find you and the girls. I've never been so frightened in my life. Lauren, you stood there, and said you didn't answer your phone because no one called that you wanted to talk to. If that statement was meant to hurt, you achieved your goal."

They both gazed at each other for a few moments, and then Lauren broke the contact. "I thought— it— it looked like you and Pam could have been having an affair."

Thad seemed dumbfounded. "An affair! Under your roof! With you in the house! What kind of dog do you think I am, Lauren?"

"What would you, given the same scenario, have done? What would you have thought if I were entertaining a man under your roof, and we were both in our pajamas?

Would you not have felt a bit threatened?"

"Why didn't you let me know that you were feeling that way when I tried to talk to you last night? As innocent as it was, I wouldn't have let it happen again if I had known how much it hurt you. I'm sorry about this whole thing. I wish we could turn the clock back thirty hours and start over again." Thad put both hands on the bed and gazed deep into her eyes. "Please understand this one thing, Lauren. If at any time I feel that I want to be with another woman for one night, one month, or one year, I would respect you enough to end the relationship with you first. That, my love, you can bet your life on."

"Thad." Lauren glanced at him through tear-filled eyes as she reached for his hand. "I'm sorry for misjudging you and for disregarding your feelings. I'm sorry. Please forgive me." She slipped out of bed and retrieved the ring from the dresser. She slipped it back onto her finger. She hugged him. "I love you."

Thad held her tight for a moment, and then led her back to the bed. "Sit down, Lauren." He pulled her down beside him and draped an arm around her shoulder. "I'm worried about you, darling. You've been under a lot of stress, and you're wound pretty tight, right now. You need a few nights of uninterrupted sleep. Let me help you. I can give you something to help you sleep." Lauren gave him a sharp look.

"You still don't trust me, do you? If need be, I'll sleep right here, in this bed beside you, fully clothed of course. I'll listen out for the girls."

"I do trust you. Give me two more days. After I hear from Lillian, I'll make plans to return to Connecticut earlier than I originally planned. Mrs. Brown can take care of the girls for me there."

"What about the next two days, Lauren? You need rest, now."

"Actually, it's only one more day." She stood, "It's almost seven o'clock. I need to get the girls up so that I can feed them."

"Let me do it, sweetheart. You have had a trying day and you haven't rested."

"Thanks, but I'll do it. What about you? What are you going to eat?"

"I'm not particular. I'll eat whatever you fix."

*****

Lauren descended the stairs in search of Thad. As she neared the den, she heard him and Pam talking. She hid in a corner so that she could eavesdrop on their conversation. "But Thad, we haven't done anything wrong. I like Lauren. I wouldn't do anything to hurt her."

"I know that, but listening to her side, I can see how it looked to her, and quite honestly, I would have felt the same way had the situation been reversed. Lauren has been through a lot this past year, and she's very vulnerable. She's a strong, brave, intelligent woman, but this is taking a toll on her."

"I'm sorry if I hurt her. I wouldn't do that on purpose. I guess she's going to have me replaced."

"I doubt that, but it's her call to make. She is my priority. Anything that will reduce the amount of stress in her life will be done." Breathing a sigh of relief, Lauren smiled, and then retraced her steps up the stairs. *Thanks for relieving my mind, Thad. Maybe now I can get a good night's sleep.*

*****

Thad stood at the bedroom door staring at Lauren. "Good morning, darling. How are you feeling today?"

"I feel great." Lauren lifted her arms and stretched. "I really feel like going to church, but it's too late now. Morning worship starts at ten."

"Mama, Mama," cried Brianna, as she toddled into the room.

"Mama," echoed Brittany, as she followed her sister.

"Good morning, Angels." Lauren rose from the bed and encircled both girls in her arms. "How are you this morning, Brad?"

Thad, relieved that she was calling him Brad again, grinned at her. "Brad is just fine. You look absolutely radiant, Lauren. What happened to you overnight?"

"I fell in love again; with the same man of course" she smiled.

"You wear it well. There is barely a trace of stress on your brow this morning."

"Prayer works." She smiled.

"Thank God. It appears that both of our prayers are answered. I'm going out for a paper. We can have brunch when I get back, but I don't want you to cook."

* * * * *

Later in the morning, Pam knocked on Lauren's door. "Lauren, may I come in?"

"Sure, come in. How are you today?"

"I'm okay," Pam answered. "Lauren, Thad had a talk with me last night. I'm so sorry if I hurt you. I really didn't mean to. He is an attractive man, easy to talk to, witty, and kind. I enjoy being around him, and I may have flirted with him, but that's as far as it went. I know that the two of you are in love with each other, and I find it refreshing to see. I've grown to admire you in these past few weeks. Please, forgive me."

Lauren stood from the floor where she had been playing with the girls and embraced Pam. "Everything is okay, Pam. You're forgiven, and your job is secure. I appreciate what you're doing for my daughters and me."

"Thank you." Pam returned the hug.

Thad, in addition to the newspaper, had brought a full brunch of scrambled eggs, waffles, sausage, bacon, mixed fruit, biscuits and gravy, hash browns, gelatin, rice and toast.

Lauren eyed the spread. "Are you expecting the Army to join us?"

"No ma'am." Thad said grinning. "Just the five of us. I feel as if I could eat all of this by myself. I'm famished."

"Eat," said Brittany.

"I'm pretty hungry, too," declared Pam, as she placed plates on the table.

"I hope you're hungry too, sweetheart." Thad eyed Lauren.

"I am, a little." Lauren smiled and began putting food on the girls' plates.

* * * * *

Lillian O'Hare arrived at Lauren's house early Monday afternoon with the confirmation that Lauren's adoption of the girls was legal, and that there were no grounds for contesting it from any source. She went on to say that, Walter Burke had been approached by a lawyer, and told that he might have a case, telling him that rather than to go to court, Lauren might decide to settle with him. Burke, not knowing where Lauren lived, had been watching his sister's house periodically to see if anyone showed up.

Lillian told Lauren that she should not feel any financial obligations towards him either because he's an addict who had gotten a tidy sum of money from Lydia over the years.

"Anyway, that's the story. No matter what anyone says or does, no one can take the girls away from you. Now, you go on, live worry free, and marry this man before he gets away from you. When are you leaving for Connecticut?"

"I'm leaving as soon as I can get a flight out. Thanks for everything. I now have one less thing to worry about."

"Glad to be of service. Congratulations, again. Let me know when you set the date. You all take care."

* * * * *

After calling the airline, Lauren replaced the receiver and turned towards Thad. "We're in luck. There's a flight leaving Thursday morning that'll get us to Connecticut at twelve-thirty in the afternoon."

"Are you ready to face all of that again, baby?"

"I'm going to have to face it sooner or later. Taking a break from all of that drama has strengthened my resolve."

"I'm proud of you, sweetheart, but remember, no matter what, we're in this together. Okay?"

"I hear you sir."

CHAPTER EIGHTEEN

Lauren and Pam sat at the table enjoying a glass of tea. "You know Pam, in spite of everything, I am glad to be back. This is the only place that I can call home."

"I'm going to miss you, Lauren. I'm sorry about that incident in Michigan. I think you're one class act."

"That's as they say, water under the bridge. I've enjoyed your company, too. Thank you for putting your life on the line for my daughters and me. I've learned to respect your agency, now that I've had a positive encounter with it. You will always be in my prayers."

"I would like it if we could stay in touch. Your little darlings have really grown on me."

Lauren stood and moved towards the door. "We'll be in touch. I just hope that I won't need your services anymore."

"I hope not. Well, Wendy will be here soon. After I brief her, she'll have to stay with you until the case is officially closed."

"I appreciate it. Now, if you don't mind, I'm going to stretch out for a little while. Mrs. Brown, the housekeeper, will be arriving soon. She has her own key, of course. I just don't want you to be alarmed if you hear her come in."

*****

Lauren awakened from her nap to find that Mrs. Brown had returned from her trip. "How are you Mrs. Brown? Wow! You look great. What have you been up to? By the looks of things, I might have to start looking for a new nanny." Lauren sat on the sofa.

Mrs. Brown straightened a picture on the wall. "No way, at least not any time soon. I had a wonderful time in New York. We also visited Maryland and Virginia. Now, tell me about you. Other than not eating, how have you been?"

"There's not much to tell. Thad visited for a week. He came back yesterday."

"Have you decided when you're going to marry that man and put him out of his misery?"

"I'm afraid that if I marry him now I'd be putting him in misery."

"Please tell me that that mess didn't follow you all the way to Michigan."

"No it didn't, but I see that several calls came here. There aren't any messages, though."

"That's good. Oh, look at my little girls." Mrs. Brown squealed as she spotted the twins. "They've really grown in three weeks. Walking and talking too. They're getting prettier by the minute. Did they enjoy themselves?"

"They had a good time playing outside in the back yard. We visited a couple of parks where they had a chance to play with other children."

"Excuse me, Lauren." Pam interrupted. "Wendy and I are finished." Wendy had come in while Lauren was resting. "I'm glad that I had a chance to say goodbye."

"It's not goodbye, but so long." Lauren stood and embraced the agent. "Thanks, again. Be safe." She walked Pam to the door, and then turning to the other agent, she greeted, "It's nice to see you again Wendy. As much as I like you, I was hoping that I wouldn't have to see you again under these circumstances."

Wendy smiled. "Let's hope that it won't be for long."

"Yes, lets. I do want you to know how much I appreciate what you're doing for us." They ringing of the telephone interrupted them. "I'll get it. It's Thad."

"How does it feel to be home, sweetheart?"

"It feels absolutely wonderful. I'm ready to start living my life again, and I need to start by going through what looks like a mountain of mail. I'll wait until tomorrow to tackle it though. How was your day?"

"Same old routine except I didn't have any surgeries scheduled for today. I have two scheduled for tomorrow, though. Did you eat dinner?"

"We did. We finished about an hour ago."

"But, did *you* eat?"

Lauren mimicked a little girl's voice, "Yes, daddy. I ate all my food, baked chicken, mashed potatoes and mixed veggies. No bread, but I did have raisin rice pudding for dessert."

Thad laughed. "Good girl. You didn't have to rub it in about dessert."

"That'll teach you, but you do know that I wouldn't make dessert without making enough for you don't you?"

"I think that's the number one reason I love you."

"Why? Because I can cook or because I make dessert for you?"

"Neither. It's because you care so much about others. By the way, Gene and Joan invited us to come for a visit on Saturday."

"Oh Brad, I don't know." Lauren sat in a nearby chair. "I hate to leave Mrs. Brown home alone. You know that Wendy has to go wherever I go."

"Why not bring her with us. You know she'd be welcomed."

"You go, sweetheart. I really wouldn't enjoy myself, looking after Mrs. Brown and the girls while I'm being looked after by Wendy. An alternative would be for me to invite them here."

"That's a good idea. I'll call them now and extend the invitation. I'll call you back, later."

After lunch the next day, Lauren began tackling the mail. Among the bills, magazines, periodicals, and the like, were a letter and pictures from Jennifer, two invites to Fourth of July celebrations as well as graduation announcements, and a wedding invitation. Near the bottom of the pile was an official looking manila envelope. Wondering what it could be, Lauren opened it, and then screamed.

Agent Green and Mrs. Brown raced up the stairs and into the study where they found Lauren standing over her desk, shaking and staring at a sheet of paper, which contained a drawing that depicted two little girls swinging from a hangman's noose.

Wendy called her office while Mrs. Brown attempted to calm Lauren who had run out of the study and down the hall to the girls' room.

It was surprising that both girls had slept through the scream.

Mrs. Brown stood beside Lauren. "Ms. Jeffries, do you want me to call Dr. Bradford? Ms. Jeffries. Ms. Jeffries." Mrs. Brown shook Lauren's shoulder.

"What is it?

"Do you want me to call Dr. Bradford?"

"No. Don't bother him. I think he's in surgery."

"Are you sure, Ms. Jeffries? I'm sure he would want to know about this."

"I'll call him, later. He needs to concentrate on his work. He should be finished soon."

"What can I do? I'll watch the girls for you if you want to lie down."

"Thank you, but I'll stay with them." Lauren sat in the rocker. After several minutes of waiting in shear agony, she pulled the cell phone from her pocket and dialed Thad's office. "Hi Carol, this is Lauren Jeffries. Is Dr. Bradford available?"

"He's just finishing a family consult, but he should be walking in any minute. Do you want to hold or do you want him to call you back?"

"I'll hold thank you."

"Hi, sweetheart," Thad answered after a minute. "How are you?"

"I need you." Her voice caught on a sob.

"What is it, darling?"

"Can you come? I need you, now. Please, come."

"I'll be right there, love."

*****

Thad didn't take time to change out of his scrubs. He grabbed his medical bag, informed Carol that he could be reached by pager, and headed for the door. The fifteen minutes ride to Lauren's house seemed to take hours.

He noticed several cars parked near her house when he turned into the driveway. His heart began to beat faster when he noted that one of the cars belonged to Alan Wilcox and another belonged to Dan Coles.

Almost before he had applied the brakes, he was running into the house. "Where is she?" he asked of no one in particular.

Mrs. Brown answered, "In the nursery."

Thad bounded up the steps and into the nursery. "Darling," he said, pulling Lauren into his arms. "Darling, what is it?"

"They threatened the girls, Brad. My babies are in danger." She cried.

"Tell me what happened." He whispered as he continued to hold her.

"There was an envelope in the stack of mail that I was going through." She sniffed, "It had a drawing of two little girls swinging from a hangman's noose."

"My God, darling!" Thad tightened his embrace. "What kind of sick-o are we dealing with? Did you see where it was mailed from?"

"I think California."

"California! What did the police have to say?"

"I don't know. I haven't talked with anyone except Wendy. I'm scared, Brad."

"I know you are sweetheart. I'm feeling very anxious about this, too. I'm going down to talk to Coles. Are you going to be okay?" Lauren nodded. "I'll be back shortly."

*****

The girls woke up while Lauren waited for Thad's return. She changed their diapers, but didn't leave the room.

"Dink mommy," Brianna said.

"Dink mommy," echoed Brittany.

"Okay, angels. I guess we need to go downstairs. You must be hungry, too."

All eyes turned to Lauren and the girls as they entered the kitchen where Agent Coles, Wendy, Mrs. Brown, Captain Wilcox, two other policemen, and Thad were talking.

Thad lifted one of the girls into her highchair while Lauren lifted the other into hers.

He whispered, "Okay, sweetheart?"

Lauren nodded and proceeded to fill the girls' cups with juice. She moved as by rote preparing a snack for the girls.

Thad moved quickly to remove the bowls, which were in danger of falling from her trembling hands and placed them on the highchair trays. She fought hard to stop the tears that had formed in her eyes from falling. Thad put an arm around her shoulder as they both stood watch over the girls.

Dan turned to Lauren. "Lauren, I don't think I need to tell you how sorry I am about this. I thought it was over. This is Agent Bill Wheeler and Agent Dan Jensen. As soon as you're ready, we have to talk to you."

Thad squeezed her shoulder gently in a show of support.

"We can talk now."

"We are very concerned about this latest threat, Lauren, and that's what we're calling it–a threat. We need you to take this very seriously and..."

Lauren's head snapped up. "You think I'm not?"

"Yes, I believe you are, Lauren. I just feel the need to reiterate how serious we think this is. Agent Wheeler is a profiler with the bureau. From all of the information we've gathered, he has concluded that either the perps are having fun scaring you out of your wits or is operating at the behest of someone else. We're going to have to take you all the way back to your college days, and maybe beyond, to see who might have a grudge against you.

The fact that they are crossing state lines, and using the U.S.P.S. for a terrorist act makes this a federal offense–a major felony.

Agent Coles sat across the table from Lauren. "I know that you have been vigilant, and we're asking you to keep it up. Mrs. Brown has to be careful, too. Now that they have threatened your children, there's a chance that they will threaten her as well. Agent Greene will be staying with you."

"In addition, we'll need a list of any visitors you may be expecting and the names of family members who might be calling or visiting on a regular basis. Anyone wanting to gain entrance to the house will need identification. You'll be under the protection of law enforcement at all times.

We need your cooperation in letting us know where you are at all times. Are there any questions?"

"Not at this time," Lauren answered with a sigh. "I do want all of you to know that Brad, Dr. Bradford, has my permission to speak on my behalf at any time that I'm unable to speak for myself."

"Duly noted, Lauren. We'll need that in writing too."

"Agents Wheeler and Jensen are going to talk with you for a while to see what if anything we've left out."

* * * * *

The agents followed Lauren into the den. There, they spent the next hour perusing reports to make sure nothing had been over-looked. After cautioning her to log any questions or events of interest, they left. Lauren re-entered the kitchen. Thad held her chair as she prepared to sit with her daughters. "You need to eat, darling."

"I know. I'm just not hungry, right now."

"I understand, but you need to eat a little, love. Remember the girls are depending on you. You can't afford to get sick."

CHAPTER NINETEEN

By the time everyone else arose on Saturday morning, Lauren had already fixed breakfast for them all.

After breakfast, she took the girls outside to enjoy what was promising to be a beautiful, warm, sun drenched day. The girls seemed to enjoy the feel of the grass under their bare feet, and being pushed and pulled on their riding toys.

Brittany spied Thad standing on the patio. "Fen."

Lauren glanced towards the patio to see Thad leaning against a pillar, observing them. "Good morning."

"Good morning, sweetheart. You look well rested. How are you feeling?"

"I feel great."

"Really? What happened? You were pretty stressed out when I left you earlier this morning."

Lauren grinned, and then winked at him. "I'll tell you about it later." She brought the girls onto the patio so that they could continue their play. "May I offer you breakfast?"

"No thanks to breakfast, but I would enjoy a cup of coffee and conversation."

Lauren went inside and returned with a mug of coffee. Thad reached for the coffee mug. "Not so fast, sir," Lauren said. "You haven't greeted me properly." Thad planted a tender kiss on her lips.

"That's better. Let's sit over here so I can keep an eye on the girls."

"What gives?"

"I feel so much better today. I'm so ashamed. I forgot my refuge, my strength, and my present help in times of trouble. I had a long, soul bearing talk with God after you left. I'd been leaning and depending on you and law enforcement instead of Him. Don't get me wrong, I still need you. He put you and the others here for me, but He's my ultimate protector. Do you understand what I'm saying?"

Thad smiled tenderly. "Yes, darling, I understand. I prayed long and hard this morning, too. Ah,...Lauren, you said that you still need me. Do you need me enough to marry me sooner than September?"

"I do, but I can't do this to you. They've threatened the girls. You might be next."

"If they are planning to threaten me, they'll do it anyway. Our being married will not cause it, nor will it stop it."

"I don't want to take that chance."

"But, if I'm threatened now you'll marry me? Let me be selfish, Lauren. I need to be with you. I made a vow not to be sexually intimate with you before we were married. I can't sleep under the same roof with you without the benefit of marriage for a number of reasons. My respect for you heads the list. I need to know that you're all right." Thad stared at her. "The hardest part of my day is when I leave you at night. I want to be here to hold you when you're frighten.

I want to be the go between so that you don't have to answer all of the questions from law enforcement. I want to take care of you and the girls

. Since we're planning to get married anyway, why not now? I'm more stressed being away from you than I could ever be with you. I love you so much. Don't you think God would want us to marry?"

Lauren laughed, "Thaddeus Bradford! You're pulling out the big gun, now."

"Well? Trust Him, love.

"I don't know— well, I— okay."

"Okay? Are you saying that we can get married soon?"

"Yes, I am. Will you give me time to tell my family? We won't have time to plan a big formal wedding, but we can have a very small ceremony, just our families and those who attended our engagement party."

"Let's not forget your protectors. What date do you have in mind?"

"What about two weeks from today. July twelfth."

"Perfect. We can tell Gene and Joan tonight, but I don't look forward to telling the rest of my family."

"I'm so very sorry. I..."

"Darling, don't," he interrupted. "I love you. My family can accept it or reject it. I'm planning to spend the rest of my life with you and the girls. So, wipe that frown from your brow. Okay?"

"Okay. I just want them to be happy for you."

CHAPTER TWENTY

Gene and Joan arrived in Dalton as planned. They now sat with Lauren and Thad discussing the harassments. "Are you guys serious!" exclaimed Joan. "You mean to tell us that you have been going through this for over a month and haven't said anything to us about it?"

"Joan, we needed everything to appear as normal as possible. We didn't want anyone else to get hurt in anyway," Lauren said.

Gene scowled. "What do the police say?"

"Not much." Thad interjected. "The calls and letters are coming from three different states. That makes them hard to pin down. Several of the calls were made with pre-paid cells or calling cards. They're either very crafty or they watch a lot of television."

Turning to Lauren, Gene asked. "How are you holding up, Lauren?"

"As of today I'm very well. I think Thad has something to tell you guys."

Gene glanced at Thad. "What's up, brother? Not more bad news I hope."

"Not bad. The best. Lauren and I are getting married July twelfth."

"You are? I thought the wedding was scheduled for September. What gives?"

"In light of recent events, I need to be with Lauren and the girls."

"I'm happy for you both, but you know what you're in for.

You are aware that Joan and I are the only family members who'll attend the ceremony don't you?"

"I'm assuming that that's the case. I'll invite them all. It's their choice to attend or not." Thad paused for several moments. "I think I'll attend the family dinner tomorrow. Alone" He glanced at Lauren.

"You'll get no argument from me, Brad."

"Good for you, brother-in-law. I'm proud of you for choosing to be happy. We know that I wasn't your parent's choice for Gene, either."

"Yeah, but you weren't a slut with two sniveling brats trying to get your hands on the Bradford fortune."

Thad seemed shocked. "Lauren! You heard that!"

"Of course, I did. So did everyone else within a half mile radius."

Gene laughed. "And you didn't run for the hills?"

"What! And leave all that money?"

The four of them laughed.

"You are going to be okay, sis." Gene continued to laugh.

*****

Thad visited Lauren after the trip to his parents' house. Lauren noticed his pensive mood and reached for his hand. "I'm here when you want to talk." He squeezed her hand gently, but firmly, and led her to the sofa. He sat and pulled her into his lap and held her tight.

CHAPTER TWENTY-ONE

When Lauren called family and friends to give them the news of the pending nuptials, Vivian Reed not only offered her house for the ceremony, she offered to be the wedding planner.

Lauren's sister, Michelle, and Gene accepted the honor of attending for their siblings. Pastor Jenkins was available to perform the ceremony. They had but to wait for the next ten days to pass.

*****

Mrs. Brown had just put the girls down for their afternoon nap, and Lauren and Agent Greene were chatting amicably in the kitchen as Lauren prepared dinner, when they heard a very authoritative banging on the front door.

Wondering who could be pounding on the door instead of ringing the doorbell, Wendy, with her hand resting on the weapon that she wore on her hip, unsnapped the holster and moved to open the door. "May I help you?"

"I'm L.C. Bradford. I want to see Ms. Jeffries."

"Is she expecting you?"

"Young lady, I'm here to see Ms. Jeffries, not to be interrogated by you. Now, are you going to get her or do I have to do it myself?"

"The name is Agent Greene, and I wouldn't try that if I were you, Mr. Bradford. Now, you can stay right here while I see if Ms. Jeffries wishes to see you." Wendy closed the door, and then informed Lauren that L.C. Bradford wanted to see her.

Oh, aren't I privileged, she thought as she headed for the door. "Mr. Bradford, I understand that you wish to see me?" Lauren stood in the door.

"I do. You have the rudest guest."

"And visitors, Mr. Bradford. What can I do for you?"

"I would like to speak to you in private."

"Do come in." Lauren led him into the living room. "Wendy will you excuse us, please?" Turning to Mr. Bradford she said, "We're alone now. State your business."

"I'll come straight to the point. My wife and I don't want you to marry our son. We don't want your kind in our family."

"Whatever my kind is. You and Your wife are hypocritical snobs who are trying to get away from your entangled roots. You stand here, in my house, passing judgment on me. Yet, you feel its okay for your son to sow his wild oats with me, while reserving marriage for the rich, society tart who has aborted a child that she couldn't possibly know who fathered. And what about you, Mr. Bradford, are you still housing your little harlot?"

Mr. Bradford's face paled. "Oh, what's the matter, Mr. Bradford? You think you're the only one who can hire a detective? Now, state your business and get out of my house."

Mr. Bradford was fuming to the point of trembling. He reached into his breast pocket. "I have a cashier's check here for one hundred-fifty thousand dollars. It's yours if you tell my son that you won't marry him."

Lauren was so enraged that she had to hold on to the sofa for support. "You're shameless. You think you can sell your son's happiness. Let me tell you what you can do with—"

"Two hundred thousand and that's as high as I will go."

"They haven't minted enough money to buy me off. I love Thad and I know that he loves me. He's the only one who can stop me from marrying him.

"You'll never be a Bradford. There's no way our society or our family will accept you and those little brats that you're trying to pass off as adopted. Don't ever set foot in my house again. You're not welcome."

"That's your wish Mr. Bradford. The wedding will still take place on July twelfth. Believe me, I'm just as reluctant to own you as my father-in-law as you are to own me as your daughter-in-law. Good day, Mr. Bradford." Lauren led him to the door.

"You'll rue the day you marry my son. I'm well connected. If I can't break you, I can have you broken." Bradford stormed out of the house. He turned to her just as he stepped over the threshold. "I'll give you three days to change your mind. After that I'm..."

"July twelfth, Mr. Bradford." Lauren slammed the door in his face.

Wendy entered the room. "Wow! Am I dreaming? Is he for real?"

"He's for real. Darn! I hate to tell Thad about this, but he'll be very angry with me if I don't. They have no idea how much they are hurting him."

"He loves you, Lauren. Any man who chooses a woman over family, money, and prestige is a rarity."

"I know. He is quite a man, and I love him so much."

"I'm sorry, but you know that I have to report this incident, don't you?"

"I know. Please let me be the one to tell Thad. He is going to be just as furious as he will be hurt."

CHAPTER TWENTY-TWO

Thad smiled from the door where he stood watching Lauren and the girls romping on her bedroom floor. "Hello, my beauties."

"Hi." The two girls chorused.

Lauren turned to him. "How are you today, my love?"

"I'm very well. All three surgeries were successful."

"Thank, God. Have you eaten dinner?"

"Not yet. I was hoping that you will have pity on me and feed me."

"Spoiled brat. Let's go downstairs and see what I can scrounge up."

"Dessert first." He caught her hand to help her up, and pulled her into his arms for a passionate kiss. "Eight more long days before I don't have to stop at a kiss." Thad released her and reached for one of the babies. "Come on, little one. He picked Brittany up from the floor.

"Lauren, have you eaten yet?"

"No. I was hoping that you would come by for dinner so I waited to eat with you."

They sat down to dinner. "This is good. Yep, you've made a spoiled brat out of me. Do you think you could stay home and become a full time wife and mother?"

Lauren stopped chewing and peered across the table. "You're kidding aren't you?"

"I am, but do you think that you could do that?"

"You mean do I think I would go stir crazy if I had to do that day after day?"

"Would you?"

"I don't think so. I'm getting used to motherhood, and I'm enjoying it. I also enjoy all aspects of nursing. I'm not quite ready to give it up. Is that what you want me to do?"

Taking a sip of coffee, Thad answered. "No, baby, at least not yet. I have thought a lot about the benefits of having you home all day. By the way, have you given any thought to us going away for a few days honeymoon?"

"What? And take Wendy and the girl's with us? No way!"

"We could make arrangements for someone, Michelle or Joan, to take them for a week or so. Mrs. Brown could go along to help with them."

"Let me put the girls to bed then we can talk about it, okay?"

"Okay. I'll make a couple of calls while I'm waiting for you."

A few minutes later they sat in the patio swing, sipping tea and holding hands. "I forgot to tell you how well you look today. I'm amazed at how stress free you seem these past few days."

"I attribute it all to God, and of course you, love. I'm not going to let this thing dictate how I live my life. I have a question for you."

"Shoot."

"Monetarily speaking, how much is our love worth?"

Thad stared at her. "There's not enough money in the world. Why do you ask such a silly question?"

Lauren met his questioning gaze. "That's what I told your father."

"That's what? What are you talking about?"

"Your father came here today. He—"

"Wait a minute! You are telling me that my father came here to this house? What the hell for?" The muscles twitched in his jaw.

"Calm down, sweetheart. You frightened me when you get upset like that."

"Baby, you know I'd never hurt you."

"I'm not frightened for me. It's you I'm concerned about."

"Sorry. What did he want?" Thad asked in a calmer voice.

"Please don't get any more upset. He offered me two hundred thousand dollars to get out of your life."

"Damn!" Thad stood and began pacing the floor. "Who does he think he is? What right does he have to come to you like that?" He stopped pacing. "What else did he say to you?"

"Oh, he had a lot more to say. Like I'd never be a Bradford, that I'm never to come to his house again, that I'm a slut, that I'm passing my brats off as being adopted, and that I will rue the day that I marry you. He also said that he's well connected, and that he could ruin me or have it done, and that I will never be accepted in society."

"Damn him! Damn him!" Thad began to pace again. The muscles in his jaws all but jumped now. "Was that all?"

"That was enough. I had some not so nice things to say to him, too. Among which was that he's a hypocrite, and that the same rules by which he measures morality in others don't seem to apply to him. I also told him that he accepted the notion of you sowing your wild oats with me, but marriage, for you, is reserved for the rich society slut, and that he, a married man, has a woman that he's keeping."

"Lauren!" Thad stared at her dumbfounded. Suddenly, he let out a side-splitting series of laughs. "How did you learn that?" He asked, wiping tears from his eyes.

"I really didn't learn it. I guessed it. He thinks I hired a detective."

Thad laughed again. "Oh, to have been a fly on the wall. That's priceless. I don't think anyone has ever stood up to him like that before."

"Oh, I forgot to tell you, I have three days to accept the offer." She smiled at him mischievously. "So, you'd better best that offer by Friday."

"Man! I sure can't borrow the money from him. Can I pay it in installments every day for the rest of my life?"

"Oh, yes. I'd love having you indebted to me for the rest of our lives. I love you Thaddeus Bradford."

Thad's face turned sober. "You, Gene, Joan, and the girls may be all of the family I have left."

"Oh?"

"My parents warned me that if I marry you, I would be cut out of their wills, and disowned as their child."

"They can't be that heartless."

"They can, and they are. I don't care about being cut out of their wills, but in spite of everything, I love my family." He sighed as he sat beside her. "Even without kicking me out of the family, I wouldn't be visiting them anyway because I wouldn't go anywhere that my wife and children are not welcomed."

Lauren caressed his cheek. "I'm so sorry about this, Brad. If there's anything that I can do to ease the pain you know that I would do it."

"I know you would, Lauren. I'm going to tell Gene about all this when he comes."

"Wendy witnessed much of your father's tirade. She had to report it to her boss."

"She has to do her job. Now, what about the honeymoon? We can plan it so that the girls will be safe."

"Let me see if Michelle is able to keep them for a week. We can ease out of here without notice just as we did when I hid out in Michigan. As long as it's somewhere cool. Then again, I guess it would be quite a challenge to find a cool spot in the middle of July."

"Not if we go to San Francisco. Their summers are colder than our autumns. Want to give it a try?"

"It's okay with me if that's what you want. A week in San Francisco can be pretty expensive, though." Lauren answered.

"It can, but I can manage it. A friend of mine offered us her loft in Marin. It's right on the bay. I think you'll like it."

"I guess that settles it then. By the way, where is this friend going to be for that week?"

"Probably in Los Angeles. She's a writer for TV, and she spends most of her time there. We have been friends since college and we still talk frequently."

"You should have invited her to our wedding."

"I did. She can't make it."

* * * * *

Dan Coles had come to the Bradford's in answer to Thad's call. Lauren recounted the conversation she'd had with Mr. Bradford. "I'm sorry about this, Thad," said Agent Coles.

"I hope you understand, we have no choice but to talk to them, especially since they have both threatened Lauren, albeit vague."

"I'm sorry too, but you have to do what you have to do. I'm sure you'll find that my parents have nothing to do with this. They don't want Lauren in the family, but I know they wouldn't do her physical harm."

Captain Wilcox turned to Lauren, You're an amazing woman. I can't get over how you have bounced back. There's such a sense of calmness about you."

"She's my role model.," Wendy declared.

"All right you guys, you're giving me unmerited credit. The Almighty is doing this for me. As soon as I gave it to Him, I felt like a new person. All of that stress lifted right off of me. I'm still being careful though. In addition to that, I have the comfort of knowing that I have the love of a man who would fight the entire world to keep me safe if he has to." Lauren cast Thad a loving smile.

Coles smiled at the couple. "Tomorrow will mark the end of the three days. If Mr. Bradford contacts you Lauren, you must let us know."

The phone rang while Coles was still talking. Wendy checked the caller ID, "It's an unknown caller, using a calling card."

"Let it go to voice mail then play it back."

"Do you know where your girls are?" followed by a child's cry played on the machine. They were unable to tell if the voice was that of a male or female.

In two steps, Thad had reached Lauren, and had taken her trembling body in his arms. Agent Coles, Captain Wilcox, and Wendy stood by helplessly.

"This is getting sicker and sicker," said Lauren. "How I wish I knew who was behind all this. I can handle them harassing me, but they are now targeting my children."

"Lauren, I'm sorry. We've exhausted every possible method we have of trying to locate this sick-o. He or she is crafty, but I guarantee you if he keeps this up, we'll catch him.

I just need him to get in front of that surveillance camera one time," said Coles. "We have a strategy that I'm sure they won't be able to get around."

Thad pulled Lauren closer. "Are you okay, sweetheart?"

"I'm okay. I'm going to read to the girls, and tuck them in. I'll be out soon."

*****

Thad smiled as he heard Lauren's footsteps on the patio floor. "They're fast asleep. Thank God they can't understand any of this mess. I want to ask you something."

"Okay, come and sit beside me." He pulled her against his chest. "I love holding you like this. Now, tell me what's on your mind."

"What do you think of the idea of me owning a hand gun?"

Thad took a deep breath, and exhaled slowly. "I don't like it."

"It was just a thought. I don't like it, either."

Changing the subject Thad stated, "I guess this new development changes our wedding plans. I know that you don't want to leave the girls now, and I can't blame you. I don't want to leave them either."

"Our wedding is July twelfth. It's not changing, but the honeymoon is a different story."

"Baby, you mean you don't...we can still get married as planned?"

"Of course we can. We'll do the honeymoon some other time. Just remember, we have to wait until the honeymoon to consummate the marriage."

Thad stared. "You're kidding aren't you?"

Lauren shook her head no, but her eyes twinkled with mischief.

"Oh you. I'm learning you're a big tease, but I like you." Thad laughed. "Seriously, sweetheart, you're so different from anyone I've dated.

You're not after anything except to be loved and to be told the truth. A breath of fresh air, and that's a rare combination these days."

"Thank you, my friend. For that, you can have a big slice of chocolate cake for dessert."

"You know my favorite dessert."

"Banana pudding?"

"No, this is." He planted a kiss on her lips.

"I'm rather fond of that myself."

"So? Do you want me to spend the night?" They headed to the kitchen.

"No. Wendy can handle everything here. A police cruiser is going to be patrolling all night. There's going to be an agent around somewhere, too. I think I'll be okay."

"I'm getting worried, Lauren. This whole thing is beginning to freak me out. What could anyone possibly think you've done that would cause them to do this to you?"

"I don't know. I've gone over the past eighteen months of my life. I can't think of anything I've done to make anyone this angry. Other than having to write-up a couple of employees, and defending a recommendation to terminate, there isn't anything that I can think of. I had no serious run-ins with anyone in Michigan. I hadn't been here a week when the busy bodies paid me a visit that precipitated the wagging tongues. We know that Sandy Yates was a bit jealous of the attention you paid me. That debacle in the boardroom relative to my morals, and the encounters with your parents are all that I can come up with. I don't think any of these would cause this reaction."

"I wouldn't think so. My parents are hell bent on stopping me from marrying you, but I don't think even they would stoop this low."

"I'd feel a lot better if I'd done something to someone and they were trying to get revenge. It's the not knowing that's so unsettling."

Thad's phone rang. "Hello? Oh, hello Mother. Mother. No, Mother! Mother!"

Sitting as close to Thad as she was afforded Lauren the opportunity to hear Mrs. Bradford's end of the conversation as well as Thad's, and she had just heard Mrs. Bradford refer to her as a slut, once again.

He gripped her arm in an attempt to halt her departure as she stood to leave, but she wrested her arm from him and entered the house.

After checking on the girls, she went to her own room and fell across the bed. Her mind raced from the part of the conversation she'd just heard to others she'd had with Thad's parents in the past. *Maybe he'd be better off if I stepped out of his life. That way he'd have his family as well as the family fortune; and I can stop being their slut.*

Thad knocked on Lauren's bedroom door. "Lauren? May I come in?"

"Yes, please."

"Are you okay?"

"Yep. Doing pretty good for a slut." She allowed sarcasm to color her response.

"Lauren! Please don't say that."

"Did you tell your mother not to say that? I'm tired of being their slut."

"Darling, I'm sorry."

"I'm tired of hearing you apologize for their behavior, too." Lauren stared at the ceiling.

"What do you expect me to do, Lauren? I'm sorry they treat you so contemptuously. If they weren't my parents, I wouldn't feel the need to apologize for their behavior."

"Maybe we should reconsider getting married. We could save ourselves a lot of stress, and you could get your family and fortune back."

Thad stood staring at her for several moments without speaking. After a while, he ran a hand over his face, sighed and then asked, "Are you trying to tell me something, Lauren?"

Lauren turned to face him. "I'm trying to tell you that with me out of the picture, you could have the love, peace, and happiness you enjoyed with your family before you met me. You wouldn't ever have to apologize for your parents' behavior again."

"I knew what I was up against when I asked you to marry me. I told you that I love you far more than any amount of money, and that I would go against my family if I had to make that choice. I thought you and I were in this together. Now you're telling me you want to give it all up? To throw the love we have for each other in the trash? Is that what I'm hearing, Lauren?"

She ran her fingers through her hair and sighed wearily. "I'm tired, I'm frightened, and I hurt for you. I know that if I bowed out of your life, you would have your family back. You would—"

"Lauren, listen to me. I knew what sacrifices I'd have to make when I told my parents that I'm in love with you, and that I had asked you to be my wife. I work for a living. I have my own money. I don't need, nor do I depend on my family's fortune. If they cannot accept you as the woman I love, I'll just have to love them from afar."

"We." Thad pointed to Lauren. "You and I, vowed that we are in this together. I know it's not easy for you right now. I can see why you would do anything if it would result in you having a peaceful and stress free existence. I'm going to Boston tomorrow to tell my parents that if they ever refer to you in a derogatory manner again, it'll be the last time they do it directly to me or you. I told you I'd do anything in my power to protect you and the girls, and I mean it. And darling, please don't ever think of trying to save me by leaving me."

CHAPTER TWENTY-THREE

When Lauren and Mrs. Brown, accompanied by Agent Greene, exited the church on Sunday they spied not one, but two black sedans with dark tinted windows parked near her SUV.

Agent Greene told Lauren and Mrs. Brown to spend a few minutes fellowshipping with other worshipers while she placed a call to the police station.

A tall brunette, wearing a long black dress, over-sized sun shades, and a wide-brimmed hat pulled down on her face, exited the church and bumped into Lauren. Without so much as an apology, she hurried to enter one of the suspicious vehicles.

*****

Once again, Dan Coles had been summoned to Lauren's house. "I won't stop going to church, Agent Coles. I've given up just about everything that's important to me. Attending church isn't going to be one of them."

"Darling, today they showed you that they can get to you anywhere." Thad insisted.

"Thad, if they wanted to hurt me they could have easily done it today."

"Lauren," Coles changed the subject, "I know that your wedding is Saturday. We're going to assign additional agents to cover it."

"Dan, my friends don't know anything about the harassment. I don't want to get them involved in it."

"We don't want them hurt either, sweetheart. The agents will be posing as our guests." Thad added.

"We aren't giving you all the details, but rest assured, you and all of your guests will be safe."

"Thanks, Dan."

The phone rang. "Answer it Lauren. Put it on speaker."

"Hello?"

"Who's watching your back?" asked a muffled voice.

"Damn it!" Thad exclaimed.

Agent Coles scratched his head. "That's another out of state call. There is a conspiracy, which involves players from Massachusetts to California. We're missing something."

"I'm spending the night, and I don't give a hoot about how many tongues wag. I might just move in. We're going to be husband and wife in six days anyway."

"If I live that long."

"Lauren!" Thad admonished.

Thad turned his attention to the two women. "Mrs. Brown, Wendy? I'm sleeping in Lauren's room tonight– in her bed. We'll leave the door open. As a matter of fact, I'm moving the girls' cribs in there too."

"Brad, no!"

"Yes, Lauren. I promised to take care of you and the girls and I'm starting now. Nothing you can say will stop me."

Mrs. Brown smiled. "My kind of man."

"What about tomorrow? What are we going to do while you're at work?"

"Wendy and Dan are taking care of that."

"I guess there's nothing I can say since I wasn't consulted."

"Darling." Thad turned Lauren to face him. "If I'd consulted you, you would have said no. I just can't leave you anymore. I'd go crazy with worry. I love you, and I've got to do all I can; all I know how, to keep the three of you safe." He pulled her close to him. "I'm an expert in hand guns, and I'm licensed to carry a weapon."

"But you don't want me to carry one."

"I'm experienced, you aren't."

"I could learn."

"Maybe some other time."

"I love you, Brad."

"I love you too. Trust me."

*****

Thad leaned over the bed and kissed Lauren on the forehead. "Good morning, sleeping beauty."

"Good morning, Brad. Did you sleep well?"

"I did. But not as well as I will this time next week." He smiled. "Gotta go. I have a minor surgery at eight. Go back to sleep. I'll call you later."

"Okay, love. There's a key on the table in the foyer for you. Have a blessed day."

"You too." He kissed her again.

Later that day, Lauren looked up from feeding the girls to see that Thad had returned from work. "How was your day, love?"

"Long and uneventful. I was anxious to get back here to you and the girls."

"How are you going to concentrate on surgery if your mind is here instead of in the OR?"

"So far, I've been able to separate the two. Don't worry, if at any time I feel that what's happening with you and the girls will impact my ability to give my patients the care that they deserve, I'll step aside." He patted Brittany's head. "You know, I hadn't noticed until now how fast these little angels are growing." Thad sat opposite Lauren and began feeding Brianna. "Do you think that you would like to have a baby someday?"

"I've thought about it. Why? Do you want us to have children together?"

"You mean more children, don't you? I would like to adopt Brittany and Brianna."

Lauren gushed. "You have no idea how it makes me feel to hear you say that."

"Did you think I would have it any other way? They're part of the package. I love them, too."

"Someday, God willing, we'll give them a brother or sister or both."

Thad smiled. "Both sound nice."

"You know, we've been so wrapped up in this threat that we haven't had time to plan beyond the wedding. We haven't decided where we're going to live yet."

"Where do you want to live?" He spooned food into Brianna's mouth. "Do you want to continue living in Dalton or move? I know this town has not been kind to you."

"Since I have a choice, I'd rather not stay in this house. It has too many bad memories. I like your house, and it's large enough for a family of four, with room for growth."

"That's fine with me. We can always buy another one later if we need to. Are you going to sell this one or lease it?"

"I think I should lease it for now."

"Good idea. When do you want to start moving your things into my, oops, I mean our house?" He smiled.

"Let's wait until after Saturday. I'm hoping by then all of the threats will be gone. I hope whoever is doing this doesn't know where you live."

"Maybe not. You haven't been to my house since this all started."

Lauren glanced at him. "Are you ready to eat?" He didn't say anything, but sat grinning at her. "Okay, okay." She smiled, and continued looking at him. "What's that big grin all about mister?"

"I love it."

"You love what?"

"This whole domestic scene. I can't wait to make it permanent. Where are Mrs. Brown and Wendy?"

"Discreetly absent. They're so considerate. I'll ask them to join us for dinner."

The four adults enjoyed a delicious dinner in the dining room. For the first time since her return to Connecticut, Lauren was relaxed and able to enjoy a stress free evening.

After dinner, Mrs. Brown and Wendy washed dishes while Lauren and Thad put the girls to bed. Later, they played a few hands of cards before calling it a night.

* * * * *

Lauren woke and stretched with lazy effort. *Oh, that felt good. That's the best sleep I've had in weeks.* She spied a note on Thad's pillow. She picked it up, read it, and smiled. *In just four more days I'll be Mrs. Thaddeus Bradford–Mrs. Lauren Bradford. Oh, I can't wait.* She continued to smile as she headed for the stairs.

"You look well rested this morning, Ms. Jeffries," said Wendy as Lauren joined her and Mrs. Brown in the kitchen.

"You surely do," Mrs. Brown added.

"Thank you, ladies. I slept better than I have in weeks. Not a single dream and I didn't wake once during the night."

"Uh huh," teased Mrs. Brown. "I wonder what brought that on."

"Mrs. Brown!" Lauren blushed. "The door was open all night. You know that."

Mrs. Brown laughed, "I do know. We're just joshing you. I'll be glad when the two of you are married. That man is good for you."

"I agree," added Wendy. "You are much more relaxed when he's here. He loves you and the girls so much."

"And I love him and the girls so much. I'm quite fond of the two of you too."

CHAPTER TWENTY-FOUR

Thad was minutes from winding up a family consult when his pager went off. "Dr. Bradford here."

"Doctor, your father is waiting in your office." His secretary announced.

"Thanks Carol, I'll be there as soon as I can. I'm with a family right now."

Thad made his way to his office after the consult. *Now what is he up to? It can't be good if he came this far unannounced.* Thad entered his office. "Hello, Father."

"Thaddeus."

"I'm surprised to see you. What can I do for you?"

"I came to try to talk some sense into you. You can call off this farce of a wedding, come home, and marry a decent girl. Abigail said that she's willing to forgive you."

The muscle twitched in Thad's jaw. He took a slow, deep breath and even counted to ten before he answered his father.

"Father, I told you, I'm in love with Lauren. I am going to marry her in four days. I'm telling you the same thing I told Abigail. I don't love her, and I won't marry her. Even if I didn't marry Lauren, I wouldn't marry her. You don't have to accept that fact if you don't want to, but that's the way it is."

"You stupid, ungrateful fool. How can you turn your back on all that we've given you for some low—?"

"Watch it, Father. I told you I won't stand for you calling Lauren names."

"That's it! I wash my hands of you. You're no longer my son. As of today, I'm cutting you out of my will. As long as you're with that woman, don't set foot in my house. If you come to your senses before you make a bigger fool of yourself, you can come back and all will be forgiven." He turned and walked out of the office.

Thad buried his face in his hands as he sat trembling in the chair behind his desk. His eyes burned with unshed tears as he mourned the loss of his family.

I'm an orphan, he lamented to himself. *No father, no mother, no sisters. All I have left is my brother, no other family. But, I could resurrect my family if I denied my one true love; If I denied the one person who loves me unconditionally, if I denied my only chance of true happiness.*

Instead of going to Lauren's house after work, as he had planned to do, Thad went directly to his house. *Lauren doesn't need to see me like this.* Once home, he headed straight to the cabinet where he sought the one bottle of alcoholic beverage he had in the house. He fixed himself a stiff drink and then called Gene, his only link to the family that he had just lost. "Are you still coming to my wedding, Gene?"

"Of course I am. What's up with you, Thad? Why are you asking such a silly question?" Thad told him about their father's visit.

Gene let out a long whistle. "Man! I'm sorry. I didn't think he'd really go through with that threat. I think he's sick on power. He can't stand anyone going against his wishes. But, to disown you! That's low even for him. I'm willing to bet that Mother is going along with him, too. They're both sick." Gene hesitated a moment before asking, "You still have that trust fund that Grandmother Beavers left for you, don't you? That's worth half a million."

"It's still intact. I don't care about the money, Gene. I earn a hefty salary, and I have investments. It's more important to have someone who loves me just as I am."

"Thank, God for Lauren. Have you told her yet?"

"No, I haven't. I came directly home and called you. I'll call her later. I've been staying at her house since Sunday."

"More threats?"

"Yes."

"How is she holding up?"

"She's doing very well as of this morning."

"Hang in there. You know that Joan and I will always be here for you. When they find out that I'm sticking by you, they'll probably disown me, too."

"No they won't. You have the only male Bradford heir.

They're depending on him to continue the Bradford dynasty. To carry on the Bradford name."

"Not in the tradition they've set. You and Lauren have shown me what snobs we are. I'm putting an end to that now while Timmy is still young enough to be molded." Gene said of his five year old son. "Is Lauren taking the Bradford name or is she keeping hers?"

"She's a brave lady, she's taking ours. I should say that is the plan. I don't know what she'll do once I tell her about today's events." He drew in a deep breath and let it out slowly before continuing, "I think I'd better go and call to tell her I'm staying home tonight."

"All right, Thad, you take care, and I'll see you on Friday. I love you, brother."

"Thanks Gene. I love you too. Goodnight."

*****

Lauren answered the phone with a laugh in her voice. "Why, hello, Mr. Bradford. How are you?"

"Hello sweetheart. How are you?"

"I'm good. I'll be much better once you get here. Are you on your way?"

"No. I'm at home. I think I'll spend the night here."

After a short pause Lauren asked, "Are you all right?"

"I'm okay. How are the girls?"

"The girls are okay, but you're not. Please, tell me what's wrong."

"Just a little tired, and I have some things I need to think through."

"You're not getting cold feet are you?"

"No. I'm going to marry you on Saturday come hell or high water. I love you."

"I love you too, but I feel that you're keeping something from me."

"Stop fretting, love. I'll see you tomorrow. Good night."

That woman is too perceptive. If I had stayed on the phone with her any longer, I might have started bawling. As much as I need her, I can't breakdown in front of her. Not with what she's going through.

*****

Lauren stared at the receiver in her hand. *There's something bothering him, and it's not me, because if that was the case, he'd be here with me. He sounded so weary and drained. Something is weighing heavily on him.* Lauren dialed his number, but got no answer. She waited five minutes, and then dialed again. There was still no answer. Fifteen minutes later there was still no answer on either of his phones. Checking her watch, she noted that it was six forty-five. Lauren spied Mrs. Brown and Wendy on the patio with the girls. She grabbed her purse and keys and slipped out to the garage. When she was a few minutes from Thad's house, she called to let Wendy know where she was, and to say that she would call her again before she returned home.

She rang the doorbell, but there was no answer. After a few moments, she tried again without results. She began pounding on the door with her fists. Suddenly the door swung opened.

Thad stood in the doorway shoeless, shirt unbuttoned, eyes blood shot, and reeking of alcohol. "What in blazes! Lauren? What are you doing here? Did you come alone?"

"I came to see about you. And, yes, I came alone."

"Putting yourself in danger again, are you? I thought we had gone through this once before. "His voice held anger.

"I'm safe and sound. From the looks of things, I'm in much better shape than you are. Are you going to invite me in?"

He sighed and stepped aside.

Lauren called Wendy to tell her that she was at Thad's, and that she was safe. She added that she'd call her again before she headed home.

Lauren put on a pot of coffee, and then joined Thad at the kitchen table. While holding his hand in hers; they sat quietly waiting for the coffee to brew.

When the coffee was ready, Lauren fixed Thad a cup. "Here you are, darling?" She placed the mug in front of him.

He took a couple of sips of the steaming hot brew before leaning forward on the table with his face buried in his arms.

Lauren stood behind his chair and leaned over his back to hug his neck. "Talk to me. We're in this together."

For a while, neither of them moved nor spoke. Several minutes later, he sat up and leaned his shoulders into her, reaching for her hands as he did so.

She kissed the top of his head. "Tell me."

Thad squeezed her hands and kissed the knuckles one by one. "They disowned me, Lauren. My parents said that I'm not their son anymore. I've been banned from their house."

"Oh, God. I'm so sorry." She hugged him close before moving around to kneeled in front of him and wrap her arms around his waist. "Tell me what happened."

He drew in a deep breath, let it out, and placed his hands on her shoulders. "I had to choose between you and my family. When I chose you, I lost them. My father came to my office this afternoon and gave me an ultimatum. As long as I'm with you, I'm not their son, and I'm not to set foot in their house. He also said that Abigail is waiting to forgive me, and that we can still be married. As of today, I've been cut out of their wills."

Lauren held him for a while longer then stood and led him to the den. She sat on the sofa, pulled him down beside her, and invited him to rest his head in her lap. They remained in that position for the better part of an hour. Except for the gentle caress of her fingers against his temple, there was no movement or speech.

Lauren continued to caress his temple. "What can I do, sweetheart?"

" As always, darling, just continue to love me. You and Gene are all I have now."

"Have you told him what happened?"

"Yes, I talked with him just before I called you. He's thinking that he might be an outcast by association, but he's not concerned about it. He also thinks that our parents are sick, and I agree with him. He said that he and Joan will be here Friday evening."

"Thank, God for them, darling. Do you need more time to think about this? About us getting married?"

"I've thought and thought about it and I keep coming up with the same answer.

I want to spend the rest of my life with you. I've told you before that my parents can't take anything from me that I need. In the past weeks, I've come to realize that I never really had their love. The only thing that I'm losing is a sense of family, no matter how dysfunctional it is." Thad squeezed her fingers. "Anyway, I'll have my own family in a few days." He gave her a faint smile. "By the way, I'm a little perturbed with you for coming here without an escort. You may have put yourself in more danger."

"I know, but I needed to know that you were okay. Why didn't you answer your phones?"

"Actually, I never checked to see who was calling. I thought it may have been my parents. I was scared sober when I saw you standing at the door without Wendy."

"How long or shall I ask how many drinks have you had?"

"I don't know. I got home around four-thirty, and I went directly to the cabinet. I may have had three or four. I'm sorry, baby. I just needed something to dull the pain."

"I understand, but the next time you need to handle something, anything, please come to me. You know as well as I do, that drinking doesn't solve anything."

"You don't need any more stress."

"Together, darling. Remember?"

"Yes, ma'am. I remember. Excuse me for a few minutes I need to get cleaned up."

Thad stood in the door, fresh from a shower with his overnight bag. "Are you ready to go?"

"I will be as soon as I get my dessert and call Wendy."

Michelle and Amy, Lauren's sisters, arrived on Thursday afternoon, as did her brother Alvin. With a house full of family, Lauren told Thad that she felt safe enough for him to return to his house until after the wedding.

The families met at Lauren's house on Friday evening for a get acquainted dinner. When asked if any of his family, other than Gene, was attending the wedding, Thad answered that they weren't able to make it.

The phone rang while they were eating. Mrs. Brown beckoned to Lauren, "Telephone Ms. J."

"Hello?"

"Call it off and you'll have a cashier's check for one quarter of a million dollars in your hands at eight o'clock tomorrow morning. Just say the word."

"No, thank you." Lauren replaced the receiver. *Darn him! He's certainly not going down without a fight.* She fought to regain her composure before she returned to the table.

"Okay, ladies, let's get these dishes cleaned so that we can put this little girl to bed." Michelle gave Lauren a teasing jab. "She has a big day ahead of her tomorrow."

Thad took her by the arm and asked, "May I have a word with you before you turn in?"

"Sure. Let's go into the study." Lauren closed the door, and turned to him. "What's up?"

"You tell me. Who was that on the phone?"

"Oh, Thad." She attempted to embrace him, but he caught her hands in his.

"Together Lauren." His gaze bore into hers.

"It was your father. You're now worth a quarter of a million dollars."

"Damn him!" He pulled her into his arms and held her tight. "Hold out until noon, and I bet you could get half of a million."

"Kiss me, darling."

"With pleasure, Miss Jeffries." He kissed her long and with passion. "This is the last time I'll be able to kiss a single woman."

"And me a single man. Are you sure you want to give up all of the benefits of being single? She kissed him again. "I love you, Thad."

"There are more and better benefits in being married. I love you, Lauren. You mean everything to me. Let's go check on the girls before I leave. I missed seeing them today."

* * * * *

Amy poked her head in the door. “Lauren, may we come in for a few minutes?”

"Of course, come in.”

Lauren’s siblings entered the room, and then closed the door behind them. “What’s going on, sis?" Alvin asked. “Who is Wendy and why is she carrying a gun? And why are the twins sleeping in your room?”

“I was wondering how long it would take before that question came up. I'm not going to lie to you. I just don’t know where to start. Well." She sighed and sat up in the bed. “Some one or more than one have threatened mine and the girls’ lives. Wendy is FBI, and she's been staying here for a month.” Lauren told them the story from the beginning, including the busy bodies and the Bradfords.

“I didn’t tell any of you because I didn’t want anyone to know anything about you all. Whoever this is might be sick enough to go after those that I love. None of my friends know what’s going on either. So far, it’s just the girls and me. We didn't announce our wedding, and except for the handful of people we invited, the hospital and university aren't aware of the pending nuptials. There'll be a dozen or so agents at the wedding, posing as waiters, guests, valets etc. We will all be well protected.”

“I don’t like this at all,” Alvin said.

“Nor do I,” Michelle added.

“Listen. If they wanted to do me bodily harm, they’ve had ample opportunity. I think, as does the FBI, that they are trying to frighten me. We just can’t figure out why. I haven’t done anything to anybody that I’m aware of.”

Michelle sat on the bed. “I take it that’s the reason you decided not to go away for a honeymoon.”

“Once the girls were threatened, I couldn’t leave them.

The original plan was for us to get married in September and honeymoon in Hawaii, but after all of this, Thad insisted that we move the date up. He wants to be able to stay here every night without compromising my reputation.”

Alvin spoke up. "How's he taking the situation with his family, Lauren?"

"He's devastated. He shouldn't have been forced to make that choice."

"Well." Alvin continued, "He's proven how much he loves you, sis. It took a lot of courage to walk away from all of that. Love is the only incentive he needed."

"Girl, if you're offered a half mil tomorrow, take it, and give it to me. Better yet, since we look so much alike, I'll sign for it in your stead."

"Alright Amy, it's time for you, and us, to get out of here so that Lauren can get some sleep," Alvin said affectionately. "Good night sis."

"Good night. I love you guys. Sleep well."

*****

Lauren decided to call Thad to say goodnight. "Hi, baby. How are things?"

"Everything is fine, love. I just wanted to hear your voice again before I go to sleep. How come you're still up?"

"I was filling Gene and Joan in on the latest."

"How did they react?"

"Same as I did. Disgusted."

"I had to tell my siblings the whole story, too. They questioned Wendy's presence and the fact that she wears a gun. They're uncomfortable with the situation, but are very happy that you will be here with us. They have a lot of respect and love for you for wanting to take care of me."

"That's good to know. Maybe I can depend on them to help keep you in line." He chuckled.

"No, you didn't just try to use that bit of information against me. Half a million is beginning to look pretty good about now."

"I give, I give." He laughed. "I love you, Lauren. Get some sleep now."

"I love you, Brad. Good night."

CHAPTER TWENTY-FIVE

Michelle stared at Lauren, who stood before her arrayed in her wedding gown. "What a beautiful day for a wedding; looks as if it's a special order for a special lady."

"Oh, Michelle, I'm so happy. I did pray for a cool sunny day. You look so pretty. Mauve is your color."

"And you're beautiful, little sister. We'd better get a move on. Wendy and Mrs. Brown are waiting downstairs with the girls. All of us are going to ride in the limo with you."

"I'm ready, Michelle."

"Another picture, Ms. Jeffries," the photographer said.

Lauren gave him a bright smile. "This is the last photo I'll take in this house as Lauren Jeffries."

*****

Vivian escorted Lauren and Michelle to a room that she had deemed the bride's room.

"You can relax here for a few minutes while I get everyone settled. Everyone on your guest list has arrived. And so has Thad." Vivian winked.

Lauren embraced her friend. "Thank you, Vivian–for everything."

"The pleasure is all mine. I had a ball putting it together. You have about fifteen minutes."

"Ready, Ms. Jeffries?" Alvin called to his sister as he pushed open the door.

"Ready, sir." She smiled.

Vivian had done a marvelous job of transforming her back yard into a beautiful wedding chapel. Everything was dressed in mauve and cream. The guests sat at the ten round tables placed on either side of the aisle.

Brittany and Brianna sat in high chairs surrounded by Amy, Mrs. Brown, Agent Pam Thatcher, and an un-identified man.

A keyboard player provided music. Michelle and her husband, Joe, marched in, followed by Thad and Gene.

Everyone stood for the bride's entrance as the musician played Here Comes the Bride. Lauren wore a long, white, strapless gown with a veil that sat on the crown of her head and flowed to her waist. Thad wore a white tuxedo with mauve cummerbund and bow tie. Their eyes met and held for several seconds before she began her march down the aisle.

The reception lasted for two hours after which Lauren, very reluctantly, left her daughters in the care of her sisters, brother, Mrs. Brown, and Wendy while she accompanied her husband to a nearby hotel for a three-day honeymoon.

CHAPTER TWENTY-SIX

Everything went smoothly for the three weeks, following the wedding.

Thad insisted that Lauren and the girls move into their new home before he returned to work. He lived in a four year old, two storied house that consisted of five bedrooms, four bathrooms and a three-car garage. The house was located on two acres of land in an up-scale neighborhood of young professionals.

Lauren and Thad spent several evenings surfing the internet and perusing decorator magazines in the pursuit of finding the perfect furnishings for the unfurnished living room, dining room, sitting room, her office and the breakfast nook.

The walls in the house were painted soft earth tones, and still looked freshly done. All of the floors on the first floor as well as the stairs were of hardwood while all of the stairs had neutral toned carpet.

After they were assured that the ordered items would be delivered by the end of the month, Thad reluctantly returned to work.

Not once, during the following three-week period did anyone spot any suspicious vehicles or people, nor were there any harassing phone calls or dead animals.

Agent Coles decided that now was a good time to end Wendy's assignment. So, with a plea for them to call immediately if any more incidents occurred, Wendy was reassigned.

*****

Lauren returned to work in the middle of August with a greater sense of security than she had left with in May.

There were several new faces at the faculty get acquainted luncheon. Mr. Hennesy and Leland Bland had accepted positions out of state. Their replacements were Dr. Amanda Stanton and Dr. Greg Long respectively.

Dr. Mason, who still held the position of chancellor, appeared to be just as uncomfortable in her presence as he had been during their last meeting.

While Thad and Lauren were talking with Vivian Reed and Amanda Stanton, Dr. Mason joined them. "Congratulations, Thad. You and Dr. Jeffries sure pulled a fast one on us. I guess I'd never have known, had I not run into your parents," he added with a smug tone. He turned to Lauren. "So, Dr. Jeffries, are you taking on Dr. Bradfords' name or are you keeping yours?"

"My name is Lauren Jeffries Bradford. I answer to both. Now that Thad has made an honest or shall I say respectable woman out of me, your job should be a lot easier."

"Excuse us, Dr. Mason." Thad touched Lauren's elbow and led her away. "Let it go, love."

"That's easy for you to say. Even now, he's goading us, letting us know that he's connected, and that he can get any information he wants. I bet he knows that your parents disapprove of me, too."

"He probably does, and he's probably told others. I just don't want you to let him pull you down to his level. He's angry because you told him off, and then snubbed him by not attending his holiday affair. The fact that others witnessed it is unforgivable."

"He doesn't intimidate me. Anyway, I'm going to work. I'll see you when you get home."

"I like the sound of that, sweetheart." Thad smiled and gave her a peck on the cheek.

"Kind of partial to it myself, partner." She joked. "But, you'd better watch that peck on the cheek stuff. We haven't been married that long. Have we?"

"Just be glad that we are at work, young lady."

*****

Later in the evening, Lauren and Thad sat down to dinner. Lauren dabbed her lips. "I miss Wendy sitting here at the table with us."

"I do, too, but I'm happy that she's not needed anymore. It's been a stress free month and I'm enjoying it. I love being married, Lauren."

"Oh, so do I and I love you. I'm happy we got married when we did instead of waiting until next month."

"I'm happy to hear that. I was afraid you might resent my pushing you for an earlier date."

"Never. I'm happier than I could ever have imagined."

*****

The newlyweds invited Vivian, Wendy, Linda, Agent Coles and both sets of Wilcoxes to a Labor Day cook out. Including twelve children, there were thirty-one adults, enjoying the sumptuous food off the grill as well as other cookout fare.

The temperature reached a blistering one hundred degrees in the shade with no breeze, but thankfully, without humidity.

Everyone, Brittany and Brianna included, were enjoying refreshing dips in the pool when Mrs. Brown summoned Lauren; telling her that she had an urgent phone call.

Lauren ran into the house and picked up the receiver. "Hello? Hello?" The connection went dead.

"Was the caller male or female?"

"It was a man." Mrs. Brown stated. "He asked, is Ms. Jeffries there? It's urgent that I speak to her."

"There aren't any details on the call. I'm going to call my family and see if one of them called."

Lauren's investigation revealed that Michelle and Amy were together. Alvin and his family were in the park with his in-laws and Bernie was still at Camp LeJeune. Gene and Joan were in Hawaii.

Why would anyone say the call was urgent then not stay on the phone? Oh well, he'll call back if it was important, she thought as she returned to the pool.

Coles reclined on an adjacent lounger. How's it going, Lauren? Any more harassment?"

"No. Not really."

"What's not really?"

"I got a call a few minutes ago. The caller said he had an urgent call for Ms. Jeffries, but when I got to the phone, the line was dead. No one in my family called. The only person in Thad's family who'd call us is Gene, and he and his family are in Hawaii. They would have asked for Thad, anyway."

"That's the only unexplained call you've gotten in the past five weeks?"

"That's it."

"I need to talk to Mrs. Brown." Coles stood and walked into the house.

*****

Lauren climbed into bed beside Thad. "Thad, did Dan Coles talk to you today?"

"No. Was he supposed to?"

"I thought he would. I received a strange phone call today." She retold the story.

"And you're just telling me?"

"What was there to tell, love?"

CHAPTER TWENTY-SEVEN

Lauren, Amanda, and Vivian founded *Women of Substance*, a support group for young women between the ages of eighteen and thirty-five–a place where there was no pressure to compete. The main focus was on relationships with a special focus on family dynamics.

The center was located in a renovated office building several blocks from the university, and was opened on Tuesdays and Thursdays.

Although there were no drugs, medical or educational services provided on site, the participants, if needed, were given referrals to the appropriate agencies.

By the middle of October, there were twenty-one participants in the group. Many of these women were coping with self-esteem issues, stemming from as far back as their childhood.

Except for the once a month potluck, no meals were served at the center. There were, however, fruit snacks, juices, and water. The last thirty minutes of each meeting was dedicated to a member led exercise routine.

Lauren petitioned the police department to have a cruiser in the area between nine and nine-fifteen on the evenings of the meetings.

All the participants were having a wonderful time, shedding the stresses that constantly pulled on their life strings. Everyone seemed to embrace one of the most important themes of the program-we are all equal.

At the end of October, two more participants enrolled in the program. They brought with them a spirit of nonconformity. Their mission seemed to be to upset the smooth flow of the program.

During the second week of their arrival, there was an altercation between Amanda and Doris, one of the new participants. Amanda had asked her to put out the cigarette that she was smoking in the ladies' room.

When she refused to comply, the woman was asked to leave the premises. Although, Lauren was not involved in any of the proceedings; as she was escorted out of the building, Doris shot her a threatening look and yelled. "You'll be sorry. You'll pay for this."

Two of the program's participants drove vehicles of the same make and model as Lauren, but differed slightly in color.

On, Thursday, the second session after Doris was expelled; Lauren and the other two ladies exited the building to find all four tires on each of their vehicles slashed.

Lauren knew instantly that this incident had nothing to do with the other two women. The culprit couldn't distinguish the cars in the dark, so slashed the tires on all three to get to hers. It was unanimous, everyone at the center believed that Doris, angry because of the expulsion, was behind the tire slashing, but Lauren knew better.

When Lauren arrived home, Mrs. Brown had already put the girls to bed, and had retired to her room. Thad was in the study.

"Hi, sweetheart," she greeted as she hung her coat in the closet.

"Lauren," he said, without looking up from the paper in his hand.

"Lauren? What kind of greeting is that? What's the matter with you?"

"Enjoying your sessions at the center?"

"I am. Did you talk with Dan?" Lauren sat in a chair opposite Thad.

"What has he got to do with the center?"

"Okay. What's going on, Thad? What do you have stuck in your craw?"

"Maybe you should take a look at these, and then answer your own questions." Thad thrust an envelope into her hands.

"Thad!" Lauren glanced at him in alarm as she grabbed the envelope before it fell to the floor. She opened the envelope and gasped as she eyed four photos. One was of her hugging a man, and three which looked like a man kissing her.

"Well?"

Lauren held up the photo of her hugging a man. "I can explain this one. But, I don't know about these. Where did you get them?"

"They were mailed to me at the hospital. You're still saying that you don't know anything about them. A man kissing you and you don't know anything about it. Do I really look like that big a fool?"

Lauren felt as if he had slapped her. Tears burned her eyes. "In this photo," she said huskily, as she pointed to one of the photos, "is Gary Bronson, the high school classmate I told you I had seen over a month ago.

The same one that you told me I should have invited to dinner. These others, I don't know about. Take a closer look. It looks like my face, but have you ever seen me wear clothes like that? Or is it that you're buying into the notion that I'm a slut, too? That's exactly what this looks like, a picture of a harlot."

She hesitated briefly before she went to stand before him. "You listen to me Thaddeus Bradford. As you know, I was a virgin when you married me. You're the only man I've been sexually intimate with. I love you with all my heart and I have absolutely no reason to be slumming around. I have been faithful to you. If I wanted to be with someone else, I would have left you four months ago, and been a quarter of a million dollars richer for it. I don't know who sent you those pictures, or who has had the time to follow me or who wants to hurt me that much. I suggest you take a good look at those pictures, and then take a good look at our marriage, because if you ever accuse me of being unfaithful again I promise you, I will walk out of this house and never look back. Now that, my dear husband, you can bet your life on." Lauren stormed from room before the tears could fall.

The doorbell rang while she was half way up the stairs, but she didn't bother to go back to answer it. *Let him get it.* She continued up the stairs.

A few minutes later, Thad knocked on the opened bathroom door.

"Lauren, Alan Wilcox wants to talk to you. He's downstairs."

"I'll be down shortly." She splashed water on her face, and headed back downstairs and into the kitchen. "Hi, Alan."

"Hi, Lauren. You know I'm a little peeved with you, don't you?"

"No. But I'm not surprised. You aren't alone. What brings you out this late?"

"Why didn't you tell me about what's been going on at the center? Given the history of harassment, you could be in danger."

"That's exactly why I didn't tell you. I'm not going through that again."

"You aren't the only one involved in this, Lauren," Thad said just as the doorbell rang again.

"My. My. Aren't we popular tonight? Who else have you invited to this soiree?"

With his hand on the knob, Thad turned to her. "Lauren! They have your best interest at heart. The least you could do is cut the sarcasm." He opened the door. "Come in, Dan. Alan and Lauren are in the kitchen."

Coles shook hands with Alan and nodded in response to Lauren's nod. "So?" he said to Lauren. "Since the call on Labor Day you've had two women disrupt your support center, a verbal threat, slashed tires, and now, these photos. Have you left out anything?"

Lauren's "Isn't that enough?" earned a warning glance from Thad. Dan fingered the photo. "Lauren, if I didn't know you, I'd be inclined to believe that this is a photo of you, too."

"At least you gave me the benefit of the doubt." She glared at Thad.

"We're going to take these photos to the lab to examine them more closely. The harassment could be starting all over again. Lauren, we have to depend on you to tell us if there are anymore incidents."

"I'll tell you, but you're not going to station an agent at my house, again."

"Lauren, be reasonable. You aren't the only one in this. Have you forgotten about the girls?" Thad asked, urgency lacing his voice.

"How dare...?"

Coles spoke up. "It hasn't gotten to that point. This could be something altogether different."

Lauren sounded annoyed. "I know you don't believe that, Dan. And, you don't have to sugar coat anything for my benefit."

"Well, I think that's all we can do for now. We'll let you know what we learn about these photos. Remember Lauren. Call us."

"Goodnight Alan, Dan." She headed for the stairs, leaving Thad to see the men out.

Thad was sitting on the side of the bed when Lauren entered the room after her shower.

"Lauren, I'm so sorry for accusing you of being unfaithful. Please forgive me. Those pictures scared me to death."

Lauren continued towards her side of the bed without comment.

Thad pulled her roughly against his chest and held her. "I'm sorry, Lauren. I'm sorry." Lauren stood unresponsive. He eased his hold on her so that he could see her face.

Tears streamed down her face. Thad lifted her in his arms, and sat on the bed, holding her close as the tears continued to fall. After the tears subsided, he handed her a box of tissue. "Talk to me, Lauren."

"How could you?" She sniffed. "You sounded just like your parents. I would never dress like that nor would I ever cheat on you."

Thad gestured as if his heart had fallen to the bottom of his stomach. "Lauren, I would never think of you that way! Baby, I never saw the clothes until you pointed them out to me. All I saw was what looked like a man kissing my wife. And in the other, you were embracing a man, and you seemed to be enjoying it. I was scared Lauren. I didn't know if I was losing you or sharing you.

I do know that I didn't want to do either. I love you sweetheart. Forgive me. No matter how long I stared at those pictures, I still saw the same thing; a man kissing my wife. I never saw clothes. Can you understand how I could feel that way? Please, please don't compare my love for you with the contempt my parents feel for you. You are my friend, my wife and my lover. I love you so much and I'm so sorry."

"I'm sorry, too, Thad. I forgive you. Somebody almost got their wish. They're trying to break us up."

"We aren't going to give them the satisfaction. We made a vow to each other and we are sticking to it, together."

"Yes, we are."

CHAPTER TWENTY-EIGHT

The next day, Thad called home to inform Lauren that he had to go out of town on an emergency. "How's everything there, darling?"

"Everything is fine. Are you on your way home?"

"I am, baby, but I won't be able to stay. I have an emergency in Hartford. It's a doctor patient confidential issue, and given all that has transpired in recent months; I don't want to talk about it on the phone. Would you pack a bag for me? Five or six days' worth of clothes? No suits. I'll be home in about thirty minutes."

*****

Lauren zipped the bag. "What's the emergency? What is it that you couldn't talk about on the phone?"

"The governor has taken ill, his physician is out of the country, and I've been called in for a consult. Anything other than that, I guess you'll have to find out through the news media. I don't know how long I'll be gone." He made a dash for the shower.

At the sound of the car horn, Thad slipped on his coat. "Take good care of yourself and the girls, sweetheart. You mean everything to me. Please don't take any chances. Tell Dan if there are any more incidents. I love you." He kissed her. "I'll call as soon as I can." Thad hurried to the waiting car.

*****

Lauren answered her office phone. "Lauren Jeffries."

"Lauren, this is Dan Coles. I'd like to stop by if you have a minute."

"How did you know I'd be here on a Saturday?"

"I called your house. Mrs. Brown told me you were at work. Can I stop by?"

"Okay, but I have a teleconference in forty-five minutes."

"I can be there in ten."

A few minutes later, Dan arrived at Lauren's office. "What's up, Dan?" Lauren asked as she motioned him to sit.

"We got the report back on the pictures. Your face was definitely superimposed. Do you have any idea how they may have gotten a picture of you?"

"No. I don't. I don't remember those head shots. If the whole photo was intact, I might be able to tell when and where it was taken."

"I've never been so baffled by a case before. We've gone over everything dozens of times and we still can't come up with a plausible reason for all of this."

Lauren stood peering out the window. She sighed deeply, and without facing the agent said, "I don't know why you haven't figured out who is behind this. I have."

"What! You have?" He sounded astonished. "Who do you suspect?"

Lauren emitted another deep sigh, and then whispered. "Thad's parents."

Coles stared at her. "Are you serious? Do you really believe that they would stoop to this? This is incredible. Have you told Thad that you suspect them?"

"Yes, I truly believe it. And no, I haven't mentioned my suspicion to Thad." Lauren faced the agent. "I would appreciate it if you didn't either. Not to him or any of your agents until you have thoroughly investigated it. If you investigated on my word, and my suspicions are unfounded, it could mean the end of my marriage."

"What makes you think they could be involved?"

Lauren unlocked her desk drawer and pulled out a journal. "This is a chronological log of every encounter I've had, directly and indirectly, with the elder Bradfords. And this," she flipped the page, "is how these events fit into the entire list of events surrounding the harassments. The Bradfords have friends in this area, even on the board at the university; my boss included. Money can buy loyalty and position, and enough money can buy murder. What isn't written there, are conversations between Thad and his parents relative to their feelings about me, and his being married to me?"

Coles flipped through the journal. "Whew! Would you consider working for the agency? I wish we had agents as methodical as you are. How is it that you haven't shown me this before now?"

"I had to know that I could trust you. But most of all, I don't want to hurt my husband."

"What was the deciding factor in you telling me?"

"That photo supposedly of me kissing some man. That person is dressed like a low-life. That's how his parents regard me, especially his mother. I believe now that things are going to get worse. Now, for the first time, I believe they'll try to have me killed, just so I can't carry the Bradford name."

"Good God, Lauren! I hate to admit this, but what you're saying makes a lot of sense. We might need to assign an agent to you again. At least to the twins. I don't think anyone would stoop to harming Thad."

"Only if he stays married to me."

"Maybe I should stop by and talk to both of you this evening."

"Thad's in Hartford for a few days."

"I'll take this." He patted the journal.

"No Dan. I'll make you a copy."

"You still don't trust me do you?"

"Ninety-nine and nine tenths." She smiled.

"Be very careful, Lauren. I know you believe that those participants at the center were working with whoever has been harassing you, and now I do too."

"I don't want anyone else getting hurt. I might have to quit the center."

"Don't quit yet. Let's see what we can do. We're going to add extra marked and unmarked patrols in the area. I'll call you later this evening."

*****

Lauren answered Thad's call later that evening. "How are things, Brad? You sound tired. "

"I'm beat," answered Thad. "I guess you heard the news reports."

"No. I haven't watched any news today. What's up?"

"The governor had quadruple by-pass surgery. It was touch and go there for a while. He's critical, but I'm optimistic."

"Did you perform the surgery?"

"Yes. We were in there for more than six hours. There were some complications. How was your day? How are the girls?"

"We're all fine. I spoke to Dan today, and he confirmed that my face was superimposed onto those photos."

"I knew it would prove that, sweetheart."

"He said that they're going to step up the patrols around the Center and around here."

"Please be careful, Lauren. I can't wait to get home, but I have to be sure that the governor is out of danger before I leave."

"Do what you must. We'll be okay and I'll be careful. I love you."

"I love you, Lauren. I'm going to shower and go to bed."

"Did you get a chance to eat?"

"I ate a sandwich earlier. I'm much more tired than I am hungry. I'll call you tomorrow. Love you."

"Love you back."

Lauren turned the television to the late news as she prepared for bed. *"Dr. Thaddeus Bradford, a renowned heart specialist at Parkdale Medical and Research Hospital in Dalton, was summoned to Hartford to perform the surgery. Dr. Bradford stated that, "although the surgery was a success, the governor is still critical, but we are very optimistic. He's resting peacefully."* The story was also carried on the national news.

At nine minutes past midnight, the ringing of the telephone awakened Lauren. "Hello?" All she heard was what sounded like the recorded cackle of an old woman. She checked the caller ID, and noted that there was no data.

Lauren picked up the phone and dialed. "This is Lauren Jeffries Bradford. May I speak to Agent Coles, please?"

"How are you Lauren?" Dan answered.

"I'm a nervous wreck. I received a call. It was a recording of what sounded like a cackling old woman. The kind you hear in movies."

"Did you get a number?"

"No. There was no data. I didn't think too many people had this number. We do know who does have it. Don't we? The call came about an hour after the late news carried the story that Thad is in Hartford tending the governor."

"That's too much of a coincidence. I'll check into it, and I'll make sure that the cruisers are on patrol as ordered. Try to get some sleep. I'll check with you tomorrow."

* * * * *

There were no calls or other disturbances during the next five days. Thad appeared at Lauren's office door. "Hey, sexy lady."

"Brad!" Lauren squealed, and dashed from behind her desk into Thad's arms. "I'm so happy to see you. That was the longest six days in history. How is the governor?"

"He's recovering nicely. No more complications. How are my girls?"

"They're good. They missed you, too."

Thad glanced at his watch. "It's three-thirty. Can you slip out a little early?"

"I think so. Let me get this report to Janet and make a phone call." She dialed the phone and spoke for a few minutes before hanging up and joining him at the door.

"I'm ready, sweetheart." They walked down the hall.

"Is everything okay? No calls or any other mischief?"

"There was one call. Where would they have gotten your number? You aren't listed."

"I don't know. What did they say?"

"They didn't say anything. It was just a recording of a cackling old woman."

"Did you report it?"

"I did. Right after it happened."

"Good. May I ask a favor of you?"

"Of course you may. What is it?"

"Don't go to the Center tonight."

Lauren glanced at him and smiled. "I wasn't planning to. That's what that phone call was all about."

*****

Lauren called as they entered the house, "Mrs. Brown, we're home!"

Mrs. Brown entered the room with the twins in tow. "Welcome home, Dr. Bradford, Mrs. Jeffries."

"Hello, angels." Lauren bent to kiss her daughters. "Daddy is home."

"How are my little girls?" Thad asked.

"Dada," Brittany babbled.

"Dada," Brianna echoed.

Thad's mouth fell open. "My stars! Did you hear that? They called me daddy." Thad lifted both of the girls and gave them each a kiss on the cheek. He glanced at Lauren. "Thank you darling. What a wonderful welcome home."

"Thank Mrs. Brown, too. She helped me teach them."

"Thank you, Mrs. Brown. Thank you."

Lauren teased, "And for that, Mrs. Brown, you can have the weekend off starting right now. Now, go and call that young man of yours."

"Mrs. Jeffries!" Mrs. Brown blushed.

"What? You think I can't spot a person in love? I do have a little experience you know."

"What are we going to do with her, Dr. B.? She sees too much." Mrs. Brown laughed.

"I don't know, but I'm sure I can think of something."

Thad's cell phone rang a couple of times during the evening, but he opted not to answer. After the second call, he turned the phone off. They played with the girls for a while before putting them to bed.

*****

The next morning Thad stared across the table at Lauren. "How would you like to visit Michelle for the weekend?"

"What a good idea. When do you want to leave?"

"As soon as you can get packed. I'll call Hartford to check on the governor while you get ready."

By ten a.m. they were on their way to New Jersey. Lauren cast Thad a loving smile. "Thank you, sweetheart."

"Thanks for what?"

"I know what you're doing. And you're right. I do need this."

He grumbled good-naturedly. "You're too smart for your own good."

Thad's phone rang again. He checked the caller ID and chose not to answer it. He glanced at Lauren to gauge her reaction.

"It's okay. You'll tell me when you're ready." She smiled.

"I love you, woman."

"I know you do."

CHAPTER TWENTY-NINE

The week before Thanksgiving, Lauren and Michelle sat in the den talking. "Lauren. Thanksgiving is next week. Why didn't you all wait until then to visit?"

"We're having dinner with Vivian and her family on Thanksgiving. Plus, you know I don't like traveling on holidays. In addition to that, the forecast calls for snow and sleet."

"Amy and her family are coming tomorrow. Did you know that Bernie and Alvin will be joining us at Amy's for Christmas? It seems that you're the only one who's not going to be there."

"Thanks. Make me feel guilty, why don't you. Anyway I don't know what we're doing yet. I'll be out of school for three weeks, but I don't know how much time Thad can take off."

"How's everything else going, Lauren? Have you gotten anymore threats?"

"We've gotten a couple." Lauren picked up a pillow.

"I'm worried about you. Aren't you afraid?"

"Not for myself, but for the girls. They're protected while we're at work, and there are patrols at night. As long as Thad is home I feel pretty safe."

"I'm glad you do, because I don't. The police still have no idea who's behind this?" Michelle asked.

"No. I think they're following some new leads. Can we please change the subject? I want to escape all of that—for the weekend at least."

*****

Lauren offered to drive as they prepared to return home.

"You can drive if you like, but I'm not tired. That was the most relaxing weekend I've had in a long time. I hadn't been fishing since college."

"I'm glad you had a good time. Ray and Don are good people, and they enjoy their fishing no matter the weather."

"It appears you enjoyed yourself, too. You seem so relaxed and stress free. Maybe we should consider moving."

"What good would that do? Remember, the calls were coming from three different states.

Some of the no data sent calls could have come from yet another state. We're not going to let whoever is doing this have us hopping from state to state."

Thad's cell phone rang.

"Go ahead, answer it. She's not going to stop until you do."

"You know who it is?" He looked surprised.

"Not exactly. It's one of two people or both."

"What are you, some kind of seer or something?"

"No, sir. I'm just an intuitive female so, be careful." She winked.

"It's both, and I don't feel like being bothered with either."

*****

There were two messages on the answering machine when they arrived home. The first was an unknown caller and the other was a cryptic message from Velma Bradford. "Thad this is your mother. Call me."

"And here I thought you were an orphan." She grinned at him. "I told you women can't resist you."

"Very funny. We'll see how well you can resist me." He chased her up the stairs.

One of the girls called out, "Dada."

"Darn!" He stopped. "I know women stick together, but do they really start this young?"

Lauren laughed aloud and replied, "Evidently. Now go see what she wants."

The telephone rang as Lauren stood in the doorway to the nursery. "I'll get it, Dada." Lauren was still giggling when she answered the phone. "Hello."

"Let me speak to Thad."

"Oh. Hello Mother, dear," Lauren answered with mischief in her voice.

"Don't you dare call me Mother. Now, put my son on the phone."

"First, you'll have to promise me that you will be civil–no yelling at my husband."

"How dare you? Who do you think you are?"

"Why, your daughter-in-law, of course. I'll get Thad for you. Darling, Mother is on the phone." Lauren said loud enough for Velma to hear.

"Darn..."

Lauren touched her husband's lips with her fingers. "No, darling. Be nice." Thad caught her hand and led her to the phone with him. He put the phone on speaker so that Lauren could hear the conversation. "Mother?"

"Thaddeus, you need to tame that insolent little..."

"Be careful, Mother," he interrupted. "Why are you calling?"

"How could you embarrass us so? Everyone has been calling saying how proud we, and Abigail must be with you saving the governor's life and all. How could we tell them the truth, that you're married to some low—"

"Goodbye, Mother." Thad broke the connection.

"I'm sorry, Lauren."

"No need for apologies, love." She snickered.

"Lauren, what did you do? What did you say to her?" Thad squinted with suspicion.

"Besides calling her Mother dear, and telling her she had to promise to be civil toward you before I let her talk to you? Not a thing." She batted her eyelashes in mock innocence.

"What am I going to do with you?"

"We've come full circle. That's where we were before the girls summoned you, Dada."

"Uh huh. You were trying to resist me." He grabbed her and tickled her ribs.

CHAPTER THIRTY

Dr. Mason approached Thad as the board meeting was convening. "Congratulations." Dr. Mason pumped Thad's hand. "We're very proud of you. That's good publicity for the hospital and university."

"I hear you've been getting job offers from every corner of the country," Larry Wilcox goaded.

Mason kidded, "There's no chance of you leaving us, is there Thad?"

Thad stroked his chin. "I'm keeping my options open."

*****

Lauren and Thad had dinner with Vivian and her family. Vivian cleared the table. "What a difference a year makes. Huh? This time last year, you couldn't buy an invite to the season's shindigs. Now, you don't have the space to fit them all on your calendar."

Lauren raked a few crumbs onto a plate. "I need to learn not to hold grudges. I'm not planning to attend half of those affairs. Yours, of course, is very special. We're going to reenact our first kiss." She blushed. "By the way, can you believe Thad received several invitations addressed to him only?"

"I believe you. Money can't buy etiquette, diplomacy, common sense, or class, and education is a poor substitute for them all. Have you and Thad given any thought to accepting any of the job offers he received?" Vivian stacked the plates.

"We've tossed the idea around. I think he would accept a new job for me as I would for him, but both of us like what we are doing here, and I love what we're doing at the center. I especially love my friends." She gave Vivian an affectionate hug.

"And, this friend loves you." Vivian returned the embrace.

*****

With the social season in full swing, the invitations began to pile up. Thad continued to receive invitations that were addressed only to him.

Lauren, who felt that she'd been deliberately snubbed, decided she wasn't going to attend certain affairs. This decision caused tension between them. Today her refusal to attend a specific affair ignited yet another argument.

"No, Thad. I'm not going. That invitation was addressed to you. They know full well that you're married. I view that as a blatant slap in my face. If you want to go, then go."

"Lauren. Please," he begged.

"No."

"How would it look if I showed up without you?"

"It would look the same way it looked when the invitations read: Dr. Thaddeus Bradford. It would be expected."

Thad didn't try to mask his displeasure. "All right, this is the third affair you've refused to attend. Why don't you go through all of the invitations and tell me which ones you're not going to attend. That way, we won't have to go through this again."

"Okay, I can do that." Lauren picked up the invitations and sifted through them. She handed several envelopes to Thad. "Here are three addressed to you; one from Dr. Mason; one from the Floyds, and one from the Canters."

"So, you're telling me that if I want to go to any of these, I would have to go alone."

"I'm not going."

"If the situation was reversed, I would go for you."

"If the situation was reversed, I wouldn't ask you to go."

The tension between them appeared obvious to Gene and Joan who were spending the night with them. "Maybe it was an oversight, Lauren. Maybe they intended for Thad to bring a guest."

"Oh, come on, Joan! I'm not a guest. I'm his wife. All of these people know Thad's married."

"Maybe you should go to remind them."

"I'm not going. This is their not so subtle way of letting me know that I'm out of my league, but it's okay with me. I wasn't raised to be a society lady; I'm very comfortable in my station.

Thad, you were invited to these same parties last year when you *were* single. Did you tell Gene and Joan that a guest card was included in your invitation at that time?"

"Thad, is that true?" Gene asked.

"Yes it's true. Are you ready to go?" Thad's voice held a terse tone.

"Lauren, I'm sorry. I think I'll stay here with you."

"No, you're going, Joan." Gene chimed. "We're ready. Good night, Lauren."

Joan hugged her sister-in-law and whispered, "Good night, sis."

Thad gave Lauren a kiss on her cheek. "Good night, Lauren."

"Enjoy," Lauren replied.

*****

Only a few guests had arrived ahead of the Bradford siblings. Thad spotted their hosts, Edwin and Janice Canter, and asked if he could have a word with them. The trio followed Edwin and Janice into the library. "Have a seat. We're happy that you all could make it. What's on your mind Thaddeus?"

"Mr. Canter, given the fact that our families have been friends for many years; it pains me to know that the two of you would treat this friendship with such callous disregard."

"Thaddeus, whatever are you talking about?"

Gene interrupted, "He's being tactful, Mr. Canter. I don't feel the need to be. Both of you know that my brother is married, yet you sent him an invitation as if he's a single man. Last year when he *was* single, you were courteous enough to enclose a guest card. Did you really think that Thad would accept your invitation when you have treated his wife so contemptibly? And, do you think Joan and I would excuse your callous treatment of our sister-in-law?"

Thad stood to his feet. "And, Mr. Canter, you should know that I would never go any place or accept any invitation that excluded my wife. Good night, sir."

As the brothers and Joan were leaving the Canter's they encountered L.C. and Velma Bradford.

"Gene, Joan," Velma called. "Where are you going? The party is just beginning."

Gene walked out the door, never looking back. "Enjoy yourself, Mother."

*****

Lauren hadn't moved from the chair where she was sitting before the trio left. "Anyone for Chinese?" Thad whispered in her ear.

Appearing perplexed, Lauren asked, "What are you doing home?"

"Bringing dinner to my wife. I love you, Lauren. Gene and Joan are here, too."

"What happened? What about the Canter's party?"

"They have to go on without us. It's much more important that I'm here with my wife. Come to the kitchen with me." He pulled her to her feet. "I almost made a big mistake tonight." Holding her close he added, "I'm so sorry."

Lauren joked as she and Thad entered the kitchen. "My, oh, my. Look at this. All dressed up to eat off paper plates. You all didn't have to miss your party you know."

"Yes we did," They answered in unison.

*****

Thad climbed into bed and gazed at Lauren. "Can we talk for a minute?"

"Sure." She lowered the book she was reading.

"I owe you more of an apology than I've given you. I'm sorry for my behavior tonight. I didn't realize how much my accepting that invitation affected you. Then, I saw your face. By the time I reached the car, I knew I couldn't go. When I told Gene and Joan my reason for not going, Gene insisted that we go and confront the Canters, which we did.

We both let them know how we felt about the way they'd treated you. I told them I would never go anywhere that my wife is not welcome. By the way, my parents were arriving as we were leaving. They acknowledged Gene and Joan, but ignored me.

I hate to think that Mr. and Mrs. Canter are snobs. Although, they're part of the elite society, they've never, to my knowledge, portrayed such blatant snobbishness. They all seem to forget that you're now a part of me. I almost forgot that tonight, myself." Thad stared at Lauren. "Sweetheart, except for the past year," Thad continued, "I've lived my entire life in that world. Going to these affairs had been second nature to me. I never had to consider anyone else's feelings. I just went. I was upset with you for not wanting to go; I couldn't understand why you wouldn't want to. To be invited to the Canter's affair is quite a coup. Now, I think I understand why you didn't want to attend."

Thad kissed her cheek. "Please forgive me, Lauren. Don't change who you are for me or anyone, but please bear with me while I learn what is really important. It scares me to think of how much damage I would have done to our marriage if I had gone tonight."

"Thad, remember our slogan, together. There's nothing to forgive. I'm happy for us that you came to this conclusion on your own. However, I'm sorry for your loss. No one should have to pay such a price for love." Lauren caressed his face, and then kissed him.

The next morning, the phone rang while the two couples ate brunch.

"Mr. Bradford, telephone," Mrs. Brown announced. "It's your mother."

"Tell her I'm not available," Thad answered.

"She wants to speak to Mr. Gene Bradford."

"Tell her—"

"I'll handle it, Gene," Lauren interrupted. "I don't want Mrs. Brown in the middle of this."

Lauren entered the den and picked up the phone.

"Hello, Mother. We're in the middle of brunch. I'll let Gene know that you called. Have a nice day."

After Lauren returned, Thad pushed himself away from the table. "Ladies, will you excuse us for a while?" The two men retired to the study.

"They're really hurting," Joan stated.

"I know they are, and it's so needless. I've heard and read about the dynamics of the rich and want to be famous, A.K.A. Blue Bloods, but I've never seen it up close, and I must say, very personal. I don't understand the obsession with it."

"I grew up on the fringes of it myself," Joan acknowledged. "My parents craved that life too, but they weren't obsessed with it as our in-laws are. They act as if they've been charged with keeping the bloodline pure. I squeaked in, but I'm afraid they'll never accept you. They will, however, do all they can to break you and Thad up. Be very careful. Gene and I love you. You've made Thad very happy. And," Joan giggled. "You've added some spice to our lives." They began clearing the table.

"Be that as it may, Joan. I think things are going to get pretty rough for me; and for the three of you by association. I think Thad's going to pay the highest price."

"Girl, you're giving me the chills. Do you really believe that?"

"They want me out of this family."

"Lauren!" Joan whispered, in a shocked voice. "Do you think our in-laws are behind the harassment?"

"I take the fifth."

"Oh, my God! You do believe it! Oh, my God!" After a long pause Joan whispered, "Are you going to tell Thad you suspect his parents?"

"I have no intention of telling him. Eventually he'll find out on his own. It might be at my funeral when he does, though."

"Lauren!"

"Joan. You do know I was offered a quarter of a million dollars *not* to marry Thad. Don't you?"

"What! Please tell me you're kidding. Does Gene know?"

"I don't know whether he knows or not. That offer came the day before our wedding.

The first offer had come a week or so before when Mr. Bradford came to my house and offered me a hundred and fifty thousand dollars, which he raised to two hundred thousand dollars before he took his leave.

Thad and my family knew about it. He never said whether or not he mentioned it to Gene."

"Lauren, I'm so sorry. I wonder why I was never harassed. There isn't much difference between you and me."

"Gene didn't have an Abigail waiting in the wings. And unlike you, my family is comfortable, not wealthy." Lauren started the dishwasher.

"What shallow people."

"Those are my sentiments exactly. Don't be too defensive of me, Joan. I don't want you to suffer because of your friendship with me."

"Don't worry, my friend." Joan smiled. "Gene is just as protective of me as Thad is of you. I'm not as feisty as you, but I can hold my own."

"Mama." Brittany and her sister had toddled into the kitchen ahead of Mrs. Brown.

"How are my angels?" Lauren put an arm around each of the girls.

"They're getting prettier and prettier. How old are they now?"

"Say, we're nineteen months, Auntie Joan."

"Daddy."

"Daddy will be out in a little while, Angel."

"They call him daddy. That is so precious."

"Uh huh, and his head swells every time he hears it." Lauren smiled. "He loves them as much as they love him."

"Are the two of you planning to have any together?"

"I would like to, but not until this mess is cleared up. It's taking all of the creativity we have just to keep these two safe." They moved into the den.

"I understand. Oh…" Joan changed the subject. "I meant to tell you last night that I like your Christmas decorations.

You don't have a problem with the girls pulling on the tree?"

"Are you kidding? We've had to re-hang the same bulbs several times. For some reason they don't go near the tree when the lights are on."

Lauren glanced at Joan, "I guess since Megan and Drew are older you don't have that problem anymore."

"No, they just want to decorate everything, inside and outside. I can't wait for your Poor Man's Christmas party. It sounds like it's going to be a lot of fun."

"Daddy, Daddy." Spying Thad and Gene, the girls ran into Thad's arms.

"Hey, Pumpkins." Thad grinned as he picked up both girls and swung around with them. They squealed with joy.

"Fatherhood suits you, brother."

"I love it. I wouldn't have it any other way. I would like to have four or five more just like them."

"What did the two of you have to drink in there?" Lauren kidded. "My husband's senses are impaired." They all laughed.

"Well, you guys, as much as I enjoy your company, we must head north. Joan wants to stop and do some shopping along the way. We'll see you on Friday. Take care."

"Be very careful, sis," Joan whispered as she embraced Lauren. "I won't say anything."

"Thanks, Joan. Be safe."

Lauren slipped an arm around Thad's waist as they waved a final goodbye to Gene and Joan before closing the door. Thad turned to his wife. "How are you feeling, love?"

"I'm feeling better."

* * * * *

During the next week, they received several anonymous phone calls where they heard only heavy breathing on the line. Lauren received several calls at the office, as well. On one such call, she was summoned out of a meeting because the caller said there was an emergency at her home, and on yet another call, the caller said Merry Christmas, followed by the canned cackle of an old woman. Thad received a call at the office asking him if he liked the pictures, and how did he like sharing.

CHAPTER THIRTY-ONE

The invitations listed attire as very relaxed. Each guest was to bring a wrapped gift suitable for a child between the ages of newborn and eighteen years old.

Instead of a live band, a CD player provided music. There wasn't a sit down dinner, only a buffet. They danced the electric slide, bunny hop, and the two-step. There was a stage for karaoke and a piano for Christmas carols.

"Lauren, this is one of the best holiday galas I've ever attended," Linda declared. "Everyone seems to be having a good time."

"Thanks, Linda. I thought this would be a nice change from all of the stuffy affairs we get bogged down with, and we get to do something good for others as well."

The party was touted as one of the best celebrations of the season, and it earned honorable mention in the local paper's society page.

Lauren and Thad attended four parties between the one they hosted, and Vivian's New Year's Eve Celebration, including one hosted by her sister, Amy, and one hosted by Gene and Joan. At each of these parties, they were congratulated on the success of their party. Thad and Gene's parents were noticeably absent from their party as were their sisters.

* * * * *

At Vivian's party, Lauren strolled onto the patio. There was no moon, and it was much colder tonight than it had been a year ago. But, just as it had happened a year ago, a sudden chill shook her body. Then Thad slipped a jacket over her shoulders.

He stroked her back. "Better?"

"Better." She snuggled against his touch.

"I love you, Lauren Bradford."

"I love you, Thaddeus Bradford." They shared a passionate kiss.

"Lets' get inside, darling, before you freeze to death."

"It's supposed to be, before Vivian sends a search party for us."

"Such a stickler for details." He gave her a light peck. "Now, get inside, woman."

*****

Lauren and Thad relaxed on the sofa, watching the game and discussing the holiday parties. "Sweetheart," Lauren grimaced, "you mean to tell me you've endured at least twenty-four years of attending party after party for six weeks straight?"

"Uh, huh. I never thought about it. It was expected of me, so I did it. I never paid any attention to whether or not we were having fun. When we were younger, the young adults always had their party within the party. You don't want to know about that."

"Oh. Who says I don't." Lauren grinned.

"Believe me baby, you don't."

"I know you were used to attending at least fifteen parties during the season, but this year we only attended six-seven including ours. Do you miss them? Did you enjoy yourself?"

"Lauren, trust me. This has been, by far, the best season to date. I've really enjoyed all six of them. You pulled off one of the best parties I've ever attended. Everyone is still talking about it. I'm so very proud of you."

"Thank you, kind sir. I, for one, am glad it's over. Once in a while a party is okay, but every week for six weeks in a row is a little much. What if we'd attended all of them?" Lauren chuckled. "You may have guessed by now that you married a bore."

"Ha! You a bore? I've had more excitement in the last year with you, than I've had my entire life."

"Yeah, I can imagine. Most of it, I'm sure you could have done without," Lauren lamented.

"None of which you are to be blamed for. Let's hope all of that is behind us. This is a new year."

"We can always hope. Want some ambrosia?"

"Need you ask, my love?"

CHAPTER THIRTY-TWO

After the season, they took down and stored all the decorations. The house was restored to its original order. Thad resumed his work at the hospital, and the unpredictable life of an ER surgeon. Mrs. Brown returned from a week's vacation with the news that she had accepted her beau's marriage proposal.

Lauren raised an eyebrow. "Should I begin the search for a new nanny?"

"Not yet, Mrs. B. We won't be getting married for at least another year. He has some things to work out, and I still need to work."

"That's a relief. You've spoiled us. We'd be hard pressed to find anyone as capable or as trustworthy as you."

"That's nice of you to say, but when, and if the time comes, I'm sure you will. For now, I'm still taking care of you, and my precious little ones. Mr. B. does a pretty good job of that himself." She smiled.

*****

Lauren returned to work at the university, and at the Center. So far, there were no disruptive participants or slashed tires. Thankfully, the sense of camaraderie and trust among the participants had returned.

When she returned home Thursday evening, Lauren noticed a strange car in her driveway. As was her custom, she went directly to the downstairs bathroom and washed her hands. Then she went to the girls' room to check on them. Afterwards she went back downstairs to greet Thad. "Hi, darling," she called, as she entered the den.

"Oh, good evening." She noticed the middle-aged couple sitting on the sofa.

The man stood. Thad approached her, giving her a kiss. "Hello, darling. This is Mr. and Mrs. Edwin Canter." To the Canters he said, "This is my wife, Lauren."

Oh no! What now?

Mr. Canter extended his hand. "Mrs. Bradford, it is indeed a pleasure to meet you."

Mrs. Canter stood beside her husband and extended her hand as well. "It's a pleasure for me as well." Lauren raised an eyebrow at Thad.

Thad placed his hand in the small of Lauren's back. "Let's all have a seat. The Canters have something to say to us." As they resumed their seats on the sofa, Thad seated Lauren in a chair, and then perched himself on its arm.

"Mrs. Bradford," Mr. Canter began. "As I told Thad, my wife and I came here to offer you both our deepest apology. Our treatment of you was reprehensible, and we are ashamed of our behavior. We allowed ourselves to be misled, and in doing so, we have damaged the life long relationship we've had with two fine young men—men we've grown to love and respect."

Thad stroked Lauren's shoulder. "Lauren, you weren't invited to the Canter's holiday celebration because my parents told them you were caught cheating on me. They said, I had kicked you out. My parents also said you were making trouble for me in the courts—trying to get your hands on the Bradford's fortune."

Lauren widened her eyes. "I see."

"Mrs. Bradford, when Thad, Gene, and his wife showed up to tell us how they felt about us excluding you, we were baffled. We questioned Thad's parents and all they said was; that stupid boy took her back. I ran into Gene last week, and I begged him to tell me what was going on. Gene told us what a lovely person you are, and how much you and Thad love each other." Mr. Canter leaned forward and continued.

"After my talk with him, I felt like the scum of the earth. I could not wait to apologize to the two of you. I can't imagine why L.C. and Velma would do this to their own son. We thought they were telling the truth. We had no reason to doubt them. Believe me, that's the only reason we sent the invitation to Thad alone. Please, forgive us for our ignorance and any pain we have caused you."

Lauren sat in silence, digesting what Mr. Canter had said. Thad squeezed her shoulder. She took a deep breath and began to speak. "Mr. Canter, Mrs. Canter, coming here today is one of the greatest acts of courage I've witnessed in quite some time. However, be very clear, the only pain you or anyone, may have caused me, has been through the pain it has caused my husband. He's been ostracized because he dared to love someone outside the circle. He's been hurt badly, and it angers me that people can be so superficial. It angers me more to know that these same people would trust him with their lives on an operating table, but won't give him credit for having enough sense or discernment to choose a woman to be his wife.

I don't like having to explain how I feel about certain aspects of my husband's life. You see, I'm not, nor do I wish to be, a socialite. I hold no ill feelings towards those who are, or those who aspire to be. On the other hand, I have no tolerance for those who are, and use their positions to hurt others.

My husband does his best not to let me know how his parents and others have hurt him through the way they've treated me and him, too, for that matter." While Lauren released her feelings, Thad squeezed her shoulder again, this time letting his hand remain in place.

"I feel and share his pain, Lauren continued. "When and where ever I can spare him any grief, I'm going to do it, and if that means not being socially correct, then so be it." She smiled in the direction of the Canters. "The two of you have earned my respect today. You could have made a phone call or sent a letter of apology. Instead, you added degrees of sincerity by doing this in person. I'm sorry you were made a party to this ugliness. I thank you for coming, and I pray the little snag in the relationship you've enjoyed with Thad over the years, has been mended.

The final thing I have to say to you, on this matter, is—no matter what you've heard about me, know that I love Thad with every fiber of my being. I know he loves me equally as much, and I won't let any external force come between us." Thad slid his hand down her arm.

"Now, I don't think either of you need to be forgiven for anything, but if you need to hear me say it, I forgive you." She smiled.

"Thad." Mr. Canter cleared his throat. "You are a blessed man. This is some lady you have here."

"She sure is," Mrs. Canter added.

That smiled. "I know that. She's a good cook too." Thad kissed her cheek. "How would you like some coffee and dessert?"

*****

After a wonderful evening, Thad closed the door behind the Canters. "Thanks sweetheart. You're quite a ...Oh, just thank you for being you. I love you so much."

"They're a nice couple." Lauren slipped her arm around Thad's waist for a quick hug. "I really do respect them for what they did."

"So do I, sweetheart." Thad led her into the kitchen. "I've always admired Mr. Canter, and it hurt to think he would deliberately treat us that way. My parents are in for a royal dressing down from them. The fact that someone as powerfully connected as the Canters is defending us is going to push us even farther away from them. I can handle that. With you by my side, I think I can handle anything."

"Together, love. Now, let's clean these dishes and go to bed."

CHAPTER THIRTY-THREE

Word of the support center traveled throughout the university and the surrounding community. By the end of January, several more participants had enrolled in the program, which brought the total to thirty-seven. Two more facilitators, Su Yeong, a high school principal and Julie Page, a police officer, also joined the staff.

In spite of the tire slashing incident, the women still looked forward to the sessions. Several who struggled with weight issues, had lost a few pounds since the program began. Others seemed to have gained more self-confidence.

Unknown to the others, Lauren had received one anonymous call at the Center. She answered the phone where the caller had asked to speak to Ms. Jeffries. She pretended she was going to get Ms. Jeffries and asked the caller to hold. She counted twenty seconds, then said hello. The caller hung up. She later logged the call in her journal, but didn't tell anyone about it.

* * * * *

Due to the governor's illness, the inaugural ball, slated for January, twenty-second, had been postponed until February, sixteenth. Thad greeted Lauren with excitement as she entered the den. "Hi, babe." He kissed her, then spun her around in a dance step.

"Whoa! What's gotten into you? Did you hit the lottery or something?"

"No. I just feel good. Everything went well at the hospital today. We haven't been harassed of late and," he held up an envelope. "We've been invited to the governor's ball. Dr. and Mrs. Thaddeus Bradford."

"Are you accepting?"

Thad stopped abruptly. "You don't want me to? You don't want to go?"

Lauren laughed. "Of course, I want to go. I'm just teasing you."

"Girl, one of these days I'm going to learn to read you. Much of the time I can't tell when you're serious, and when you're not."

"That's my ace in the hole." She tickled his ribs. "Don't ever think you'll always know what this woman is up to."

"I know you better that you think I do, Mrs. Bradford." He pinned her arms to her sides "Now, tell me you're sorry for teasing me."

"No." She laughed.

He squeezed her arms. "Tell me," he ordered with mock anger.

"Okay. Okay. I'm sorry."

"That's better." He grinned and released her, with a swat to the derriere.

"I still have the upper hand." She laughed and dashed up the stairs. The phone rang just as she reached the top step.

"I'll get it," Thad called from the foot of the stairs. "Darling, pick up the phone. It's urgent."

Lauren answered, alarmed, "Hello?"

"Lauren, how are you?" Jennifer laughed into the phone.

"Jennifer, how are you?" she cried, as Thad entered the room with a huge grin. "Jen, would you hold a minute. I need to smack my husband?"

"Gotcha," he whispered in her ear.

"Lauren you sound so happy."

"I am, Jen. I'm happier than I could ever imagine. I love married life, most of the time." She glanced at Thad and stuck out her tongue. "How's everything with you? I miss you and the kids. Thanks for the pictures. The children are really growing."

"We're all doing very well. John is so relaxed. He's getting to know the children, and they adore him. I'm also very happy. Are they leaving you alone there?"

"Yep. They finally got the message. I'm not going anywhere, at least not yet."

"How did the season go? Did you get many invites?"

"Oh, yes, many. We accepted six of them. And, my dear friend, we hosted a Poor Man's Christmas Party. We even received honorable mention in the Hartford Tribune."

"Well, excuse me, Miss Thang. I guess I'll have to find myself some new friends; more befitting my station." Jennifer laughed.

"Girl, don't start that mess. Anyway, when are you coming this way again?"

"We'll be there in June. Perry is getting married in New York."

"That's great. Please plan to spend a few days with us."

"Thanks. I'd love that. Oh, oh there goes Missy. I'll be in touch again soon. Kiss the girls for me, and give Thad and Mrs. Brown my love."

"You do the same for me on that end. I'm looking forward to seeing you in June."

Lauren hung up the phone. "Now, mister," she said, turning to Thad. "What were you saying?" She pounced on him.

CHAPTER THIRTY-FOUR

Thad and Lauren celebrated Valentine's Day at the same restaurant as the year before. They also had flowers delivered to Mrs. Brown. Thad had flowers delivered to Lauren, and the girls. Early Friday morning Thad and Lauren drove with the twins and Mrs. Brown, to Hartford, where they'd be attending the governor's ball.

Thad slipped an arm around Lauren. "Are you excited?"

"Not overly. Although, I am a little curious about what happens on the other side of these events. The side the cameras don't show. I want this, for you."

"You really don't like that life, do you?"

"Nope. I like to keep my feet on terra firma. But, I'm very proud of my husband. Because of him, we're going."

* * * * *

Thad stared as Lauren stepped into the room. "Lauren. You look absolutely sensational. That's your color. I love it."

"Thank you, sir." She spun around, showing off her gown. "I'm glad you approve because I bought it with you in mind. And you, my dear husband, are handsomer than handsome."

"You're going to wow them tonight, love. Are you ready? The car is waiting."

"Good night, Mrs. Brown. The girls are sleeping. You can go to sleep when you're ready, too. Please don't open the door to anyone. If we need to, we will call you on your cell phone."

"Okay, Mrs. B. The two of you look so elegant. You're going to be the best looking couple there."

"Thank you Mrs. Brown. Have a good evening."

* * * * *

As Thad and Lauren entered the ballroom, a young man approached them. "Dr. Bradford?"

Thad acknowledged, "Yes, I'm Thaddeus Bradford."

"Governor Standis would like to see you. Would you follow me, please?"

"Dr. and Mrs. Thaddeus Bradford, sir," Announced the aide he opened the door to the grand room.

"Ah. Dr. Bradford. It's nice to see you again." The governor grasped his hand. "You remember my wife, Maureen." The governor turned to Lauren. "Mrs. Bradford. It's a pleasure. This is my wife, Maureen."

"Governor, Mrs. Standis. I'm pleased to meet you both."

"Please, have a seat." Mrs. Standis offered. "Dr. Bradford, my husband and I are forever in your debt. We wouldn't be here now if it weren't for you."

"I'm sure, ma'am, that had I not been able to perform the surgery, someone else would have. I was just doing what I signed on to do."

"You're very humble," the governor said. "You were requested because of your reputation. I understand that you didn't hesitate when the request was made.

I, we..." He glanced at Mrs. Standis, "appreciate your dedication. I wouldn't insult you by offering any kind of payment, but I would be honored if you and Mrs. Bradford would sit at our table tonight as our honored guests."

*****

At the reception, the governor stood before the crowd. "Thank you. Thank you very much." The governor responded to the standing ovation he received as he stepped to the podium. "Ladies and gentlemen, before I deliver my address I want to introduce my honored guests. The man who saved my life, Dr. Thaddeus Bradford, and his lovely wife, Lauren."

Thad stood and waved to the crowd. When he would have asked her to stand, Lauren threw him a kiss. He smiled and resumed his seat.

Lauren leaned over and kissed him, "I'm so very proud of you."

Thad smiled and patted her hand.

*****

The steak and seafood dinner was scrumptious. After dinner, there was dancing in the grand ballroom. The governor danced first with his wife, then his daughter, and then with Lauren.

Thad danced the first dance with Lauren, which was good because several other partners claimed her hand before he had a chance to dance with her again.

"Now, Mrs. Bradford," Thad teased," Tell me you're not enjoying all of this attention." They moved gracefully across the dance floor.

"Oh, it's okay, for tonight, but tomorrow I want the attention of my children and my husband. Only."

"Your picture is going to be on the front page of the paper tomorrow."

"Darn! I forgot about that part of this gala."

*****

On the way home, the next day Thad treated the women to lunch. Mrs. Brown was anxious. "Okay, Mr. and Mrs. B., I can't wait another minute. Please, tell me about the ball."

Lauren feigned distress. "Oh, Mrs. Brown. I thought I was going to have to hang a *taken sign* on this hunk here. There were about four hundred or more women there, and I believe each of them danced with him, at least once. I did manage to get the first and last dance with him, though."

"Don't believe her, Mrs. Brown. It was the other way around. I was getting a little jealous. Some of those men had the nerve to tell me, you have a gorgeous wife. You must be very proud of her. The waiters had to walk around with towels to wipe up the drool."

Mrs. Brown laughed aloud. "In other words, the two of you had a good time. I have something to show you." She reached into her oversized bag and produced a newspaper that she passed to Lauren.

"Oh, no." Lauren moaned. There, on the front page, in living color, was a full-length photo of Thad and her with the governor and his wife.

"The handsome Dr. Thaddeus Bradford and his lovely wife, Lauren, were the honored guests of Governor and Mrs. Standis..."

The story of the ball filled four columns.

"What's the matter Mrs. B? The two of you looked great."

"I just don't like having my picture splashed all over the paper."

*****

Lauren sighed. "It is good to be home. I feel as if we've been away for a week instead of a weekend. I did have a good time, though."

Thad deposited their bags in their room. "I did too, sweetheart. I know you're not fond of these affairs, and I was afraid you might be bored. But, no one would have known by your actions, that you hadn't been doing that all your life."

"I have no problem adapting. I think you misunderstood me. It's not the partying and fellowshipping that I don't like–it's the pretense that turns me off. I'm not going to like the fall-out from this, either. We're going to be flooded with invitations. Those invites will subtly draw us into the political arena. You know, I have no love for politics." Lauren wrapped her arms around Thad. "But I have lots of love for you, darling, and if that's what you want, I'll do my best to accommodate you."

"What more can I ask?" Thad kissed her on the forehead. "Don't worry. I have no political aspirations. I'm learning that many things I deemed important before I met you, are not important at all."

CHAPTER THIRTY-FIVE

At a staff meeting, Lauren eased into the seat between Linda Abrams and Larry Wilcox. "Shall we bow?" Larry teased. "You two have made us very proud. There was more written about the handsome doctor and his charming wife than there was about the governor."

"Good morning, handsome doctor," Vivian greeted as Thad slid into the seat beside her.

Dr. Mason rushed into the room. "Morning, everyone. Sorry I'm late, but I had to meet with the media. Everyone wants a word on our two celebs here."

Lauren whispered to Linda. "I thought you were PR."

"So did I. I don't think the media called him. He called them. He's trying to hitch a ride on your popularity."

"Parasite."

"Dr. Bradford, Dr. Jeffries, I can't tell you how proud the staff is of you both."

"What a difference a year makes," Lauren said sarcastically. Thad favored her with a naughty girl look.

"Dr. Jeffries." Dr. Mason cast an annoyed look her way. "You've been vindicated. I'm hoping we may be forgiven for our past mistakes."

Lauren felt her face redden in anger. "I've been what? Vindicated? Dr. Mason, did I just hear you mentioned a desire to be forgiven? It's been more than a year since my name was dragged through the mud, and this is the first time I've heard anything close to an apology come out of your mouth." Lauren stared at Mason.

"A year ago, you had me tarred, feathered, and poised to be run out of town. Even after I presented written proof the rumors about me weren't true, you still didn't offer an apology.

As a matter of fact; until now, you never mentioned the incident to me or in my presence again.

We both know you've mentioned it to other people.

Now that my husband has the ear of the governor and a few other VIPs, you want forgiveness—a free ride in the name of the hospital. I don't speak for my husband, but as for me? I'm out of free passes.

All of this media madness is about my husband of whom I'm very proud. We all know that had he not operated successfully on the governor, we wouldn't be having this conversation. No half-baked apology would have been forth coming."

Dr. Mason's face turned beet red. He sputtered a reply, and then called the meeting to order.

As the meeting ended, Thad turned to his wife. "Lauren, will you walk with me to my office?"

"Do you want Lauren Bradford or Dr. Lauren Jeffries Bradford?"

"Why don't both of you come?"

"What is it Thad?" Lauren asked, as he closed the door behind him. "Did I embarrass you?"

"No. You didn't embarrass me, Lauren. You embarrassed Dr. Mason. You didn't have to do that."

"You're right. I didn't. I could have said nothing, just like I did seventeen months ago. He asked for forgiveness for an on-going travesty. Did he offer an apology then or today? No, he didn't. He wants vindication, but he wants to keep me under condemnation. You're aware of the things he'd said about me, and about our marriage. You know too, that his tolerance of me has been by default–my marriage to you. If he could, he'd get rid of me in a heartbeat. No matter how well the nursing program is flourishing."

Thad pulled her into an embrace. "You're right. It's just that you have a way of cutting a person to the core. Having been a victim of it myself, I guess I have a tendency to feel sorry for them. We deserved the tongue lashings."

"You've always been quick to apologize, even for things that you weren't responsible for. I didn't set out to embarrass Dr. Mason. He purposely says things in the presence of others, so he can get away with it.

Our past mistakes, indeed. You've been vindicated. That infers absolution for some wrong I did. He's the only current member of the board who has not apologized for that mess last year. Leland Bland is the other."

"I wasn't aware of that."

"I know you weren't. Although, we work for the same company, I try to keep our business life separated from our personal life, so I don't bring office mess home."

"I love you, doctor. Will you have lunch with me?"

"As long as my husband approves," she joked.

Lauren returned to her office and called Vivian. "Hi Vivian, this is Lauren. I'm returning your call."

"What did you do, go into hiding after the meeting?"

"I received a mild reprimand from my husband, and then he took me to lunch."

"He has to admit you were right. All you did was to expose Mason for what he is. He needles you every chance he gets. We've all noticed it. I think he'll be less inclined to do so now."

"Whatever. Vivian, I was going to call you later, anyway. Do you have a few minutes? I have something that I want to discuss with you."

"I'm free. What's up?"

"I'll come to your office."

In her office, Lauren told Vivian about Mrs. Standis' interest in the center. "Are you kidding? She's interested in our center? Wow!" Vivian gushed over the news that the governor's wife was interested in hearing about the work that they were doing at the Center.

"I'm glad you're enthused about it. I think you'd be the perfect person to work with her. Amanda agrees. As a matter of fact, she's on her way over here to tell you that."

Amanda peered into the room. "Hey, you two."

"Hi, Amanda," Lauren and Vivian answered simultaneously.

"Come and join us," Vivian invited

"So, Lauren, did you tell Vivian the news?"

"I was just telling her we think she would make a great liaison."

"What about it Vivian?" Amanda asked. "Do you accept?"

"I'm honored. Thanks for the vote of confidence. What do I do now?"

"Call Mrs. Standis' office," Lauren replied. "They'll guide you from there."

"Lauren, the Center was your idea, why don't you want to work with her?"

"That's just not my thing. I'm a behind the scenes person. Amanda and I will concentrate on finding a larger facility for our current group. Plus, starting a new group on the other side of town will require our attention."

"This is exciting." Amanda giggled. "As long as we have you backing us up, Lauren, we can do anything."

"Be nice ladies, my bark is worse than my bite."

"Are you kidding? Were you in that board room this morning, or was that just a figment of our imagination?"

CHAPTER THIRTY-SIX

Hearing the phone ringing, Lauren entered the den. After noticing the caller ID, she picked it up. "Hello Joan."

"We're just checking on you guys." Joan then asked, "Is everything going okay?"

"Thankfully, everything is settling down. Is there something we need to know?"

"You and Thad are the envy of our in-laws. They were afraid you would embarrass the family. You have no class, you know," Joan teased.

"I'm sorry to have disappointed them."

"Has there been any more harassment?"

"Not since the Canter's visit. That somewhat validates my suspicions. I'm sure our in-laws received a tongue-lashing from them. They probably pulled their people back. I'm surprised they haven't been in touch with Thad, riding on his popularity like they're doing at the hospital."

"Do you think it's over, Lauren? I pray that it is."

"Other than a call coming to the Center, asking for Dr. Jeffries, nothing has happened. I'm still being cautious, though."

"Good thinking. Are you all still coming up for the weekend?"

"That's the plan. I'll talk with you before then."

*****

"Daddy. Daddy," Brianna squealed.

Lauren looked over her shoulder to see Thad standing in the doorway. "Hello sweetheart. How was your day?"

"Hey, baby. How ya doing angels?" He stooped, pulled the girls into an embrace, and then glanced over their heads at Lauren. "Has Mrs. Brown left already?"

"Yes. She left about an hour ago. Did you need her for something?"

"No. I'm going to take a shower."

"Dinner will be ready in fifteen or twenty minutes."

After their meal, Thad complimented Lauren on the dinner then helped her with the dishes. When the dishes were done, they bathed the girls and put them to bed.

"What's the matter?" Lauren asked, as she lay curled against him on the sofa.

"A little tired."

"That's not all."

They sat in silence for a few minutes. Lauren began singing *Together, Together* to the tune of *Tomorrow*.

Thad chuckled. "Smarty." He sighed again. "My father called me today." Lauren remained silent. Thad pulled her tighter against him. "He'll never change, Lauren. Is it foolish of me to keep hoping he would?"

"No, darling, it's not. What is life without hope? Do you want to talk about it?"

"I know I need to, but darn it, it hurts me to come to you with something my parents said about you. If you weren't so perceptive, I wouldn't tell you anything. I just can't lie to you. You always know when something's bothering me."

"I can take whatever they say about me. What bothers me is the effect their comments have on you."

"How did you learn so much about me in eighteen months, yet I haven't figured you out, yet?"

"Yet? You aren't expected to figure me out. I'm a woman."

"That you are my love. That you are." He squeezed her in a loving hug. "Anyway, he called to say he'd seen us on the news with the governor. And, while you looked decent enough, I need to be careful you don't do or say something that would embarrass me, or the family name—you aren't well bred. Of course, if I had stayed within my own class and married Abigail, I wouldn't have that worry. We've been married almost nine months and they still won't give up."

"Darling, I'm going to say something, and I hope you'll accept it in the spirit in which it is said." Lauren sighed, and sat up to face him. "The state of your relationship with your parents is beginning to take an emotional and physical toll on you.

Sometimes, for the sake of mental and physical health, we have to sever the ties with the source of the unrest—even if it is family. Your parents have already told you that as long as you're with me you aren't their son. They set the conditions under which you could remain in, or return to the family. Unless you are planning to get rid of me, you need to tell your parents, once and for all, to stop harassing you, or suffer the consequences.

You've done and said all you can. It wasn't out of concern for you that your father called today. It was for himself. They can't stand the idea that we, not them, have the governor's ear. Who am I, a low-life, that I should have my picture splashed all over the papers, and television with the governor? It's more embarrassing to them. They can't explain this phenomenon to the same people they've low rated me to."

She took Thad's hand. "You see darling, I'm not their stereotypical low class. Because your parents couldn't find fault in my character, they did their best to bad mouth me, even using untruths to further their goal of severing your relationship with me. So, it's up to you now. I know you love your parents, and I have no problem with that. You have to decide how much more of this you're willing to take."

Thad sighed. Before he could say anything, the phone rang. "Hey, Gene. What's up? What! Are you serious? When did this happen?" He paused while he listened. "How are you doing? Well thanks for calling. I'll see you tomorrow."

"What's the matter?"

"Uncle Lewis died a couple of hours ago."

"Oh, no. I'm so very sorry."

"I can't believe this. I spoke to him and Aunt Charlotte just yesterday. I forgot to tell you they sent their love. Man! He was only sixty-seven years old. I'm going to call Aunt Charlotte. She must be devastated."

"Okay. Please extend my condolences. Let me know what I can do for her, and for you." She hugged him tightly and left the room.

*****

Uncle Lewis Parker wasn't really Thad's uncle. He and his wife, Charlotte, were Thad and Gene's godparents. They too, were mega wealthy blue bloods, but they never exhibited the snobbishness the Bradfords did.

Their only child, a son, was killed in a skiing accident sixteen years ago. At the time, he was only twenty-two years old. Since then, the Parkers had transferred their parental attention to Thad and Gene.

Uncle Lewis, a former stockbroker, was founder and CEO of Parker Financial Inc., and Aunt Charlotte was a society lady who unselfishly devoted her time to charitable causes.

They had both challenged the elder Bradfords on their views relative to Thad's marriage, telling them they admired Thad for choosing to be happy.

*****

Early Saturday morning, Thad and Lauren left the girls with Linda and her family, and drove to Boston to be with Aunt Charlotte. Several visitors were in attendance, including Velma Bradford and her daughters. Thad and Lauren each greeted Aunt Charlotte with a long, warm embrace, which she returned in kind. Thad's mother and sisters ignored them.

Aunt Charlotte, having noticed the snub, asked Mrs. Bradford and her daughters to follow her to her bedroom. Loud voices carried from behind the closed door, but they weren't discernible.

Shortly thereafter, Mrs. Bradford and her daughters left without a word to anyone.

Aunt Charlotte then summoned Thad and Lauren into the bedroom. "I'm sorry," said Aunt Charlotte. "I don't like what I just saw, and it won't be tolerated in my home.

Lewis and I tried to talk some sense into your parents, but they wouldn't listen. Lauren, you continue to hold your head up. You're a lovely young woman with nothing to be ashamed of, and my god-son is blessed to have you as his wife. I hope that someday L.C. and Velma will come to their senses. It is a shame Elaine and Anna feel they have to emulate their parent's behavior.

Now, Gene and Joan will be here in a few minutes. We're going to finalize the arrangements. Thad, I would appreciate it if you went with us. Lauren, would you be kind enough to house-sit for me until we return?"

*****

Several visitors stopped in to pay their respects while Lauren was minding the house. She was washing dishes and putting order to the kitchen when L.C. Bradford strolled in.

"I guess Charlotte is too distraught to be aware of who she is leaving unobserved in her house. She seemed to trust you not to lift anything."

"Oh, put a sock in it, Mr. Bradford. I've had about enough of your pompous ass. You walk around here with your chest pushed out as if you're somebody. You are just a figment of your own imagination. You'd better watch yourself. I have the ear of the governor and some US senators, you know. One is even from your state. It wouldn't do to have them find out about what you and your wife have been doing to me. They will if you ever call Thad again with any more of that nonsense you've been spewing." Lauren put her hand on her hip. "If you've disowned him as your son, leave him alone. I'm Mrs. Thaddeus Bradford, and I intend to be for the rest of my life. I don't make idle threats, Mr. Bradford. You'll find I'm better at your game than you are. I know people, too; some just as ruthless as you. Now, if you will excuse me, I'll get back to the task at hand. By the way, the governor's wife and I talk every week."

Mr. Bradford shot her a look of pure evil. "Who in hell do you think you are, talking to me like that?"

"I told you. I'm Mrs. Thaddeus Bradford, your daughter-in-law." Lauren smirked.

L.C. Bradford spun on his heels and stormed out of the house mumbling to himself.

*****

After the funeral, many of the well-wishers returned to the Parker house for a repast.

Although, the elder Bradfords had attended the funeral service, they were noticeably absent from the fellowship.

Thad and Lauren extended Aunt Charlotte an invitation to spend some time with them. She graciously accepted, but said it would have to be later in the year because she and Uncle Lewis had planned to take a trip to Europe with friends during the Easter holiday, and she explained that Lewis would want her to keep her plans.

CHAPTER THRITY-SEVEN

Lauren sat with her legs curled under her. "Thad, I've been thinking that this would be a good time for us to go on our honeymoon."

Thad lowered the book he was reading to look at her. "Is there any special reason to do it now?"

"Well, I'll have a week off at the end of the month, and since you're in a position to take off almost any time you want, I thought it would be a good time to go."

"Do you have a place in mind?"

"Hawaii."

"Oh, you've been thinking about this haven't you?"

"I need to get warm. Normally, I like the cold weather, but for some reason it seems to be hugging my bones this year. Hawaii would be ideal, not too hot and not too cold."

"If that's what you want, we'll go. What about the girls?"

"I'll ask Michelle to take care of them for us. I'll do that before we make reservations, but, sweetheart, you don't seem to be too enthused about going. I don't want to go if you don't want to."

"Make the plans. I would love to go. I'm just tired that's all. It doesn't seem as if I can get enough sleep."

That's exactly the reason I want us to get away.

*****

Lauren leaned back into Thad's arms as they stood perusing the scenery from their hotel room. "Ah, eighty-four degrees," she cooed. "This feels wonderful. Just what the doctor ordered. How would you like a nap before dinner? I know you didn't sleep well last night, and it didn't help that we spent the better part of today traveling."

"That's not a bad idea. I could use a couple of hours shut eye."

Lauren was concerned about Thad's emotional state. He'd had a strenuous week, having performed at least one surgery each day.

Two of these surgeries were long and complicated, and one of those patients died of complications, following the surgery. Thad seemed to have become depressed over the death of this patient. Although, he was going to bed early, he wasn't sleeping well. He was beginning to look tired.

Although a contributing factor, Lauren, felt that the death of the patient, wasn't the true source of Thad's depression. She had encouraged him to seek medical advice to obtain a mild sleeping aide.

Vowing that they wouldn't take any work related materials on their trip, Lauren had brought along a novel by her favorite author. She walked out to the connecting patio and settled into the lounger to enjoy her book while Thad napped.

She chuckled to herself when, at six o'clock, she woke from a refreshing nap to find her book had slipped to the floor, and the sun had slipped behind the buildings.

Lauren peeped into the room and saw that Thad was still sleeping. Deciding to let him sleep she returned to the lounger and began reading, again.

Shortly thereafter Lauren heard Thad calling her name. She entered the room. "Here I am, sweetheart. Did you sleep well?"

"I did. Why didn't you wake me? It's eight o'clock."

"That should answer your question. You slept four and a half hours because you needed to. I wasn't about to interfere with your rest."

He stretched lazily. "What am I going to do with you?"

"What you've always done. Don't mess with success. Are you ready for dinner? I'm famished."

"So am I. I'll be ready in a sec."

*****

Thad glanced at Lauren who was curled-up in a chair reading. "Wow! I feel great today. That's the best I've slept in quite a while. How are you this morning, love?"

Lauren smiled. "I'm fine, but it's almost noon Hawaiian time."

"What! How long did I sleep this time?"

"It doesn't matter. We have no clock to watch or schedule to keep. For the next eight days we're going to do what we want to, when we want to."

"Not if it means keeping you cooped up in this room."

"To see you wake up like this every morning, I'd do anything, including staying cooped up in this room."

"Come here." He held her in a tight embrace. "I love you." He kissed her. "Now, I'm going to shower, get dressed, and then we're going to play tourist."

* * * * *

As planned, no schedule was set for the remaining days, but Lauren and Thad found themselves going to bed early and sleeping late. They didn't venture off the island, opting instead to explore the shops and gardens in the surrounding area. Every day, after a late dinner, they took long walks along the beach talking and holding hands as they went.

On the fifth night, as they sat in the sand watching the moonrise over the beach, Thad slipped an arm around Lauren's waist and pulled her closer to him. He kissed the top of her head. "Thank you, darling."

"You're welcome."

"How did you know?"

"I put myself in your shoes. Superman would have had a difficult time trying to walk with the load you've been carrying around these past months."

"You are so perceptive, so in tune with me."

"I'm just so in love with you. You needed to clear the forest so you could see the trees."

"You're right. Thanks to our talks this week, I'm beginning to see clearer already. I need to do a better job of prioritizing. I need you to know that you and the girls will always come before anything else in my life."

"You've proven that. Oh, I forgot to tell you, the girls' new birth certificates came Friday. We're now officially the Thaddeus Bradford family."

"Lauren, that's wonderful. They're now officially my daughters. You have no idea how happy that makes me."

"I do."

"Sorry, I forgot," Thad said, referring to Lauren's adoption of the girls.

*****

Eight days later Lauren and Thad returned home. "Welcome home, Mr. and Mrs. Bradford. Oh, look at my little girls, trying to grow up while they were away from me," exclaimed Mrs. Brown.

"How are you, Ms. Dora? You look as radiant as ever after a week with Mr. Bill."

"Look who's talking. I need sunshades just to look at you and Dr. B. Hawaii is a wonder medicine. The two of you look great."

"Thank you, madam. I, for one, feel great."

"And I for two," chimed Thad. "When did you get back?"

"Yesterday afternoon. Bill was going fishing with the boys, so I decided to get an early start."

"Thank, God whoever was behind the harassment has given up. It's been a couple of months since we've gotten a phone call."

"Actually it's been closer to four months. There hasn't been an incident of any kind since the first of January. Believe me, I don't miss it."

"Neither do I. Are you ready to turn in, Mrs. Bradford?"

"Yes, I am. I've been spoiled. But, after tomorrow we won't be able to sleep in. It's back to the salt mines."

CHAPTER THIRTY-EIGHT

Janet looked up to see two women approaching her desk. "Ms. Jeffries?"

"No. I am Janet Mosley, her secretary. May I help you?"

"We're looking for Ms. Lori Jeffries. I'm Detective Jill Evans, and this is Ms. Jane Landis from Children's Services."

"Ms. Jeffries is in a meeting. Can I help you?"

"We need to speak directly with her. Can you get her back here or tell us where she is?"

"I'll page her."

Lauren stepped into her office. "I'm Lauren Jeffries. How can I help you?"

"Ms. Jeffries, I'm Detective Evans and this is Ms. Landis. We need to talk to you about your daughter. We've gotten several reports of suspected child abuse."

"What?" Lauren sat abruptly in a chair. "What— who— where did you hear that? Where is my daughter?" She pushed the button on the intercom. "Janet, call my husband. Tell him to get here, right away."

"Ms. Jeffries, your daughter is in protective custody until we have finished our investigation."

"You have my daughter? Where did you get her from?"

"We are asking the questions, Ms. Jeffries," the detective said.

"And it sounds as if I shouldn't answer them without additional information."

"You can answer them here or at the precinct."

Thad burst into the room and hurried to Lauren's side. "Lauren? What's going on?"

Lauren held up her hand to quiet Thad. She pressed a button on her phone, putting it on speaker.

"Bradford residence," Mrs. Brown answered.

"Mrs. Brown this is Mrs. Bradford. How is everything going?"

"Just fine Mrs. B. I was just getting ready to put the little angels down for their naps. Do you want to speak to them?"

"Sure. I'm missing them today. I really need to hear their voices. Put them on the speaker. Hello Brittany. Hello Brianna."

"Hi mommy."

"Hello precious. How are mama's little angels?"

Thad leaned toward the phone. "Hello pumpkins. How ya doing?"

"Daddy," the girls acknowledged in unison.

"Are you about to take a nap pumpkin?"

Brittany babbled. "Nap daddy."

Lauren touched the phone. "Have a nice nap, angels. I love you."

"Daddy loves you, too. Have a nice nap and Mommy and Daddy will see you soon. Okay? Bye bye."

"Mrs. Brown," Lauren instructed the nanny, "don't take the girls out this afternoon. We'll see you shortly."

Thad slid his hands into his pockets. "Okay. Someone tell me what's going on here."

"I'm being investigated for child abuse."

Thad turned to face the detective. "You are what! Where did you hear such nonsense?"

"They said they have my daughter in protective custody."

"Well, I guess you just heard our daughters on the phone, and we only have two children."

The detective and Mrs. Landis exchanged perplexed glances. "This is obvious some kind of mistake. The detective announced.

"Obviously," Lauren said. "Where did you get this poor child you think is mine?"

"From County Hospital. An unidentified person left a note with the child, saying that she rescued her from her abusive mother, Dr. Lori Jeffries."

Again, Lauren pushed a button on the phone and placed a call. This time she did not put the call on the speaker.

"Hello, Alan, this is Lauren. Can you and Dan meet me at my house, right away?" Lauren listened. "Yes, he's with me. What do you say to about twenty or thirty minutes? That will be fine."

Thad touched her arm. "They'll be okay, darling."

Lauren turned to the detective. "I'm not answering anymore questions. I'm sure you need to see for yourself that my daughters are safe. You can follow us or ride with me to my house if you like. Darling, are you riding with me or are you driving your car?"

"I'll drive you. I can get my car later. We're ready detective."

* * * * *

Alan Wilcox and Agent Dan Coles were standing beside his car when Lauren and Thad, followed by the detective and Mrs. Landis, drove up.

"Lauren what's up? Hello, detective." Alan greeted Lauren and the detective.

The detective introduced the other woman, "Captain, this is Ms. Landis from Children's Services."

"What's going on here, Evans?"

"We received child abuse complaints against Ms. Jeffries."

"Are you kidding? Against, Lauren? Someone's made a huge mistake," Agent Coles chimed in.

Lauren spoke up, "Captain, maybe we should take this inside."

Inside, Mrs. Landis repeated the story of how the baby was found. "We're bound by law to investigate all complaints."

"You said you received several calls. Why is this the first time you've contacted me?" Lauren asked.

"We've been investigating, Ms. Jeffries. This is the first time we've had anything solid to go on."

"You still don't have anything solid to go on. Would you and the detective like to see my daughters, now?"

"Ms. Jeffries, I'm sorry. I hope you understand, we have a job to do. We don't know until after we investigate if there is any truth to the allegations."

Lauren responded with anger, "That being the case, you should treat people as innocent until they're proven guilty. Not as if the jury just convicted them.

How many people have their reputations ruined because of lies like this? If you'd been doing an adequate job of investigating, you would have found that I have two children only a few months older than that poor girl. One should wonder why I would abuse one and not the other."

"Detective Evans, I want to see your report before you file it," Alan said, saving the detective from further tongue lashing from Lauren.

"Yes, sir. Is that all, sir?"

"That's all, detective."

*****

Lauren and Thad stood facing Alan and Dan across the kitchen. "Let's all sit down." Thad offered. "What do you make of this, Dan?"

"I'll tell you what I make of it. Our reprieve is over." Lauren stared directly at Alan.

"I think it's a case of mistaken identity. There was definitely a little girl suffering from abuse, taken to County this morning. They probably got the name mixed up."

"Good try, Dan. They said this was part of an on-going investigation of me." Lauren pulled out the metropolitan telephone directory. "In here is a list of more than one hundred thousand names. There are only two other Jeffries in Dalton spelled the same way I spell mine, and they're both men. I'm not listed. The complaint said Ms. Jeffries. Most people now refer to me as Dr. or Mrs. Bradford. Why would the name Jeffries be randomly selected, and why is it that Evans and Landis came directly to me. There's something they didn't share with us, Thad."

Alan chuckled and glanced at Dan. "I told you she should be working for us."

"I see what you mean. You're very observant, Lauren. We'll talk with Detective Evans when we get back to the precinct. You're right. This reprieve might be over. Let's hope this isn't related to the past harassments."

Thad closed the door behind Coles. "Lauren, I'm going to talk to Gene and ask him to recommend a good law firm.

There's no telling what kind of attorney we're going to end up needing. This thing is as sick as it gets."

"I know. They really need to check on that baby. Who would use an innocent child in their sick games? Whoever it is should be put under the jail."

"I agree. We're dealing with a sick mind. I'm just wondering where they got this child from."

"We can ask Alan when he calls. He said he'd call as soon as he had more information." Thad glanced at his watch, "It's almost three o'clock. There's no need in us going back to work today, but I do need to check on a couple of my patients."

*****

The next day Dan made an appointment to see Lauren in her office.

Lauren opened the door to his knock. Agent Coles stepped into the office and closed the door behind him. "We need to talk. You believe the same people are behind this, and I believe you've been keeping something from me."

"Not really, Dan. Here, have a seat. The only incident between the slashed tires and now, was a call to the Center the first part of January. I answered the phone where the caller asked for Ms. Jeffries. I told him I would get her, but when I returned to the phone, he'd hung up." Lauren sat behind her desk.

Thad has had several run-ins with his parents since then, and I had an ugly exchange with his father a month ago. I threatened to sic the governor on him if he didn't leave us alone. Thad has been officially disowned as a Bradford. They cut him out of their wills, and barred him from the house. He can return to both, if he gets rid of me. They haven't offered me anymore money to leave him, though."

"Any *more* money? You were offered money to leave him? When did this happen?"

"My father-in-law came to my house eight days before my wedding and offered me one hundred-fifty thousand dollars, which he raised to two hundred thousand before I had a chance to tell him what he could do with his money.

He called again the night before my wedding and offered me two hundred and fifty thousand dollars. All I had to do was call off the wedding."

"Gee, thanks for letting me know, Lauren."

"I'm sorry. I thought Wendy or Alan told you. Wendy was present when he came to the house. She said she had to report it. Remember, with the wedding and all, my mind was elsewhere. I'm sorry."

"I'm sorry too, Lauren. I just can't believe anyone would go to such extremes. Thad still has no idea you suspect his parents?"

"No, he doesn't, but his sister-in-law does, and she believes I'm right. I didn't tell her I suspect them, she deduced it from a conversation we had. Anyway, did you get any information on that baby?" Lauren doodled on a pad.

"It's sick, Lauren. The baby was born to a drug addict, who we now have in jail. The child is suffering from mal-nutrition, but otherwise unharmed. She's in protective custody."

"What about the report of abuse? Is my name on file?"

"No. The report was written without your name or the accusations mentioned."

"Thanks. How are we going to handle this threat?"

"How do you want to proceed? Do we tell Thad?"

"I don't know. You have no idea what he's gone through as a result of his parents' antics. These accusations against them, if true, could destroy him. I 'm willing to wait a while longer. That is, if no one gets hurt. In spite of everything, what they did with that baby is a blessing in disguise."

"You're right about that. Well, I guess we'll wait and see what happens." Dan prepared to leave. "This information about the money offer puts a new light on Thad's parents. A very suspicious one. I'm going to discuss it with Wilcox. Lauren, please keep me posted; on everything."

"Okay Dan, I will," she chuckled.

"Why don't I believe you?"

"I have no idea." She smiled. "I promise you I'll tell you everything from now on. This is getting scary."

CHAPTER THIRTY-NINE

Joan sat folding clothes in her den. "How's it going, Lauren? Is everything really as quiet as it looks from the outside?"

"So far, so good. We've been very busy at the Center. The new building will be ready for us to move into in another two weeks. Mrs. Standis is very excited about that. I think she's going to attend the grand opening. Needless to say, Vivian is very excited too."

"Have our in-laws been behaving themselves? No more harassment?"

"No. There hasn't been anything since Uncle Lewis' death."

"What happened then? I didn't know there was an incident."

In response to Lauren's recap of the incident between Mr. Bradford and herself, Joan laughed. "Remind me never to cross you. Did you tell Thad?"

"No, I didn't. He has enough to contend with. I'm sure Mr. Bradford wouldn't dare tell him the truth about our conversation. I have the upper hand for now. That doesn't mean I'm letting my guard down though."

"Smart lady. Gene and I have been getting the cold shoulder too. Sunday dinners are now held in a restaurant with only Alana and Elaine and their families."

"I'm sorry about that. I hate to be the cause of a family rift."

"You aren't, Lauren. You held up the mirror for us to see ourselves. Some of us disliked what we saw and changed. Others liked what they saw, and remained the same, that's the sad part."

"So? You all had a nice time in Hawaii, did you?"

"The best Joan." Lauren rested her hands on the towel she was folding. "I was becoming very concerned about Thad. This thing with his parents has really been eating at him. He was having trouble sleeping, and he was always tired. The main reason for going at that time was for him to get some rest."

"It worked. He looks great, better than I've seen him look in months. As a matter of fact, both of you look great."

"Thank, you. All we did was eat, sleep, talk, and walk. We went to bed early and woke up late. He talked about his parents' rejection of me and how it hurts him. Their disowning has really devastated him. He also talked about how he has to maneuver around the pain. That was the first time we've spent hours talking about that one issue, and in doing so, he was able to purge. He too, had to realize we have no control over anyone's thoughts or actions except our own."

Joan placed a towel the basket. "You have a degree in psychology, don't you?"

"I do, but this had nothing to do with degrees. It was all about helping to get the man I love through a very difficult period. If we couldn't get through that intact, there's no way we'd be able to get through what's coming—and it is coming. I don't know when or what, but it's coming."

"Thanks for loving my brother-in-law. I do believe you're the only woman who would have put up with what you have from his parents. He's very happy with you."

"Love will cause you to do many things you didn't think you could, or would do. I love Thad with all my heart, and I know he loves me equally as much. There isn't much I wouldn't do for him."

Joan smiled. "We're learning that."

"Well, my dear friend," Lauren said, as she stood. "As always I've had a lovely weekend, but it's getting late and both Thad and I have an early day tomorrow."

*****

On Memorial Day, Lauren and Thad took the girls to a parade, and then joined Vivian and her family for a backyard barbeque. "Are you working this summer, Lauren?" Vivian asked as they sat watching the children play.

"No, I'm not. As a matter of fact, I have a feeling that pretty soon Thad is going to ask me to quit working altogether."

"You really think so? Do you think you'd like that?"

"He's been making subtle hints to that effect. I told him I'm not ready to give up working just yet. In spite of all the drama at the university, I really do like my job. But, I'm learning that Thad likes the domestic scene."

"What would you do if he insists?"

"He wouldn't do that."

"I guess not. I would be afraid to." Vivian laughed.

Lauren grinned. "Be nice, now."

When they returned home, a package bearing a D.C. postmark, addressed to Lauren, sat in front of the garage door. The fact that it bore the US postal stamp, and delivered on a holiday threw up a red flag. Leaving the package untouched, Thad ushered Lauren and the girls into the house, and then called Alan Wilcox.

After viewing the contents of the package, a picture of a coffin beside an open grave bearing a hand printed caption that read R.I.P., they agreed that Lauren's life was in danger.

"I think they've slipped up this time. We may be able to track this through the postal system," said Coles. "Lauren, we're going to assign an agent to you, again, and this time we are not making it a secret. We're going to flush them out."

"You won't get any argument from me," replied Lauren.

Thad breathed a sigh of relief. "That's my girl."

Lauren glanced at him. "Am I really that bad?"

All three men looked at her and nodded yes.

"You're pretty darn stubborn, my love."

"I prefer determined."

"Synonymous, but we respect that." Alan laughed, and threw his hands up, feigning warding off an assault.

Lauren chuckled. "Thanks guys. I needed that. What are we going to do now, Alan?"

"Give us some time to do some investigating and strategizing. We'll be in touch with you tomorrow. By the way, are you planning to go away at all this summer?"

"I don't know. We haven't discussed it."

Thad glanced at Lauren. "I think we should think about it, Lauren. We'll let you know, Alan."

"I'm going to check to see who we have available to assign to you, Lauren.

"It would be nice if Wendy is available. I don't feel up to breaking in a new person. I'm not the easiest person to get along with, you know." She cast Coles a mischievous smile.

"Yeah, we know." Alan winked.

*****

Thad reached for Lauren. "Are you okay?"

"As okay as I can be. I'm not going to fall apart, at least not yet. I'm not going to pretend I'm not afraid, though."

"Neither am I. I'm more concerned than I've ever been. I feel so helpless. If they knew the Lauren Bradford I know they wouldn't want to hurt you." After a pause he asked, "Have you given any thought to taking a vacation?"

"Like Hawaii?"

"I would like that if we can take the girls with us. You make the arrangements and I'll get the time off."

"I'll make the arrangements, but we're not going until after your birthday celebration. I've already sent out the invitations."

"I'd almost forgotten about that. What are we going to do about security for that?"

"It's already taken care of. We'll be safe."

*****

Thad's thirty-fourth birthday celebration was a rousing success. Among the seventy guests were several of his friends from college and med school. There was even a childhood friend, Max Stone, who grew up in the same neighborhood with Thad.

"So, you're the woman who's put the tongues in Boston in high gear." Max said as he danced Lauren across the floor. "They had me thinking you were some kind of ogre." He chuckled.

"I'm a chameleon."

"So, the person I'm seeing tonight isn't a true picture of who you are?"

"It is, for the most part."

"Good, because what I've seen, I like. Thad's a lucky man. He's also a very happy man. That's what important."

"Isn't it important that I'm happy too?"

"Of course it is. Contrary to what the grapevine reports, you and Thad make a very lovely couple. Thad is a wonderful person."

"That's nice of you to say, Max, but it sounds as if you have been privy to some ugly gossip."

"I know Thad's parents and Abigail quite well. If it makes you feel any better, even when we were in school, I never thought Thad would marry Abigail. There's always been something a little different about him. He didn't embrace the privileged life with the gusto like the rest of us did."

Max continued the conversation as he led Lauren away from the dance area to a table where they could observe the other dancers. "If I didn't know better, I'd think you'd grown up with us. You have the manner of a genteel lady." He smiled.

"I'm who my parents raised me to be. I can be whoever I need to be at any given time, but I find it less stressful just being me. I like me. Why haven't you gotten married, Max? Isn't your family expecting you to settle down, and present them with a grandchild or two?"

"They are, but not many of us meet the kind of women Thad and Gene did."

"I guess one has to be in the right place at the right time. I don't know about Thad, but I was certainly not looking for romance when I met him. We became good friends who fell in love."

"You mean to say you didn't know of him before you met him?"

"Anyone in the medical field had heard of him. When I was in grad- school I'd read an article he'd written, but I had no idea he was connected to the university."

Max changed the subject. "You have children. Don't you Lauren?"

"I have twin daughters. Please don't tell me you've heard the scuttlebutt surrounding them too."

"I did, and I confess I believed it until Gene set me straight. It's none of my business, or anyone else's for that matter."

Thad tapped Max. "Excuse me, Max ole boy. May I have a dance with my wife?"

"If you must, ole buddy. You're a lucky man."

"I'm a blessed man," Thad said as he danced Lauren away.

Later that night Thad lay in bed with Lauren enfolded in his arms. "Thanks for a lovely party, sweetheart. Everyone seemed to enjoy themselves, and you seem to have gained a few more admirers. I might have cause to be jealous."

"Are you kidding me? Jealous of whom? I must not have seen everyone who was here tonight."

"You and Max seemed to have had quite a conversation."

"Yeah, I wonder about him. He appears harmless, but part of his conversation sounded as if he was on a fishing trip."

"Are you some kind of clairvoyant? I'm beginning to agree with Dan and Alan; you should be working for the agency. Max *was* fishing. My parents told him to find out everything he could about you and your relationship with me. After he met you, he was so ashamed that he confessed everything to me. He said other than telling them what a lovely person you are, he isn't telling them anything."

"That's so sad. I thought they knew all they needed to know about me. I'm fortune hunting trash."

"Lauren, don't do that. I told you, they're sick. Don't be surprised at anything they do or say. Now, may I have a kiss to start my new year?"

"You received some lovely gifts. I especially like that desk clock Larry gave you, it's very unique."

"It is unique, but I'm partial to the fishing rods the girls gave me, and I'm going to find time to make good use of them."

"I have one more gift for you darling, but it's on special order, and you'll have to wait a few months, but I can show you a facsimile."

"No. Let me guess. Is it a boat?"

"I'm sorry. I never knew you wanted a boat."

"I like boating, but I haven't entertained the idea of owning one in the near future. "Is it an African safari, or a trip to the Amazon rain forest?"

"None of the above, daddy. I guess my little gift pales by comparison."

"Lauren? Lauren, darling." Thad tenderly turned her face toward him. "Why did you call me daddy? Are you trying to tell me something?"

"No, I'm not trying to tell you anything. I'm telling you that in six and a half more months you're going to be a daddy, again."

"Oh, Lauren. I'm so happy. This is the best present I could hope for on any day. How are you feeling? Are you happy, too?"

"I feel great and I'm doubly happy."

"Doubly? Is there another hidden message in that? Are we expecting twins?"

"That's what the doctor said."

"Are you happy about that, having twins I mean?"

"I am. Maybe we'll have a son and a daughter."

"I already have two daughters, Lauren. You mean another daughter and a son."

"I stand corrected. I'll be happy for whatever the Lord sees fit to bless us with."

"So will I, sweetheart." Thad folded her into his arms again and kissed her.

"Watch it mister, that's what got you in the pickle you're in now."

"I'm not complaining." He kissed her again. "Why did you wait so long to tell me? Did you plan to get pregnant?"

"I didn't plan or not plan, but when it was confirmed, I decided to wait and make it a birthday present. Can't you see the change in my body?"

"I noticed a little weight gain, but I thought you were just gaining back the weight you'd lost. It looks good on you."

"I hope you'll still be saying that in three more months."

"Trust me, I will."

*****

Lauren began calling family to announce her pregnancy. "Congratulations, sis. I'm happy for the two of you. I bet Thad's chest has expanded by a couple of inches," Michelle joked.

"And everyone knows he has beautiful teeth too. He hasn't stopped grinning yet."

"What about your in-laws? Have you told them?"

"I don't think Thad is planning to tell them. Let them tell it, the babies will never be their grandchildren, anyway."

"Do you realize that with one pregnancy you'll be the one with the most children in the family? Wow! Four children, all under the age of three. I love you sis, and I'm very happy for you, but I still say, better you than me."

"Okay, Auntie Shell. You'll be my first baby sitter."

"I'm happy to oblige, especially since they get to go back home. Congrats again sis, I've got to get back to work."

Lauren and Thad called Gene and Joan to give them the news. "Hey brother, how does it feel to be a year older?"

"I couldn't feel any better. Thanks again for the gift. Is Joan around?"

"I'm on the extension, Thad. How are you?"

"On top of the world. Lauren is on the phone, too. We just wanted to see how you guys feel about becoming an uncle and aunt again."

"Are you kidding? Lauren you're pregnant? Congratulations." Joan sounded excited.

"Congratulations, little brother. When is this little bundle of joy expected to arrive?"

"They should be here in time for Christmas."

"They? Are you expecting twins," Joan exclaimed.

"Yes," Lauren teased. "We had to make up for lost time. Thad's getting old you know."

"Did you know last night?"

I did, but it was Thad's birthday present, and I couldn't tell anyone until I told him."

"We're so happy for you both," Gene said. "Thad?"

Thad shook his head, anticipating his brother's question. "I'm not telling them, at least not yet. We've told everyone we want to know. The others can find out through observation."

"Good move. We won't tell anyone."

*****

"Excuse me Dr. B. The phone is for you." Mrs. Brown announced from the doorway.

"Thank you, Mrs. Brown. Hello? Why, hello Aunt Charlotte. How are you? How was your trip?"

"I'm doing wonderfully, better than I expected I would. We had a grand time in Europe."

"I am so happy to hear that. We'll plan a visit soon."

"That's the reason for the call. The reading of Lewis' will is Thursday, and you and Lauren need to be there. Could you all come and plan to spend the weekend? I would love to see the girls."

"We would love to spend the weekend. There's some good news we want to share with you, too."

CHAPTER FORTY

Although the Parker's combined worth was staggering, each was very wealthy in his own right. A fact that many didn't know until after the reading of the will.

"Good afternoon, everyone, it appears that all parties are present. For the record, I'm Thomas R. Gray, Esq., attorney for the estate of the late Lewis Medgers Parker. Let us begin. August 15, 1985 in the Commonwealth of Massachusetts, I, Lewis M. Parker, being of sound mind, do deem this to be my last will and testament…"

In addition to Aunt Charlotte, the household staff, and selected charities were also beneficiaries. Thad, Gene, and their families were bequeathed with sizeable monetary considerations. Both Thad and Gene also received holdings in the investment firm.

*****

The family sat in the parlor with Aunt Charlotte. I don't know what to say. Gene spoke up. "This was totally unexpected."

"That's putting it mildly," added Thad. "I had no idea you were wealthy. I never gave it a thought."

"I know. Very few people know. You both know Lewis and I thought of you as our sons. We're proud of both of you, and we're so happy the two of you selected, on your own, I must say, lovely young women to be your wives. Thad, I'm extra proud of you. You haven't had an easy time of it as of late, but you have stood as a man. You accepted the twins as your own, and you've protected your wife and children from all forces. Lewis and I often spoke of your dedication to your family. We also acknowledged the price you paid for this."

Aunt Charlotte addressed Joan and Lauren. We also saw how much the two of you love our god-sons in spite of the ugliness you both have endured from your in-laws. The two of you have shown me great love and respect as well. Lauren, I've not known any woman who's been treated as badly as you have, and still stayed the course."

"I'm extremely happy Lewis wrote his will the way he did. The only thing he didn't put in it is that we hope you will use the money to do the things you want to do. In other words, enjoy it. Now, let's pull off these mourning facades and have some refreshments. Lewis would like that."

CHAPTER FORTY-ONE

Amanda and Lauren were visiting with Vivian in her office when Amanda asked Lauren if she was ready to face another year with Mason. "I'm ready. Since I'll be spending less than four months, opposed to the usual ten with him, I'm almost looking forward to it. I have a feeling he'll be his usual pompous, self-righteous self at tomorrow's board meeting."

"Leopards don't change their spots" Vivian laughed. "Have you decided whether or not you'll be returning to work after the babies are born?"

"Not yet. Thad really wants me to stay home, but I like working. If I decide to continue working, I'd have to find an additional nanny. Mrs. Brown is a great nanny, but even she would find caring for four children under the age of three challenging. Added to that is the fact that Mrs. Brown is getting married soon, and she might be leaving."

Later that morning, after the board meeting, Dr. Mason approached Thad. "Dr. Bradford, are congratulations in order or has your wife put on a few pounds during the summer?"

Thad didn't try to hide his displeasure. "It could be both, Dr. Mason. I'll leave that one for you to figure out."

* * * * *

Lauren climbed into bed. "Now do you see what I've had to put up with for the past two years? He has a burr where I'm concerned."

"I know. I started to tell him to ask you, but I thought better of it; didn't want you to get upset."

"That's not it, Thad, and you know it," laughed Lauren. "You just didn't want me to get him told. Truth?"

"Truth." He chuckled. "By the way, I'm not going to be able to go to your doctor's appointment with you tomorrow."

"It's too late to reschedule now, but if all goes well, you'll have at least six more appointments."

"I'm looking forward to it. Did they say when the cribs were going to be delivered?"

"Yes, worrywart. In four to five weeks. We have lots of time."

"I know we do, but I don't want to wait until the last minute. You're due to deliver four months from Tuesday you know."

"Oh, that soon, huh? What we really need to be thinking about are names; two boys and two girls. I would like to name one of them after Aunt Charlotte or Uncle Lewis."

"Lauren, that's very thoughtful of you. I know Aunt Charlotte would be honored."

* * * * *

While Lauren drove home from her doctor's appointment, she noticed a dark green sedan had been following her for several blocks. *Please let this be a coincidence.* The vehicle seemed to accelerate just before she slowed to turn into her driveway. It advanced on her, narrowly missing her rear bumper. Lauren's heart raced. *Was he trying to hit me?* She sat in her car until she was nudged by the movement in her abdomen. She slowly entered the house and called Dan Coles.

"Lauren. How are you? Thankfully, it's been a while since I've heard from you," said Dan Coles.

"I thought I was okay, but I'm not so sure, now. I think I might have been followed today." She relayed the tale of the green sedan. "I didn't notice the car until I was about a mile from home. I don't know how long it may have been following me."

"Are you sure he accelerated before you turned into your driveway?"

"I'm positive. I could see the car moving on me before I slowed for the turn, and I felt I was going to be clipped."

"Dan?" Lauren said into the quiet phone.

"I'm here, Lauren," Coles said with a loud sigh. "I thought I'd prepared myself for this phone call. I thought, and hoped it was over. Have you mentioned this to Thad?"

"No. You are the only one I've told."

"How do you want to proceed from here, Lauren? Are you ready to tell Thad you suspect his parents?"

"Dan." Lauren crossed her legs. "I've thought and thought about it, but I haven't been able to do it. I can't bear to hurt him. Have you been able to find out anything?"

"Not a thing. We've had investigators snooping around in Boston, but we haven't been able to find anything concrete. Your in-laws are quite influential, and well respected from all we can tell."

"They're respected, but are they respectable? I'm not ready to concede that they're not involved. We just have to prove it. I would check out Dr. Sydney Mason, too, if I were you. He and I have had several run-ins."

"Have you told me everything, Lauren? You haven't held anything back?"

"This is the first incident since Memorial Day, no calls, nothing. But, Dan, this happened on the heels of Dr. Mason asking Thad if I'm pregnant. Thad hasn't told his parents about the pregnancy. Although, Thad didn't confirm it, I believe Mason told them, anyway."

"Be careful, Lauren. I have something I need to check out. I'll call you later this evening."

*****

Thad set his briefcase down and reached for Lauren. "Hi, sweetheart. How are you feeling?"

"I'm feeling fine. How was your day?"

"Until an hour ago it was great. Then, I received a call from my parents." He breathed a heavy sigh.

"I can imagine what that was all about. Let's sit in the den with the girls for a little while. I'd tell you to rest your head in my lap, but you might get kicked."

"It looks like we have a rivalry going already." He paused, before continuing. "My parents know you're pregnant."

"I know."

Thad stared at her. "How did you find out?"

"When Mason asked you if congratulations were in order, I knew he was going to call your parents. He might be one of the many reporting to them."

"You really think that, Lauren?"

"I do. His alliance with them could be the reason he's so antagonistic towards me. They're birds of a feather."

Thad held Lauren close and rubbed her back. "That feels good," she murmured. "Can I hire you to do that three times a day for the duration?"

"If the price is right, you have a deal." The phone rang.

Mrs. Brown announced. "Dr. B. Your mother is on the phone."

"Thank you, Mrs. Brown." Thad pushed the disconnect button without answering the phone. Lauren raised an eyebrow, but remained silent. He then continued to absentmindedly rub Lauren's back. "Will you excuse me for a little bit? I need to make a couple of calls before dinner."

The phone rang again as Thad was entering his study. "I'll get it," he called out. He picked up the receiver. "Hello."

"Hey, Thad. Sorry I missed your call. What's up?"

"Gene, I need to talk to you as soon as possible."

"What's going on? You sound serious."

"I am, Gene. Can you meet me this evening?"

"Sure. Where do you want to meet?"

He named a bar that was mid-way between Boston and Dalton.

Thad went back to the den where Lauren was still reclining on the sofa. Lauren, I'm leaving to meet Gene. I need to talk with him. I don't know what time I'll be back."

"You are scaring me. What's going on?"

"I'll tell you when I get back. I love you."

"I love you, too. Please, be careful."

Shortly after Thad left, the phone rang again. "Hello?"

"Lauren, this is Joan. What's going on with our husbands? Gene left in a rush, saying Thad needs to talk to him."

"I don't know exactly, but I'm sure it has something to do with their parents learning I'm pregnant. Mrs. Bradford called this afternoon, but Thad hung up the phone without talking to her."

"I guess they'll tell us when they're ready. Are you all right, Lauren?"

"I'm okay, Joan." Lauren sighed. "I think this all has to do with our in-laws learning that I'm pregnant."

"What business is it of theirs? They've already disowned Thad, so why should they care?"

"I'm carrying the Bradford name, Joan. That's the worst thing that could happen to this family."

"If they'd get their heads out of you know where, they'd see you're one of the greatest assets this family could hope for. Maybe someday—"

Lauren interrupted, "That's sweet of you to say Joan. I don't know how Thad and I could have gotten through this without you and Gene. I love you."

"We're family, Lauren, and we're friends. Gene and I love you. Oops, there's the other line. We'll talk tomorrow. Take care."

"Thanks, Joan. Good night."

*****

Thad and Gene arrived at the bar at the same time. "I don't think it'd be wise for me to sit in a bar right now." Thad pointed to a building across the street. "Let's go over to that restaurant."

In the restaurant, they sat facing each other, sipping coffee. "What's going on Thad?"

"They heard that Lauren's pregnant. Mother called me this evening, but I refused to talk to her. Gene, I'm through hoping they'll accept Lauren. Gene gazed over the rim of his coffee cup at his brother. After several sips he said, "Tell me what happened."

"Father said— he said—" Thad averted his eyes so Gene couldn't see the pain in them. "Gene, he said, "how dare you allow that slut to get pregnant?" Then he added he would wager the bastard isn't even mine. He said he'd rather see Lauren dead than to see her have a baby under the Bradford name."

"He said what? Are you serious? They've gone stark raving mad. Man!"

Thad sat back in his chair and ran a hand across his face. He then leaned forward on the table and looked intently at Gene. In a whisper he said, "I believe our parents are behind all the harassment."

Gene spewed his coffee. "Are you crazy?"

"No, they're crazy--with hate. None of this stuff started until Mr. and Mrs. Bickers saw Lauren and me together eighteen months ago. You've seen how our parents treat Lauren. Look at what they told the Canters. The way they tried to ruin her reputation. Did you know they asked Max to spy for them at my birthday party?"

"Are these really our parents we're talking about? I'm not going to say you're wrong, but I'm having a hard time wrapping my brain around the idea that our parents would do Lauren, or anyone, physical harm." Thad continued to stare at his brother.

"It's just as scary to know that they have a number of people doing their bidding. How am I supposed to tell my wife that I think my parents are out to harm her?"

"You are going to have to tell the agency about your suspicions, too. Did you say they'd already assigned an agent to Lauren?"

"Yes they have. Well she won't actually be here until this evening. Lauren thinks her boss has been feeding information to our parents."

"Do any of these people know Lauren? She's one of the nicest people I know, and she'd go out of her way *not* to hurt anyone. Why would anyone want to hurt her?"

"She *is* a wonderful person. That's why I fell in love with her. If only our parents would have taken the time to get to know her." After a moment of silence Thad said, "Gene, I'm not asking you to follow my lead. Your relationship with our parents is a lot different from mine, and I wouldn't be hurt if you maintained a relationship with them."

"Thad, you and I are brothers and best friends, and as of now, the only family I have. If they could do this to you, given the right circumstances, they would do it to me. I don't like this. As far as I'm concerned, what they did to Lauren, they could and would do to Joan."

"Thanks, Gene. I don't think I could have gotten through this without you."

"So, where do we go from here, brother?"

"As I said earlier, I've told our parents I'll press charges against them if they call or come by again. I have to meet with Agent Coles, too, but for now, I have to go home and tell my wife what's going on."

"I'll go with you if you need me to."

"Thanks, Gene, but I'm going to talk to Lauren tonight, and I think I need to do that alone. I'll call you tomorrow. Thanks again for your support." Thad stood and embraced his brother. "Drive safely."

"You do the same. Be careful, Thad."

*****

Lauren slid out of the bed as Thad entered the room. "Did you eat dinner?"

"I ate a little something. I'm not hungry." With his hands on Lauren's shoulders, he gazed into her eyes. "I need to talk with you, Lauren, about something very serious."

"What is it? What's wrong? Is someone sick or hurt?"

Thad led Lauren across the room and assisted her into a chair. He then sat on a footstool before her and held her hands in his. He told her about the conversation he'd had with his parents. "I told them if they called either of us or came near either of us again, I'll press harassment charges against them. I don't want anything more to do with them. And Lauren, "He took a deep breath. "I believe my parents are responsible for the harassment you've been going through."

Lauren stared at him, and then exhaled. Suddenly, she began to tremble.

Thad took her hand. "Come here, darling. Let me help you back to bed."

Contrary to what he thought, the trembling wasn't caused by what he had told her, but by the desolate look in his eyes. Lauren decided at that moment she'd never let him know that she too, suspected is parents.

"Will you lie down with me for a little while, love?"

"I need to shower first."

"Do that later. Lie with me, now. Please. I need you to hold me."

*****

Thad opened the door to Capt. Wilcox. "I appreciate you stopping by Alan. Lauren and Dan are in the kitchen.

"Hi Lauren, you're looking lovely today. How are you, Mrs. Brown?"

"I'm good. Mrs. Bradford, I'm going to take the girls into the den."

"Thad, you said you have something you need to tell me."

"Yes Alan, I do. I think you'd better sit down for this." Once, again Thad relayed the conversation he'd had with his parents and voiced his suspicions.

Coles emitted a soft whistle and glanced at Lauren who favored him with a subtle shake of the head. "I'm so sorry. I can't imagine how hard it must be for you to say that. As a part of our investigation, we had begun to look at your parents, too. We haven't found any links to the harassment, though."

Lauren glanced up at Thad. "I have something to tell you, too. I was going to tell you yesterday, but you left to meet Gene before I got the chance. I didn't want to burden you further when you returned home. But, I think I was followed when I left the doctor's office yesterday. It seemed as if the driver was trying to hit me."

"My God, Lauren! And you didn't call me?"

"There isn't anything you could have done, darling. I called Alan."

"None of this is your fault, Thad. I'm hoping the investigation will prove your parents aren't involved."

"Lauren, Wendy will be here in the morning. She's going to drive you to and from work—"

"That's not enough Dan. Now that Thad has distanced himself from his parents, he's in danger too. There are actually six of us in danger now." Lauren cradled her rounded belly.

"She's right," Dan admitted. "I'm going to gather my team together, and we'll all meet here tomorrow afternoon. What's a good time?"

"Four o'clock is good for me," Thad said.

"That's good for me too," Lauren agreed.

"Okay. We'll plan to meet you all then."

Thad called Gene to report the latest happenings. "We're meeting Captain Wilcox and a team from the agency tomorrow afternoon."

"Joan and I will be there, Thad, we aren't letting the two of you go through this alone."

"Thanks, Gene. I'll see you tomorrow."

*****

The next day Gene and Joan arrived at Thad's house. "Lauren is resting, but you can go on up." Thad said to Joan.

Joan knocked on the bedroom door.

"Hi, Joan. I'm sure glad to see you." Lauren sat up bed. The sisters-in-law embraced each other.

"How are you, Lauren?"

"I don't know how I am. Did Gene tell you about the meeting between him and Thad?"

"Yes he did. It sounded like a scene from a horror movie. My heart aches for them. I'm thankful they have each other. Did you tell Thad you suspect his parents?" Joan sat on the bed.

"No. When I saw the look of total devastation on his face, I just couldn't do it. I don't know if I will ever tell him. Did you tell Gene?"

"I didn't. I agree with you. There's no need to tell them. You said he would find out for himself. I'm happy it wasn't at you funeral, though." Thad stuck his head in the door. "Sweetheart, Dan and his crew are here."

*****

Everyone congregated in the kitchen. "Thad," Coles said, "I want you all to know that only those of us here know exactly what is going on. We want to keep this to ourselves just in case we're wrong about our suspicions. We're going to interview your parents again. We might have to use their own words against them. For the sake of you and your brother, we'll be as gentle as we can."

"As much as it pains me to think my parents might be involved, if they're guilty, they shouldn't be treated any differently than anyone else. You do what you have to do, and my brother and I will handle the fall out."

"I agree, but thanks for the consideration. My wife has endured this long enough. Whatever it takes to resolve it, do it."

The group strategized for a while longer before the agents took their leave. Agent Wendy Green stayed to stand guard. "Thad, what do you think about me confronting our parents? Not about the threats against Lauren, but about what they said about her?"

"That's up to you, Gene. It would be interesting to know how they try to justify what they said. They might even slip and say something incriminating. Maybe we can find out who tried to ram Lauren's car yesterday."

Gene glanced agape at Lauren. "Who tried to do what? Did you say someone tried to hit Lauren?"

Joan also stared at Lauren. "You didn't mention that."

"So much has happened that it slipped my mind. I was followed when I left my doctor's appointment, and just before I slowed to turn into our driveway, the car accelerated and missed my rear bumper by a hare's breadth. It was deliberate."

"Damn!" Gene exclaimed. "The gloves are off now. We need to work fast. I think they're trying to make you miscarry. There are only two people I can think of who want to see that happen. They'd go to this length. I'm going to confront them tomorrow."

"I'll go with you."

"You can't do that, Thad. You've already told them to stay away from you and Lauren. They could counter sue you.

Besides that, what more can you say? You've been fighting with them for almost two years and it's gotten you nowhere."

Lauren and Joan glanced at each other, and their faces mirrored the anguish they were feeling for their husbands.

*****

"Lauren, its Dan Coles. Can you talk freely?"

"Yes, I'm alone."

"How is Thad doing?"

"He's not doing too well. The thought his parents could be behind this is killing him. I've never seen anything like this in my life. I've a mind to confront his parents myself."

Alarmed Coles said. "Lauren, please don't. They could do you bodily harm if you went to their house, and probably get away with it. Let us handle it. I would never forgive myself if anything happened to you. Were you trying to tell me yesterday that you hadn't told Thad you suspect his parents?"

"I'm glad you picked up on that. Now that he's figured it out for himself, there's no need for me to ever mention it to him. How are you planning to handle his parents?"

"We're going to interview them separately if we can manage it. We've contacted the office in Boston, and we'll be meeting an agent at Mr. Bradford's office on Tuesday morning. It's best to talk with him before he gets a chance to prepare for us."

*****

Agent Coles stood by as the technicians installed surveillance devices in the house across the street from the Bradfords. These devices would give them a frontal view as well as side views of the Bradford house. Any activity within twenty-five yards of their property would also be recorded.

Coles checked the surveillance devices again before locking up after the technicians. At the door he glanced about nodding his head and thought, *yes, this will give us the edge we need to catch these perps.*

Later that same afternoon, Mrs. Brown answered the doorbell. "May I help you?" She asked from behind the locked security door.

"I have a special delivery for Mrs. Jeffries."

"Does it need to be signed for?"

"No ma'am."

"Leave it at the door."

Mrs. Brown watched the young man head to his car. Suddenly, there was the screeching of car tires and shouts of halt, police.

*****

Two weeks after Thad's conversation with his parents, and the same day the box was delivered for Lauren; the ribbon cutting ceremony for the second Women of Substance facility was held.

The ceremony was a grand affair with extensive media coverage, which carried the story of Mrs. Standis' attendance as well as photos of a very pregnant Lauren standing with her. Throughout the ceremony, Thad, Dan Coles, and Wendy were never too far from Lauren's side.

"Mrs. Bradford, you look absolutely beautiful." Maureen Standis smiled as she approached Lauren after the ceremony. "How are you feeling?"

Lauren rested her hands on her abdomen. "Please, call me Lauren. I'm feeling great, but these little munchkins must be growing like weeds. They're getting awfully heavy."

"Don't you think you should be sitting instead of walking around?"

"I should be. I'm leaving shortly. I wanted to be sure that I spoke with you before I left. Have you started your program yet?"

"The ribbon cutting is scheduled for December 12th. I was hoping you'd be able to attend."

"I'm sorry, that's three days after my due date. I'm sure Vivian and Amanda will be there."

"Well, I'm sorry that you'll be otherwise engaged." She smiled, glancing at Lauren's mid-section. "I'm happy for you and Thad. My husband and I would like to have you and your family visit for a weekend. Aside from being indebted to Thad, we like you both."

"Thank you, Mrs. Standis we'd be—"

"Call me Maureen. We don't stand on formality."

Lauren smiled. "Thank you. Maureen it is. You're asking for trouble. By the time I'm able to visit, there will be six of us, four under three years old."

"Wow. If you can all get there, we'll take care of the rest." Mrs. Standis laughed. She paused and asked, "Lauren is everything okay with you and Thad? You're not in any danger are you?"

"Why do you ask?" Lauren inquired, somewhat perplexed.

"I know Dan Coles, and that young lady there," she nodded toward Wendy, "is a police officer if ever I saw one. She's not been five feet away from you all day, nor has Thad."

"It's long and complicated, Maureen."

"Let's go inside where we can talk confidentially."

"First, I have to ask Dan and Thad if it's okay for me to divulge any information."

*****

Lauren finished her synopsis of recent events relative to the harassments.

"Lauren! I'm appalled. You can't be serious. " Maureen pressed her hand over her heart, a shocked look on her face.

"I wish I wasn't. I'm very frightened."

"You have reason to be. What can I do? Perhaps my husband can intervene on your behalf."

"Thanks, but Dan is working on a plan. I have every confidence in him."

"Stay in touch with me, Lauren. I want to know that you and your family are safe and well."

"Thanks again, Maureen. If you'll excuse me, I think I'd better be getting home. All of that standing has begun to take a toll on my back. By the way, I won't be working at the Center anymore until after the babies are born, if then."

"I understand. Vivian is a lovely and efficient woman, but I'm biased." She smiled and embraced Lauren. "I'll be in touch."

Thad walked into the hall just as Maureen was about to leave. “Lauren, are you feeling okay? Maybe we should get you home. You look exhausted.”

"I was just telling Maureen that I should be getting home. My back is killing me."

"Take her home, and Thad?" Maureen touched his arm. “Please be very careful. I’m sorry for what you're going through. You can trust me to be discreet.”

"I appreciate that Mrs. Standis. We…"

"Maureen." She smiled and took his hand. “I’ll say goodbye, for now. I'll speak with you all soon.”

"Let’s go, sweetheart."

"I need to say goodbye to Vivian and Amanda."

"I’ve already said it for you. I told them I needed to get you home."

"Thad?" Lauren spotted Wendy casting furtive glances around the area, and took a few steps closer to her. “Is there a problem? What’s going on?"

"Let’s get home, Lauren. I'll tell you then."

Lauren cried out, "Oh, my God, Thad! Is it the girls?"

"No darling, they're fine. I'm so sorry I alarmed you. The girls are fine."

"Where's Dan?"

"He’ll meet us at the house."

* * * * *

Dan, Alan Wilcox, and agent Bill Wheeler were all standing on the front porch when they arrived home. There was also a police cruiser in her driveway with a young man sitting in the back seat, guarded by a uniformed officer.

"Dan what’s going on?" Lauren asked, as Thad helped her out of the car.

"Let’s go inside, sweetheart. You need to get off your feet."

Once in the house Lauren slumped into a chair with a sigh. “All right, I'm sitting. Now, will someone please tell me what’s going on?"

The men all looked from one to another. Dan took a step to stand before her while Thad stood beside her chair. "We had an incident, Lauren," Coles said. "About thirty minutes ago a box was delivered to you. The young man out there in the patrol car delivered it. He was arrested as he was returning to his car."

"What's in the box, Dan?" Lauren asked as she spied the box just inside the door. Dan ran a hand through his hair. Thad caught her hand in his as Wendy moved to the other side of her chair. Lauren's eyes widen in fear. "What is it?" Thad gave Dan a nod of approval.

"The depiction is graphic and very sinister. I don't want you to see it, especially in your condition."

"Neither do I, sweetheart. Remember we are dealing with sick, evil people."

"Is it a threat to the girls, again?"

"No, darling." Thad bit his lip. "It's a threat to our unborn children."

Lauren rocked back and forth cradling her abdomen. "Why? Why does anyone want to hurt us?"

"We'll catch them, Lauren." Dan spoke softly as he placed a hand on her shoulder. "I promise you we will." He added, slamming a fist in to his palm. "Let's go question the suspect, Bill. We'll call you later this evening, Thad. I'm taking this box with me." He lifted the box and headed out the door.

"Maybe you should lie down for a while. I'll help you upstairs."

"Okay. I want to peek in on the girls before I lie down. Lauren pointed to a brownish red spot on the floor where the box had sat. "What is that? Is it blood?" She began to tremble uncontrollably before darkness engulfed her.

*****

Dan looked up when Thad returned to the kitchen. "I'm sorry, Thad. How is she?"

"She's sleeping. Her doctor paid her a visit and gave her something to help her relax. I don't know how much more she can take. Heck, I don't know how much more I can take, and I'm not pregnant."

"Both of you have been troopers. I hope we can get some useful information from that box and its contents. The suspect, George Chaney, claims he was paid one hundred dollars, to deliver the box. He said a white male in a black stretch limo approached him as he was leaving a barbershop on Main Street. The man had a hat pulled down over his eyes, wore sunglasses, and had gray hair and a gray moustache. That was probably a disguise because he said the man didn't appear that old.

The man told him it was a surprise for a friend of his. The limo followed him to the end of your block, probably to see that it was delivered. We checked the barbershop and several patrons corroborated his story." Dan hesitated, "Thad, I must say I was scared to death Lauren was going to insist on viewing the contents of that box."

"You weren't any more frightened than I was. I almost lost it when I saw it. It's no telling what she imagined that caused her to faint when she saw that blood smear on the floor. When are you interviewing my parents?"

"Tuesday morning."

"Tuesday! That's four days from now. My wife could be dead by then."

Coles stared at Thad. "I won't let that happen. In view of this last incident, I'll see if I can get Boston to move quicker. I'm sorry about all this. Please, believe we're doing the best we can."

"I know, and I appreciate it. It's just that I feel so helpless. My entire family is in danger and there's not a damn thing I can do about it."

Gene and Joan had arrived in response to Thad's phone call, informing them of the latest happenings surrounding the harassment.

"I'm afraid of what could happen to her if this keeps up. If she goes into labor now, she could very easily loose the babies. If that happens, I'd lose her."

Gene rubbed his chin. "I can't believe this is happening. I wish Dan hadn't asked me to hold off on confronting Mother and Father. I need to know if they're the masterminds behind this."

*****

Lauren stretched and glanced around the darkened room. "Hello there, sis. How are you feeling?" Joan inched towards the bed.

"What are you doing here? What time is it?" She rubbed her eyes and sat up.

"It's almost seven-thirty. Do you remember what happened today?"

"Unfortunately, I do. I don't remember coming to bed though. Where are Thad and the girls?"

"They're downstairs with Gene, Wendy, and Mrs. Brown."

"Did you see what was in the box, Joan?" Asked Lauren asked with a somber quality in her voice.

"I don't want to know. The fact that the box was sent, is more than I can bear. This is really becoming– I'm sorry, Lauren. We're not supposed to get you upset."

"Not talking about it won't stop me from being upset. Just knowing there's someone out there who wants to hurt us is enough to keep me unnerved."

Thad entered the room. "Well, hello, sleeping beauty. How're you feeling?"

"I'm feeling fine, sweetheart. How are you?"

"Other than being worried about you, I'm fine. Are you hungry?"

"I'm not, but I know I have to eat something for these little ones." She patted her stomach. "Where are the girls?"

"Mrs. Brown is bathing them. I'll ask her to bring them in before she puts them to bed. Do you have a taste for anything in particular? Joan fixed baked chicken, green beans, rice and salad."

"Sounds tasty, I'd love some."

Joan stood. "You stay with Lauren. I'll fix her a tray."

"I can go down to eat, Joan. You don't have to wait on me."

"Yes we do, sweetheart. You fainted, and I called Grace. She came out and examined you. You need to stay in bed for the next three or four days."

Lauren stretched her eyes in alarm. "Did I fall when I fainted?"

"No baby. I caught you before you hit the floor."

"Are the babies okay? Am I in danger of miscarrying?"

"No, darling, not at this point, but your blood pressure sky rocketed as did your pulse. Grace gave you something to relax you. You really need to be quiet for a few days."

"Don't look so anxious, sweetheart. I'll be obedient. I wouldn't do anything to jeopardize the health of the babies."

"Aha, so that's the secret to keeping you docile—keep you pregnant," Thad teased.

"Enjoy the next few months, my love," she teased back.

Gene joined the group. "Hi there, little mama. How are you feeling?"

"Hello, Gene. I'm feeling great, and I'm being spoiled. Not to mention, there's nothing little about me, anymore."

"You look great." Gene's gaze held a solemn light. "Lauren, I'm so sorry about all of this."

"I know you are, Gene, but this isn't your fault. We don't know if your parents are involved in this either."

"How can you be so charitable after what they've done to you?"

"Innocent until proven guilty, sir."

"You have a good woman, Thad."

Thad smiled. "And no one knows that better than I do, brother."

CHAPTER FORTY-TWO

Lauren recovered from the frightening experience with the box, and returned to work just in time to attend the next board meeting. The board members learned to expect Dr. Mason to treat Lauren with disdain at every opportunity so; they weren't surprised when he started in on her today.

"Dr. Reed, Dr. Stanton, I'm sorry I wasn't able to make the ribbon cutting ceremony for your new center. Although, the center isn't a part of the hospital or the university, the two of you have made us proud by association. I understand the governor's wife was in attendance."

Linda frowned at Mason. "Have you read the papers or listened to the news in the past week, Dr. Mason? Dr. Lauren Bradford's picture has been all over both, along with Vivian, Amanda, and the governor's wife. The whole concept of the Center is Lauren's idea." She sounded annoyed.

"Well, whoever it was, the hospital benefited. Now let's get down to business. We have a full agenda this morning."

Thad was seated beside Lauren. He opened his mouth to protest the blatant disregard of Lauren, but she caught his hand and gave her head a slight shake.

Larry Wilcox spoke up, "Before we move on, Dr. Mason. I think we should give Lauren a round of applause. She's done a lot to help put this facility in a positive light; not just in this community, but throughout the state. She hasn't been given the recognition she so richly deserves. The nursing program has never run more smoothly, and morale has never been higher. Yet, if it weren't for Linda's reports in *Bio-Feed* no one would even know she's largely responsible for the positive PR. I think it's long past time she's recognized for the work she does here."

"Here, here!" The other board members chorused as they stood and applauded. Dr. Mason's face turned red as he lumbered to his feet.

Vivian chimed in. "Thanks, Larry. I couldn't have said that any better. We all owe Lauren so much. It seems everyone applauds her contributions except for this facility."

"Well— well— we'll have to do it another time," stuttered Mason. "We have a full agenda this morning."

Thad, Lauren, Ryan, Amanda, Linda, Larry and Vivian were having lunch together in the nurses' conference room

"Can you believe that man? He's an A#1 you know what," exclaimed Vivian. He knows very well, you started the Center, Lauren. I think he was trying to goad you by giving Amanda and me the credit for it. For some reason he hates you."

At Vivian's declaration, Thad took Lauren's hand in his and gave it a gentle squeeze.

"We need to do something about him. He's not effective anyway," Larry said.

Ryan asked. "What's his beef with you, Lauren? He's had it in for you ever since you came aboard."

"He can't stand the fact that she stands up to him, and that she's loved and respected by everyone, and she has the backing of the hospital as a whole." Linda said, before Lauren could answer. "Even after that attempt to smear her reputation a couple of years ago, she came out smelling like a rose, and is now hob knobbing with the elite. No one person is supposed to be so highly favored."

"Don't forget, she just waltzed in here and snagged the most eligible bachelor from under all the other bachelorettes' noses. Insolent little snippet." Vivian grinned, and everyone laughed.

"Thank you all for supporting Lauren," Thad said. "She wouldn't let me say anything to Mason this morning, but I'll have my say, not only to him, but to the administrative board as well. I haven't known anyone to be treated so disrespectfully in all the years I've been here. He really didn't want to acknowledge that Lauren had anything to do with the Center."

Vivian glanced at Thad. "It's okay. We all know the brains behind it, and now thanks to the media, so does everyone else."

"It is yours now, Vivian. You did a wonderful job with the ribbon cutting festivities. In fact, you and Amanda will be taking over the entire project. I'm going to be tied up for the next twenty-five years." Lauren smiled as she rested her hand on her abdomen.

"You're beginning to fill out quite a bit, Lauren," Ryan said. "Are you sure we aren't expecting twins?"

"You didn't know? We *are* expecting twins. I thought Thad had told the whole world by now."

"Do you know the gender yet?"

"No. We want to be surprised. It would be nice to have two boys to go with our two girls."

Larry laughed. "Yeah, and maybe the next time we'll have one of each."

"How come all of a sudden you're speaking French? We. We. Who's going to do the first hours of labor?" Lauren laughed. "I love you guys. Thanks for the on-going support. I don't think I could have handled Mason these past two years without you all."

Ryan shot her a look. "You're joking aren't you? We've seen you in action lady." Everyone laughed.

* * * * *

Later, Lauren lay in bed while Thad rubbed her back. "Why did you stop me from addressing Mason today?"

"Several reasons, number one being that I've learned it wouldn't do any good, especially if it was in front of others. Second is because he's not going to change, and third, he hates me. I feel sorry for him and his kind."

"Like my parents. Huh? It brought tears to my eyes to see the way the group stood up for you today. They're all very protective of you."

"That's because you're their friend, and I'm your wife. They're all lovely people. I like them."

"They're your friends too, sweetheart. They've told me on several occasions that you're a classy lady, and I'm a blessed man. But, of course I already knew that."

"I'm blessed beyond blessed too. That's something Mason can't take from me."

* * * * *

Lauren complained of persistent back pain and an overall sense of fatigue.

Grace Elliott, her obstetrician, being very concerned about her rapid weight gain and elevated blood pressure, ordered a battery of tests to see if there was a medical cause for the change.

After the examination, Grace summoned Lauren and Thad to her office. "Lauren, Thad, have a seat. I have the results of all the tests and the sonar gram."

"Is there a problem?" Thad took Lauren's hand in his.

"I don't see a problem, but I have some very surprising news for you." She scanned the medical chart again before speaking.

Thad tightened his grip on Lauren's hand. "What is it Grace?"

"Brace yourselves." Grace smiled. "You're having triplets."

Thad and Lauren's mouths dropped opened, but no sound came from either of them. They looked at each other. Thad put an arm around Lauren's shoulder. "You all right?" Lauren nodded. "Are you sure, Grace?"

"We're one hundred percent sure. I don't understand why the third baby wasn't detected on the first sonogram. We did the first one very early in your pregnancy. We reviewed those photos again, and we still didn't see any indication there was a third baby. Except for the one time, during your fifth month exam when we heard the double heartbeat, we haven't heard anything out of the ordinary."

Lauren appeared stunned. "I just saw my entire life change in less than two minutes."

"I'm afraid it's going to change even more, Lauren. I'm going to prescribe bed rest for the duration of your pregnancy. I don't like the fact that your blood pressure has been higher on each of your last three visits. Now we know the reason for the weight gain, but it is wreaking havoc on your back, and it could be the cause of the edema. Your due date is seven and a half weeks away, but we all know the odds of carrying multiple births to term are slim. We don't want to up those odds by adding any more stress."

"Will I be able to finish out the week at work?

There are a few matters I need to clear up."

"Lauren, sweetheart, let's not chance it. Please?"

"It's only three days."

"Thad, she can do the three days, but not a day longer."

"Grace, when you say bed rest, do you mean one hundred percent in the bed?"

"You can rest in a recliner for an hour or two during the day, you can go to the bathroom, and you can shower twice a week as long as you sit while doing so, and as long as someone is nearby. There's to be no climbing stairs and no lifting or bending. Call me at the first inkling of a contraction. Are there any questions?"

"There aren't any now, but there might be some after the shock wears off," Thad answered.

Thad drove Lauren to the university. "You are looking rather pensive, love."

Lauren glanced at him. "You do realize that in less than two months we are going to have five children all under the age of three? I'm just thinking of the additional preparations we have to make."

"Don't worry about that. I'll take care of it."

"I'm not going to become an invalid, Thad. There are still some things I can do that don't require lifting and bending."

"And, I'm going to leave those to you, sweetheart. It's just that I don't want you to feel that all the preparations are on your shoulders. We've done everything together so far. When you don't feel up to doing something, let me help. "

"Of course. I'm sorry for being a bit testy. Don't pay me any attention. These hormones are going to be running wild for a while."

"I'll always pay attention to you, Lauren. I might not react, but I pay attention." He parked the car in front of the building and opened the door. "Take it easy, sweetheart," He cautioned, helping her to her office. "What time do you want me to come for you?"

"Come back about four.

I'm going to finish some reports and clear some papers off of my desk."

"I'll see you then. Be careful, darling. I love you."

CHAPTER FORTY-THREE

The department had planned to host a surprise baby shower for Lauren later in the month, but due to her leaving a month earlier than she had planned, they had to move quickly to do it before she left.

Thad told Vivian that under the circumstances, a surprise shower wasn't a good idea. Since Gene and Michelle were the only ones aware of the fact that they were expecting triplets, all the gifts given were with twins in mind, even with that, they received seven car seats, and most of the other gifts tripled or quadrupled. Given what they received from Lauren's family and the Agency, there were more than enough clothes, high chairs, toiletries and bottles for three babies.

Thad and Lauren headed home after the shower. "How long have you known about the shower, Thad?"

Thad chuckled. "From the beginning. We really had to scramble to get everything done in three and a half days. I tried to get them to call it off, but they wouldn't hear of it. The ladies seemed to have had such a good time planning it. They love you, Lauren."

"And I love them. They've been so generous. I'm glad we didn't tell them we're expecting triplets. They would have done so much more than they did."

"You're right. As it is, we shouldn't have to do any shopping until they are six months old or more."

"Will you grant me one favor before I begin bed rest?"

"I can't promise, Lauren. It depends upon what it is, and since you feel the need to ask, you're already sensing I will disapprove. What's the favor?" He cast a sideways glance in her direction.

"May I please supervise the rearranging of the furniture and the storing of the gifts in the nursery? I promise I won't do any lifting or bending. I'll sit in one of the rockers while I supervise."

Thad let out a guffaw.

"What's so funny?"

"You sound like a little girl making a case for a sleepover."

"Well, can I, Daddy?"

"Yes, you can, but only if I help."

"You don't trust me."

"I do. I just want to be a part of it. When do we start?"

"As soon as all of the clothes are rinsed and folded. The other furniture should arrive on Monday. I'll do the bed rest until you get home Tuesday."

"I know none of this is easy for you, especially with the girls. You've always been so active with them. They aren't going to understand why you can't lift or play with them the way you used to. I'll try to make up for that."

"I love you, Thaddeus Bradford. You were afraid I wouldn't comply with Grace's orders. Weren't you?"

"I thought it would take a while before you did."

"I told you I wouldn't jeopardize the health of our children. I don't want to cause you any additional stress either."

"I love you, Lauren Bradford."

*****

The next day Mrs. Brown spied a package at the door. "Mrs. Bradford, a package arrived for you. It must be another gift for the babies. There's no return address on it."

"Leave it there, Mrs. Brown. Wendy, I'm going to call Dan."

"Hello, Lauren," Dan answered the phone.

"Hello Dan. How are you?"

"I'm well. I hope the only reason you're calling is to inquire about my well-being."

"I wish that was the case. There's a box at our front door. It's addressed to me, but there's no return name or address on it. Would you please come and get it. If it contains anything other than a store bought gift for the babies, I don't want to know it."

*****

The board meeting was about to begin. "How's Lauren holding up?" Larry asked.

"She's on bed rest for the remainder of her pregnancy."

"I'm sorry to hear that. It's not unusual for bed rest to be ordered in multiple birth pregnancies.

She's due in about six weeks isn't she?"

"She surprised me." Amanda chuckled. "I didn't think she would comply with the doctor's orders so easily."

"You do know her, don't you? She really has been a trooper."

"Let us come to order." Dr. Mason tapped the table where he sat. "Before we get started, Thad let me say on behalf of the board that we are sorry to hear about Dr. Jeffries. Wasn't she in a car accident just a few days ago? She's lucky, she didn't go into labor." It appeared that Mason smirked when he made that statement. "Anyway, let us get started."

Thad felt as if the breath had been knocked out of him. *How did Mason know about the near miss with Lauren? Was it supposed to have been an accident? Is this another case of him trying to let me know that he's connected? Was Gene right? Was someone trying to cause an accident hoping that she would miscarry?*

Although unable to concentrate, Thad willed himself to sit through the board meeting. When the meeting was over, he hurried back to his office and dialed Dan Coles' number.

Coles asked, "Who knows about that incident other than Gene and his wife?"

"I don't know of anyone except for Mrs. Standis. Lauren hasn't even told her family. Mrs. Brown doesn't know either. What do you make of it?"

"I think Mason just tightened the noose around his own neck. It sounds as if he was either warning or threatening you. That incident wasn't made public, and it sounds like he was saying Lauren's car could have been hit if they wanted. It also sounds as if he's hiding behind the university in saying he was speaking on behalf of the board members. Thad, has Mason ever referred to Lauren as your wife or Dr. or Mrs. Bradford?"

"So, you picked up on that, too. I've never heard him call her anything other than Dr. Jeffries."

"He just moved himself to the top of the list of suspects. Before we question him, I'm going to need a list of all those who were present at the last two board meetings.

I have to warn you, this means the whole story of the harassment is going to get out. Do you think you and Lauren are prepared for this?"

"I hate for her to have to contend with this, especially now. As it is, I don't think she'll last another two weeks without going into labor. I guess we'll have to be ready if we want to put an end to this mess."

*****

"Thad, it's Gene. It's hit the fan now. The police interviewed Father, and he's on a rampage. He called and demanded that I come to his office. When I refused, he came to mine. He blames you for the police visit, and when I objected to the way he and Mother has treated Lauren, he said I was no better than you are, and while he wasn't responsible for the attacks on Lauren, he wouldn't shed a tear if something was to happen to her."

"Do you believe he didn't have anything to do with this?"

"He might not have been directly involved, but I believe he knows who is. I believe Mother knows, too. How is Lauren?"

"Right now she's okay. I'm expecting her to go into labor any minute. She's held on longer than we expected. If she were to get wind of these latest happenings, the stress would definitely land her in the hospital."

*****

After the board meeting ended, Dr. Mason approached Thad. "I guess it won't be long before you become a daddy, huh? I hear you're having twins."

"I'm going to be a daddy, *again,* Dr. Mason."

"I mean a baby of your own."

"You don't get it, do you?" Thad remained calm. "Brittany and Brianna Bradford are my children. My wife and I are looking forward to the addition to our family."

"Oh, you adopted Dr. Jeffries children?" Mason sounded stunned. "They're carrying the Bradford name?"

"I'm surprised my parents didn't tell you." Thad's phone rang. "Excuse me. This is Dr. Bradford."

*****

Thad grabbed the ringing phone. "Hello? Hello? Is anyone there?"

"Darling, what is it?" Lauren's voice was thick with sleep.

"Go back to sleep, love. It must have been a wrong number."

"Who would be calling at two-thirty in the morning?" Lauren glanced at the clock.

"Don't worry about it. Go back to sleep."

Thad wasn't able to go back to sleep, so was able to grab the phone on the second ring when it went off again at three a.m. *This isn't a coincidence* he thought as he turned the ringer off.

Instead of reporting the incident from his home, Thad opted to wait until he got to the hospital. He prepared to call Agent Coles from his office phone when it rang. "Dr. Bradford," he answered.

"Thad, this is Wendy. Lauren's in labor. She said to meet her at the hospital. We're on our way."

As planned, the agency dispatched an officer to the Bradford residence to stand guard over Mrs. Brown and the girls while Wendy accompanied Lauren to the hospital.

*****

Awestruck, Thad held Lauren's hand as he watched Ashton, Austin, and Rachel make their way into the world.

Thad caressed Lauren's cheek with his knuckles. "Lauren, our children are healthy and beautiful. I'm so proud of you."

"I love you, darling." She squeezed his hand.

"I can't wait for the girls to see them. We have some calls to make."

"For your protection, we can make calls, but you can't receive any. As a matter of fact, nothing will be delivered to your room, and no one can visit you unless Wendy or I okay them."

"For a few hours I'd been able to forget all of this harassment. How are the girls? Who's with Mrs. Brown?"

"They're safe darling. There's an officer with them. Michelle said she'll be here the day after tomorrow. I told her it would be best if she didn't come to the hospital."

Lauren's eyes filled with tears. "Is this ever going to end? It's been over eighteen months and I'm so tired of it. I want my life back."

Dr. Elliott called from the doorway, "Hello new mama. How are you feeling?"

"I'm feeling very well. When are we going to be discharged?"

"We're keeping the babies for four or five days. They're doing fine, but we want to get their weight up a few more ounces before we release them. All of their vital organs are fully developed and performing nicely. They're doing exceptional. That time spent on bed rest really paid off. You'll be released tomorrow."

"No, Grace. I'm not going home until my babies are discharged. Is there any reason for them not to stay in here with me?"

Thad reached for Lauren's hand. "You mean with us, Lauren. I'm going to stay here with you."

"What's going on, you guys?" Grace glanced from one to the other. "I've noticed you haven't let the babies out of your sight, and there's a woman outside the door who doesn't leave this room unless you're here. Are you in danger, Lauren?"

"Someday I'll tell you about it. For now, I'll just tell you the babies and I are in danger. That's why I don't want them out of my sight."

"How long has this been going on, Lauren?"

"Since before I became pregnant."

"Are you kidding? That could have been a factor in your raised blood pressure. You should have told me you were under a lot of stress."

"Grace, the decision not to tell you was based on our friendship. We told none of my family or friends. We didn't want you all to get caught up in this."

"My God, Lauren. This sounds like a plot out of some suspense novel. You all be very careful. What can I do to help?"

"You can write a no visitors order."

*****

"Here you are, Mrs. Bradford. These are certainly beautiful." The nurse attempted to place the flower arrangement on the credenza.

Thad shouted, "Nurse, please take them out! Orders were left at the desk not to deliver any flowers or gifts to Mrs. Bradford. She's highly allergic. I'll take the card."

"What does it say?"

"Damn!"

"What is it, Thad?"

"You don't need this, Lauren. I don't want you getting upset."

"It's too late, now." She extended her hand. "May I see the card, please?" Lauren gasped as she read the inscription on the card. "Thought you could hide from us did you? Congratulations on your litter."

Thad caught her hands in his. "I'm so sorry."

"Why are you apologizing? This isn't your doing. Is Wendy back yet? Would you check to see if the officer is still on the door? It's time for the babies' feeding."

*****

There was a commotion outside Lauren's room door. "What do you mean, I can't go in there? Ms. Jeffries is my employee."

"She's not allowed any visitors, sir."

"Where is Dr. Bradford? Get him out here. I want your name and badge number."

Thad glanced at Lauren and found her eyes widened in alarm. "Don't let him in. I don't want him anywhere near us."

"It's all right. I'll take care of him." Thad headed for the door. "Dr. Mason." He greeted the man and exited the room.

"Thad, how are you? This officer said I can't see Dr. Jeffries."

"That's right, doctor. She's not entertaining visitors. There's been an attempt to harm her. How did you know she was here?"

"Oh.— I— I think I heard someone mention it or; oh that's it. I called your office to inquire about Dr. Jeffries. Your secretary told me. Well, since I can't see her, I guess I'll be getting back to the university. Good day."

Dan came to the hospital in response to Thad's call, relative to the encounter with Dr. Mason. "Congratulations, Thad." Coles shook his hand and thumped him on the back. "You hit the jackpot." He kissed Lauren on the cheek. "How are you? They are some beautiful children." He then turned his attention back to Thad. "What's going on? Why do you need to talk to me so urgently?"

"Mason tried to get in to see Lauren just before I called you. When I asked how he knew we were here, he said when he called my office to inquire about Lauren's health, my secretary told him. That's a lie. Carol doesn't know where I am. He referred to Lauren as Dr. Jeffries. After that, he left without asking about Lauren. He didn't seemed surprised to learn that Lauren has been threatened either." Thad passed the card from the flowers to Dan. "Here. You need to see this."

"Damn! How long before you're discharged?"

"A week."

"Wendy, you aren't to leave this room for any reason. You'll be relieved by either Alan Wilcox or me, no one else."

*****

Later, that evening, a nurse entered Lauren's room. "Here we are, Mrs. Jeffries. Dr. Grace ordered something for your blood pressure and a pain medicine."

"I'm not in any pain, nurse, and my blood pressure has been stable for the past forty-eight hours. I don't want the medicine."

"Dr.'s orders, Mrs. Jeffries." The nurse approached the bed with a syringe in her hand.

"I said no. " Lauren slid off the opposite side of the bed. "What is your name?"

Thad stood and placed an arm around Lauren's shoulder. "She said she's not taking the medicine. My wife asked for your name."

"I guess I'll just have to report that you refused the medication." The nurse dropped the syringe and darted out of the room without answering. Wendy, having moved to shield the babies when the nurse arrived, realized too late that the nurse was an imposter. She exited the room to give chase, but the imposter was nowhere to be seen.

*****

Three days after the attempt to medicate Lauren, a woman dressed in a lab coat, wearing oversized glasses, and her brunette hair pulled into a bun, entered the room, and announced she was taking the babies for some lab tests. "Come on little one." She lifted one of the babies out of the bassinet. "I'll be back for the other two shortly."

"Why are they testing them so late?" Lauren inquired.

"I don't know. I just follow orders," She replied, heading for the door.

"Give me the baby, ma'am." Wendy stopped her as she stepped into the hallway.

"What? What's going on? I'm taking the baby for lab tests." She took a couple of steps backwards.

"Give her the baby," said Dan Coles, who had been watching from the bathroom inside Lauren's room. He now stood behind the imposter with his weapon drawn. There were now several officers in the hallway with their weapons trained on the imposter.

"Get back or, I'll drop it," she threatened, holding the baby away from her body,

Coles put his weapon close to her ear and cocked it. "Give me a reason," he threatened. "Now, give her the baby."

Wendy took the baby from the woman and returned her to Lauren and Thad. They watched the brunette being led away in handcuffs.

Thad, noticing Lauren's shaking hands, reached for the baby. "Let me take him darling."

Tears of fear and frustration rolled down Lauren's cheeks. "I'm so scared. Who's watching the girls?" she asked of Coles, who'd just entered the room.

Thad placed the baby in the arms of a legitimate nurse, and pulled Lauren into his arms.

“Wilcox and several officers have been at your house all day. Your family's well protected. I'm going to the precinct to question this suspect, but Wendy and several officers will be on duty here, tonight.”

"Thanks Dan.” Lauren embraced him.

"No thanks necessary.” He returned the embrace. “I’ll see you all later,” he said huskily.

Thad and Wendy exchanged quick glances.

*****

There were no more incidents during their stay at the hospital. After six days, Wendy escorted Thad, Lauren, and the babies home.

"Oh, Lauren, they're precious.” Michelle cooed over the babies as she gazed into the cribs. I’ve been waiting five days to see my niece and nephews. How are you sis? You look tired.”

"I *am* tired, Michelle. I haven’t slept well in weeks.”

"You should be able to rest well now. These people care a lot for you and Thad. By the way, all of our siblings have called. They said they‘d wait until you're all settled before they come to visit. I don’t need to tell you they were shocked when they got the news about the triplets. They're still concerned about your safety, too.”

"I can imagine. So am. Wendy, why don’t you get some sleep? We have enough protection for now. I'm going to take my own advice as soon as I see my girls.”

"Thanks, Lauren. I can really use a couple of hours.”

"No, Wendy. You need several hours of uninterrupted sleep. Why don’t you…?”

"Mama, Mama,” the twins called, running toward her.

"How are my angels?” Lauren stooped to embrace the girls.

"Mama, Mama.” They clung to her. "We miss you.”

"Mommy missed you too, angels. I went to the hospital to get you another sister and two brothers. See.” She pointed to the cribs.

"Baby, baby,” Brianna cried, with widened eyes.

"Baby, baby, baby." Brittany, pointed to each crib. "Three babies, mommy?"

"That's right, sweetheart." Lauren held up three fingers. "Three babies. That's Ashton, that's Austin, and this is Rachel. Ashton and Austin are your brothers and Rachel is your sister."

"My baby, Mommy?" Brianna asked.

"Uh oh." Mrs. Brown laughed. "Possessive aren't we?"

*****

Alan called to give Thad the report of the nurse imposter. "What have you discovered, Alan? Did you find out who's behind this or why they're targeting my wife?"

"Not really. She admits she was paid to harass Lauren, but she claims she has no idea who's behind it. She did say she was told to do whatever it took to scare her away."

"Scare her away from what? Did you learn her name? Where is she from? Did they instruct her to do bodily harm to Lauren? Where does she live?" Thad fired off.

"She has a Massachusetts driver's license with the name Darlene Tucker. We're running it to see if it's legit. She said she was just told to scare her away, so she assumed she was to scare her out of town."

"Where was she taking the children?"

"She was to hand them to a couple who was waiting in the stairwell. They figured they could easily pull it off because there's not a lot of traffic during the night shift."

"What are you going to do with her?"

"She's locked up for the night. She's lawyered up, so we can't question her anymore until her lawyer gets here. There'll be an arraignment in the morning on attempted kidnapping charges. Further investigation will probably bring more charges."

"But, she maintains she doesn't know why Lauren was targeted?"

"That's her stand. Her job was to harass Lauren, and to take the babies. She's not the same person who tried to harm Lauren. "

*****

Thad returned to work on Tuesday, the day of the board meeting. Dr. Wilcox shook his hand. “Congratulations, Thad. You and Lauren believe in doing it big don’t you? Triplets. Wow!”

"I’m surprised you're back to work so soon. I thought you’d take a few weeks off,” Vivian whispered.

"Lauren has lots of help. I'm planning to take a few weeks off, later.”

"What was all that drama at the hospital? Is it true someone tried to harm Lauren and the babies?”

Dr. Mason cleared his throat for attention. “We don’t have a full agenda today, so let's get started.”

"In that case we can spare a few minutes to find out what’s happening with one of our own.” Wilcox continued, “What happened, Thad?”

"Some woman disguised as a nurse tried to inject Lauren with a dose of digitalis. When that failed, they tried to kidnap the babies.”

"What!” Paul exclaimed.

"Oh, my God! Are you kidding?” Vivian's face paled.

"Thad, what’s going on? Were they trying to steal the babies, harm them, or both?”

"We don’t know exactly what they were planning. The police should know more when they finish their investigation. They have one person in custody, and they're following some strong leads. That’s all I know for now, but my family is safe.”

Paul stared. "My God, Thad. How is Lauren doing? How long has this been going on?”

"It’s been going on for over a year. The more it draws out, the more vicious it becomes.”

"I wonder who’s behind this.” Amanda frowned.

Thad glanced at Dr. Mason and noted that his face had taken on a sickened pallor.

*****

Thad couldn’t believe Darlene Tucker posted a one hundred and twenty thousand dollar cash bond.

"She was what? Dan, are you kidding? How could she afford bail? How could she get her hands on that much cash in such a limited amount of time?"

"Her bail was posted anonymously," Coles said.

"Is there any way to find out who posted it?" Lauren asked. "I bet if you were to get that information, you'd find the masterminds."

"I think you know where to start looking," Thad announced. "We know who has unlimited resources and ready cash."

CHAPTER FORTY-FOUR

Dan Coles drove to Boston to meet with agents from the local branch of the FBI. He now accompanied Agent Charles Munford to the home of L.C. Bradford. When they entered the home, Dan eyed the packed luggage stacked in the foyer.

“Mr. Bradford, it looks as if you're taking a trip.”

"Yes, we're going to the mountains. Our family joins other family and friends there every year at this time."

"Are you leaving before you see your new grandchildren? Triplets. Imagine that. Must be pretty exciting," Coles goaded.

"Those bastards are not my grandchildren, and I have no intention of ever seeing them. Now, why are you here?"

"We have a few questions for you and your wife."

"Questions? About what?" Bradford stood at the door.

"We're investigating the attempted murder and kidnapping of your daughter-in-law and your grandchildren."

"I told you that tart is not my…"

"Why are you questioning us about this? Do you think we had something to do with this?" Velma Bradford interrupted. “You have some nerve coming here, treating us like some common criminals. You should be questioning those low life people that she's used to. Now look at the dirt she’s smearing on our name."

Dan Coles barely contained his anger. “It doesn’t seem to faze you at all someone tried to kill your son’s wife and children."

"I have no son. When the child we raised decided to consort with that low class, money grubbing, slut, he gave up his right to be my son, and since his brother finds it necessary to defend him, he suffers the same fate. I have two daughters, no other children."

"Nonetheless, Mr. Bradford, we still have to ask the two of you some questions."

"I don’t think I'll answer any questions without my lawyer present. That will have to wait. Our plane is scheduled to leave in less than two hours."

"I'm afraid you will be delayed," Agent Munford said. "You have a right to have your attorney present during questioning, but you'll have to have him meet you at FBI headquarters. You both need to come with us now."

"Excuse me, Mr. Bradford," the housekeeper interrupted. "There's a call for you. He said it's urgent."

He took the phone. "This is Bradford." He listened for a moment before saying, "I thought that had been taken care of." He paused. "No, you do what you think is best. I'm not sinking any more money into this project. Goodbye."

*****

After they interrogated the elder Bradfords and released them, the agents sat in the squad room discussing the case. "What do you make of them?" Agent Munford asked of Dan.

"They're pretty cool customers, aren't they?" Coles admitted. "Other than exhibiting their disdain for their daughter-in-law, they didn't divulge anything. Hating your in-laws is not a crime."

"Agent Coles, you've gotten to know Thad and Lauren pretty well. What's the scoop on them? There's got to be something going on that would cause a parent to disown a child," said Agent Reva Wells.

"Agent Wells." Dan said in a controlled voice. "I've known Thad and Lauren Bradford two years. In an attempt to learn who is trying to harm her, their lives have been turned upside down and inside out. The two of them are squeaky clean. During the past fifteen years, they have one paid parking ticket between the two of them–nothing more. You can read the dossier on them at any time, and then tell me if you can withstand that kind of scrutiny."

Munford held up his hand in a defensive manner. "Hey, hey, Coles lighten up. It was just an innocent question. Why are you so protective of them?"

"You know, we run into plenty of unscrupulous characters every day. It's so common that we automatically lump the clean ones with the not so clean.

You all need to study this case so you can learn the difference. "Dan stood. "I think I'll be heading back to Connecticut. I'll be in touch."

*****

Agent Favors stuck his head into Dan's office. "We haven't been able to locate Dr. Mason, sir. We've checked his home and the hospital, but no one has seen him in the past three days."

"Dan." Wilcox squeezed by Favors. "I just got a call from the DA's office. Darlene Tucker has given them the slip."

"Darn! It seems she and Mason have both disappeared. I wonder if they're together. We'd better tighten the security around the Bradfords. Put a— be on the look-out, on Mason and Tucker."

Thad opened the door to the agent's knock. "Hey, Dan. What brings you out this late?"

"...need to talk to you. Where's Lauren?"

"She's in the nursery. I'll get her."

"No, don't bother her, yet. I'll tell you, and you can decide if you want to tell her."

"Let's go into the study. Would you like some coffee?" He led the agent to the study.

"No, thanks. I just finished a cup on my way over here."

"Have a seat and tell me what's on your mind." Thad sat behind his desk.

"We're tightening the security in and around your house. It seems Darlene Tucker and Dr. Mason have disappeared. And Thad," Dan hesitated, "your parents were supposed to go to the lodge, but don't seem to be there."

Thad sat motionless for several moments. "Are you sure?"

"We have an agent in route to the lodge now, but the lodge manager has already said they never checked in."

Thad ran a hand over his face. He stood and peered out of the window into the dark. After several moments, still peering out the window, Thad asked, "Do you really think they're involved?"

"I don't know, but to be honest, they look suspicious. I pray for your sake they're not."

"How are you planning to beef up security here?" Thad turned to face Dan.

"We're going to add an additional officer here in the house, and a car is going to be stationed in front of the house twenty-four seven until this mess is resolved. We're working on another plan too, and we'll need you and Lauren to cooperate with us."

Thad sat in the chair. "Do whatever it takes, Dan. All I want is for my wife and children to be safe, and for Lauren to regain the peace of mind she enjoyed before she met me."

"You're not blaming yourself for any of this. Are you?"

"No. Not really, but if she hadn't become involved with me none of this would be happening to her."

"Don't let her hear you say that. She loves you more than life, and it would hurt her if she knew you felt that way."

"I know. I'll never tell her that."

"Well, my friend." Dan stood. "That's where we stand. You tell Lauren what you want her to know, and let me know what you tell her, so I don't slip up." Dan headed toward the door.

Thad chuckled. "I'm going to tell her the truth. You know my wife, she'll know, something's up if I don't." He opened the door.

"I figured you'd do it that way. I'll stop by tomorrow. Be vigilant. Good night."

Thad decided to call Gene before he talked with Lauren. "Are you serious? They're not at the lodge? This doesn't look good. Do you know if the police have talked with Elaine and Anna?"

"No I don't, and I didn't think to ask. Can you call them? They haven't taken any of my calls in over a year, and I don't think they are going to start now."

"Hold on, I'll try them now." After what seemed an eternity Gene came back on the line. "Neither of them is picking up. I'll check again tomorrow to see if they're still in town. You know, they usually go to the mountains with Mother and Father, but if they're in hiding I'm sure they're not with them."

"Let me know what you find out. I'd better get upstairs before Lauren comes after me."

"Be careful, Thad. I can't get away tomorrow, but I'll see you on Friday. Love you."

"Thanks Gene. I love you."

*****

Lauren and Michelle chatted while they fed the babies. "Did you get a report on Mrs. King, yet? She seems like the ideal nanny."

"She does seem too good to be true, doesn't she? Mrs. Brown likes her, but Dan told us to hold off hiring her until they check her out. I was hoping they'd have that done before you leave."

"I could always stay longer you know."

"No, you can't, Michelle. I appreciate you so much, but you need to get home to your family. Christmas is only a couple of weeks away, and you need to prepare for Ray and the kids. We'll manage here."

"My shopping is just about finished. You have heard of the internet, haven't you?" Michelle joked.

"Yes, I have." Lauren laughed. "I'm thankful for it, too; wouldn't have gotten anything done without it. You know, it would be nice if all of us could celebrate Christmas together this year. It would give the rest of our sibs a chance to see the babies."

"Girl! Are you crazy? That's twenty-one people when you add Mrs. Brown, Wendy and the other agent. You only have five bedrooms."

"I know, but our other house is vacant, and it has four bedrooms. When the tenants moved out, we had it redone just for occasions such as this. In addition, we can always move the babies into our room to make even more room. We'll have enough."

"Enough room for what?" asked Thad from the doorway.

"I just invited all of my siblings and their families to spend Christmas with us."

Thad entered the room. "You did? And you think we're going to have enough room?"

"You're forgetting we have another house," Lauren reminded him.

"Yes, I did. Michelle, she's right. We'll have enough room. We might be a little cramped, but I think it'll be fun."

"That settles it. I'll call everyone tomorrow."

"I'll come back a couple of days early to do the cooking," Michelle said.

"You do mean to *help* with the cooking, don't you?"

"Help who? You're not planning to do the cooking are you?" Thad sounded surprised.

"Christmas is two weeks away. We'll discuss it, later." She removed a bottle from the crib. Thad and Michelle cast each other defeated glances.

Michelle extended her hand. "I'll take the bottles. It's getting late. I'll wash them, and then call it a night."

"Are you ready to turn in, Lauren?" Thad waited at the doorway.

"Yes. Let me turn the monitor on, and I'll join you."

Once in bed, he pulled her close. "How are you feeling, sweetheart? The children aren't tiring you out are they?"

"They are not. Michelle and Mrs. Brown aren't going to let me do too much. Remember Michelle is leaving in a couple of days. Anyway, women have been bringing their babies home and taking care of them all by themselves for decades.

"I grant you that, but few of them have taken care of three infants and two toddles at the same time all by themselves. Please, just take it easy. I hope Dottie King checks out okay." He pulled Lauren closer and kissed her. "Lauren." Thad sighed. "I have some unpleasant news to share with you." He related the information Dan had just given him.

"Well love, we just have to trust Dan and his crew to keep us safe. In view of what you just told me, I don't think this is a good time to bring Dottie into the house. We don't need the stress of learning to trust someone new."

"That's good thinking, but it'll put a lot of work on you, with Michelle leaving."

"It'll be okay. Please, don't mention any of this to Michelle. She'll want to stay; she really needs to get home to her family."

*****

Gene called Thad the next day to inform him that neither of their sisters was home. Their neighbors said they had left for the mountains two days ago. When Thad gave this information to Dan, he told him his sisters would be added to the BOLO.

As promised, Misti Johnson, the new agent, arrived for duty at the Bradfords later in the evening.

Michelle called to say she arrived home safely and that all was well at her house. The agent who'd been dispatched to the lodge reported the elder Bradfords had not shown up, nor had anyone matching the description of Anna, or Elaine.

*****

At three weeks old, the babies were thriving. Lauren and Mrs. Brown were kept busy caring for the five children, but they had devised a schedule that proved to reduce the stress. Wendy and Misti, neither of whom had children of their own, enjoyed hands-on interaction with the children.

Two days after Michelle returned home, Lauren received a call from a Martha Floyd, who said she'd heard that Lauren was looking for a nanny. Lauren hadn't advertised for a nanny, so she became alarmed and turned the information over to Dan. After investigating, he found that the personal information the woman had given Lauren was bogus.

Days later, as she sat reading to the twins, Wendy summoned Lauren to the phone. "It's Tri-City Employment Agency." She passed the phone to Lauren.

"Hello. This is Lauren Bradford."

"Oh, I'm looking for Lauren Jeffries."

"May I ask what this is about?" Lauren inquired.

"I'm Ms. Thomas. I understand that Ms. Jeffries is in need of a nanny. We have several very capable nannies on file, and I was wondering if I could send one out for her consideration."

"Ms. Thomas, if you'd leave your address and phone number, I'll have Mr. Jeffries get in touch with you."

Ms. Thomas gave Lauren the address. "When can I expect Mr. Jeffries?"

"He'll call you this afternoon for an appointment. Thank you, Ms. Thomas. Good day."

Lauren handed the information she jotted down to Wendy, and while Wendy called Dan, Lauren called Thad.

*****

Agent Coles met Thad at the hospital. Over lunch, they discussed the "nanny" call. Dan already learned that the address of the employment agency, as well as the agency itself, was bogus. He suggested Thad go ahead and call for an appointment anyway. When Thad called the number the recording stated he had reached a number that was no longer in service. A call to Lauren assured him he called the right number.

"Something's amiss. I'm almost certain Mason is behind this. On each of these two calls, they were trying to get someone inside the house. I don't think they're after the babies. I think Lauren is the target."

The muscles in Thad's jaw began to twitch. "You're aware I'm still carrying a piece aren't you, Dan? As much as I'm hoping I'll never have to use it, I won't hesitate if the need arises."

"You're legal. I don't know of anyone who wouldn't do the same thing." Dan stared at him. "Is there anything else you want us to do for you and your family?"

"You already have the house locked down tighter than Fort Knox. I can't ask for more."

Dan arched his eyebrows. "You know, I've been studying this case for two years now, and I've come to the conclusion that this harassment has more to do with jealousy and revenge than anything. It didn't start out that way. Those two busy bodies from her old neighborhood just added fodder. If Lauren had caved in then without a fight, you wouldn't be going through this now."

Thad smiled. "Since you have been studying this case for two years, I'm sure you've learned my wife doesn't cave in to much; and never without a fight. But, what are they jealous of, and why does someone feel he has to exact revenge?"

"I don't know. I might have a talk with Lauren. She could probably crack this case single-handed if she had the time."

"Nevertheless, the only thing she has time for is being wife and mother, so don't go getting any bright ideas."

Dan stood. "Can't blame you there, bud. I'm going to check on the situation at your house, and then go to the office. Call me if you hear anything."

"Dan?" Thad called as he stood. "Do you think Dottie King is on the up and up?"

"From all we've found, she is. Her husband was killed in a motorcycle accident two years ago. She and her fifteen-year-old son are now living with her parents. Because of night school, she wanted a day job where she could leave early."

"Sounds perfect, but we'll still wait until after the first of the year to hire anyone. Thanks for everything." The two men shook hands and went their separate ways.

A few days later, Thad was driving home from work when two shots rang out, one hitting his left rear tire and the other shattering the rear window. Thad lost control of the car, and it smashed into a guardrail.

Law enforcement personnel, including Agent Coles and Captain Wilcox, converged on the scene of the accident. After Thad was transported to the hospital, Dan sped to the Bradford house to inform Lauren of her husband's accident before the news media could.

With a heavy heart, Dan knocked on the door. "Agent Coles." Wendy opened the door. "How come you knocked instead of ringing the bell? What is it? Agent?"

"Where is she, Wendy?" Dan appeared bone weary.

"She's in the nursery. Dan, please tell me what's going on," Wendy pleaded.

"Thad was in a terrible car accident. He's in surgery as we speak. It looks bad. I guess I have to go and tell her. Where's Misti?"

"She's with Lauren. Do you want me to call her?"

"Yes, I need you to be with me while I tell Lauren. Misti can keep watch down here."

Dan and Wendy entered the nursery. "Dan, what a pleasant surprise. Have you gotten new information on my in-laws?"

"No, Lauren. I—" Dan massaged the back of his neck, and turned away from Lauren. "Lauren." He sighed. "I have some bad news." He approached her and grasped both of her hands in his. "Lauren, Thad's been in a car accident. He—" Dan put an arm around Lauren's shoulder to support her as she swayed.

"Is he— Dan, is he—? Oh, God," she moaned.

"Lauren he's at the hospital. They rushed him into surgery just as I left to come here. I haven't heard anything since."

"I have got to go to him." She glanced toward the cribs. "What am I going to do? I can't leave my children." Lauren swayed. Dan held her close in an attempt to console her.

"Lauren, Wendy, and Misti are going to stay here with Mrs. Brown and the children while I take you to the hospital. I've called Alan and asked him to send over a couple of officers to assist Wendy and Misti. I'll wait until they get here before we leave. They should be here by the time you're ready."

"Thank you." Lauren sniffed. "I need to call Gene. Excuse me." She extricated herself from Dan's arms, and went to her bedroom to make her calls while Dan went to the twins' room to tell Mrs. Brown.

By the time Lauren had called Gene, Michelle, and Aunt Charlotte, Alan Wilcox arrived with the two officers. "Excuse me, while I make two more calls." Lauren left the room to call Mrs. Standis and Vivian Reed, whom she asked to call the other board members.

* * * * *

With trepidation, Lauren allowed Dan Coles and Alan Wilcox to escort her to the hospital. Vivian Reed and Linda Abrams met Lauren and the police at the ER waiting room.

Vivian informed them that Larry Wilcox and Ryan Dunlap were in the OR with Thad. "Have you heard anything yet?" Vivian asked.

"No, nothing, yet. We just got here."

"What happened," Vivian asked. "Alan? What caused him to lose control? Thad's a good and careful driver."

"We'll know more when the investigation is complete. All we know is what we've told you."

Linda was anxious. "How long has he been in there? Someone should have let us know something by now."

Alan began to pace. The accident happened about an hour or so ago. I would say that he's been in there about forty minutes."

The group lapsed into silence. Captain Wilcox broke it. "Can I get anyone a drink or anything?" Everyone declined the offer and settled back into the uneasy silence.

A short time later, Gene arrived.

"Gene!" Lauren ran to her brother-in law. "How did you get here so fast?" She threw her arms around him.

"I came by chopper. The hospital allowed us to land on its helipad. How are you doing Lauren? Have you heard anything?"

"No, not yet. Is Joan with you?"

"No, she'll be down tomorrow. I needed to get here as soon as I could. I…"

"Mrs. Bradford," a doctor called as he and Larry Wilcox walked into the room.

Lauren turned. "I'm Lauren Bradford, and this is Thad's brother, Gene." Gene kept an arm draped over Lauren's shoulder.

"I'm Dr. Stanley Jordan. Your husband and I are friends and colleagues." He glanced around the room at the others.

Lauren, followed the path of his glance. "You can speak freely, doctor. These are all friends."

"Well then," Jordan continued, "Thad came thru the surgery quite well.

He sustained three broken ribs, a dislocated shoulder, and a long, deep gash on his left thigh, which is very serious. In addition, he suffered multiple bruises and lacerations. He has a hairline fracture of the skull and a badly bruised left ankle. In other words, he was pretty banged up. He was unconscious when they brought him in. I'm sure he sustained a mild concussion. Now, the most serious injury is the gunshot wound to his..."

"Gunshot! Thad was shot?" Lauren widened her eyes, and her hand covered her mouth as a look of fear and shock ravished her face. Gene tightened his hold on her.

Dr. Wilcox continued, "I'm sorry Lauren, Thad was shot. The good news is that while the injury is serious, it is not life threatening. The bullet fragmented when it hit the shoulder blade, but we think we got it all. There is a small fracture to the shoulder blade."

While the doctor was still talking to the group, an officer beckoned to Agent Coles and Captain Wilcox. The captain and Coles stepped out of the room. "What is it Sergeant?"

"Sir, we have secured the accident scene. There's nothing more we can do until daylight, but Captain, preliminary investigation shows that this was not just your everyday single car accident."

"Why do you say that, sergeant? What did you find?" Agent Coles asked.

"There's evidence that at least two shots were fired into the doctor's vehicle." Dan and Alan exchanged glances. "The vehicle has been towed to impound. From what we've learned, there wasn't much traffic in the area at that time, but we have three witnesses who said they heard what sounded like gunfire before the vehicle went out of control. And Captain, the news media is all over this story."

"Thanks sergeant. That's to be expected, but we'll let PR handled them. Keep me posted on any new developments." Coles and Wilcox stared at each other. "How are we going to tell her, Dan?"

"Truthfully," Dan replied. "Damn! How much more can she take without going off the deep end? First, her, then her children, now her husband. She's one strong woman. I really like her."

"Be careful my friend, don't let yourself like her too much," Wilcox warned.

Dan looked at him as if he'd been caught with his hand in the cookie jar. He gave Alan a sheepish smile. "Anyway, it appears we have to post twenty-four hour security on Thad, too. Are you ready to face, Lauren?"

"I don't look forward to giving her any more bad news, but it's unavoidable. Let's go." They headed back to the waiting area.

"Dr. Bradford," Dr. Jordan was saying as the duo returned to the waiting room, "I'm sorry we had to meet under these circumstances. I need you to know Thad is getting the best care possible."

"I know he is, doctor. Please, call me Lauren. When can I see him?"

"He's being transferred to a private room. You can see him as soon as he's settled in."

"Lauren." Larry touched her shoulder. "May I suggest that after you see him, you go and get some rest? He's heavily sedated, and will likely sleep for several hours."

"I need to be here when he wakes up."

"Lauren." Gene laid a gentle hand on her arm. "You go home and rest. I'll stay here tonight. Go take care of the children; and yourself. Thad's going to need you to be strong."

"He's right, Lauren," said Dr. Jordan. "You do need to rest. You're still in a delicate condition yourself. We'll contact you if there's a need. If you don't have any questions or concerns right now, I'm going to check on Thad."

Coles and Wilcox approached Lauren and Gene as Jordan left the room. "Lauren, Gene. We just got some news you need to know about." Everyone looked at Dan in anticipation. Lauren could tell by the look on his face that the news was not good.

"What is it Dan?"

Dan met Lauren's gaze. He glanced at Gene then back at Lauren. "Lauren, preliminary investigations show that at least two shot were fired, and hit Thad's car before the accident."

Gene seeming to sense the agents were reluctant to impart more bad news to Lauren, stepped in. "Agent Coles, we just heard about the shots. One of them hit my brother."

"Damn!" Coles slap his forehead. "Lauren, Gene I'm so sorry. How is he?"

"His condition is serious, but not life-threatening." She covered her mouth with a trembling hand. Gene wrapped both arms around her.

Linda asked in a disbelieving whisper, "Alan, what's going on here?"

"Please don't keep us in the dark," Vivian pleaded. "We're Lauren and Thad's friends, and the closest thing to family they have living in the area. We love them, and we're concerned about them."

"Tell them, Dan. Tell them everything. I just can't do this anymore. I can't protect anyone anymore." Lauren sniffed.

"Come and sit down." Gene led her to a chair. "Would someone please get her something to drink?"

"Dan, did you let Wendy know that Thad made it thru surgery?" Lauren asked. She accepted the glass of water from Larry.

"I did, Lauren. She'll let Mrs. Brown and Misti know. Now," he paused, "If you all have two or three hours, I'll fill you in."

Vivian Reed, Linda Abrams, Larry Wilcox, and Ryan Dunlap listened in disbelief as Agent Coles and Captain Wilcox told them of the nightmarish conditions under which their friends had been living for the past two years.

"This is outrageous," Ryan declared.

Vivian grasped Laurens hand. "It's downright criminal. Lauren, why didn't you tell us? We could have been there for you."

Tears rolled down Lauren's cheeks. "You have all been here for me. I couldn't have made it this far without you.

You've been my support from the beginning, when I didn't have a single friend. I love and appreciate you all so much."

"Gene, I'm so sorry for what you and Thad must be going through. If there is anything we can do, don't hesitate to let us know. I understand why you kept this from us, but I know I speak for the group when I echo what Vivian said. We're all family. When one hurts, we all hurt."

"Thanks, Larry," Gene said. "It's going to get worse when the news media gets wind of the whole story. Speaking of which..." He nodded toward the TV monitor where the late news was just airing.

"This just in," said the news anchor, "local doctor escapes death?" Let's go to Norman Day, reporting from the scene of a one vehicle accident. "What can you tell us, Norman?"

"Yes, Dean. Dr. Thaddeus Bradford, a prominent surgeon at Parkdale Medical Memorial Hospital, narrowly escaped death this afternoon when his vehicle careened out of control as he exited the freeway onto Mars Lane, and hit a guardrail. At airtime the doctor was undergoing surgery at Parkdale Memorial. Witnesses told this reporter that they heard several gunshots just before the car spun out of control." There were photos of the accident scene and of Thad's car as it was towed away.

"Dr. Bradford and his wife, Dr. Lauren Jeffries Bradford, had just become parents to triplets three weeks ago. The couple also has two year old twin daughters. We'll bring you more on this breaking story as it unfolds. Reporting live from Mars Lane this is..."

"It's going to get even worse." Dan flipped the off switch. "Wendy said the media is parked in front of your house. They're also grouped in front of the hospital."

"Lauren, do you want me to go to the house with you?" Gene asked. "If you like, I can make a statement on behalf of the family."

"You can make a statement if you like, Gene, but I'd rather you stay here. I have to go to my children now."

"We're ready when you are, Lauren." Alan turned toward the door.

"I'm ready, Alan. Will you call me later, Gene?"

"Of course, I will." Gene nodded as the trio headed out the door.

*****

Larry Wilcox greeted Gene as he entered the waiting room the next morning. "How are you, Gene?"

"Good morning, Larry." Gene stood and stretched. "Have you seen Thad?"

"I just left him. He's awake, but groggy. Dr. Jordan will be out to see you as soon as he examines him."

Later in the morning Dr. Jordan reported that Thad was doing very well. "There'll be some discoloration and swelling for a while, and you can expect him to be very sore for a few days."

"Thanks, doctor, I'm going to visit him for a while."

Gene approached the bed. "Hey, brother." There was a bandage wrapped around Thad's head, his arm was in a sling, and his chest was bandaged.

"Hi." He whispered, fixing his eyes on Gene. "Lauren?"

"Lauren is fine. She was here until late last night, but went home to take care of the kids and get some rest. Are you in any pain?"

"Quite a bit, but they just gave me something for it. Have you talked to Dan or Alan? Did they say what happened?"

"I saw them last night. You need to rest now. I'm sure they'll be in to talk with you soon. I'm going to stay here until Lauren comes back, and then I'm going to take a shower and rest."

"Who stayed with the children and Mrs. Brown while Lauren was here?"

"Alan added two more officers to help Wendy and Misti, and Vivian sent her housekeeper over to help Mrs. Brown with the children."

Alan stepped into the room. "Did I hear my name?"

"Good morning Alan," Gene greeted. "I was just telling Thad you should be here soon. He wants to know about the accident."

"I'm not going to try to tell you to wait to have this discussion." Alan chuckled. "You're too much like your wife in that regard." Alan told Thad the accident was still under investigation, and that he would give him all the details once it was completed.

*****

At eight o'clock Wednesday morning, a young man arrived at the police station, stating he needed to talk with someone about the accident on Mars Lane. He was escorted to Alan's office by an officer. After hearing the man's story, Alan had him wait while he summoned Dan to come to his office.

Upon Dan's arrival, Alan introduced the young man. "Dan this is Mr. Lenny Grayson. He has a story you need to hear. Mr. Grayson, this is Agent Coles with the FBI. Why don't you tell him what you just told me? We'll be taping this conversation."

"Yes, sir." Grayson paused and took a sip of the coffee placed in front of him. "I— ah— I saw the story about the accident on the news. My sister, Annie, ah, I stay with her and her children.

Well, anyway, Annie said that that doctor in the accident was the husband of the

Dr. Bradford who had helped her get back on her feet after her husband left her and the kids.

I— ah— I had some trouble with the law, and I, ah, I been trying to find a job. About three weeks ago, I was coming out of the unemployment office. A man drove up beside me and asked if I was looking for work. When I told him I was, he told me to get in the truck. He drove to a bar out on route eight. He asked how I would like to earn five thousand dollars. I said I sure would. W, what do I have to do? He said all I would have to do is shoot into a car to scare somebody. At first, I said okay. Then he told me I would have to do it while someone was driving the car.

Then I said no. I was afraid I'd kill somebody. He tried to talk me into it, but I said no. He got mad; and told me if I mentioned this to anybody, he was coming after me, and he wouldn't be trying to scare me. He left me out there, and I had to walk ten miles back home. I never saw him again."

Dan checked his notes. "Can you describe the man?"

"He was about five feet ten inches tall, white, about two hundred thirty pounds. He had mostly gray hair, some black. Cut short. He wore glasses and had a mole by his right ear."

Dan and Alan exchanged quick glances and then Dan asked, "How did you know who you were supposed to shoot at?"

Grayson rubbed his chin. "He described the car and told me when, where, and what time to be there."

"Did he indicate he would get someone else to do the job?" Alan asked.

"No sir. Once I said I wasn't going to do it he just got mad and left."

Alan continued, "Do you think you could pick him out of a line-up?"

"Yes sir."

"I'm curious, Mr. Grayson," Dan inquired, "what made you come in today?"

"Like I said…ah… Dr. Lauren Bradford helped my sister get back on her feet. If it wasn't for her, Annie and her two children might be sleeping on the street right now.

Annie doesn't even know I'm here. I knew that when they said that shots were fired it had to be the same car because that was the area where the man told me to be. Captain, I had a bit of trouble with possession, and I served thirty days, but I'm not a criminal. That's the only time I've ever been in trouble. I, ah, coming here was the right thing to do. I should have come three weeks ago, but I'd just gotten out two days before. You know how that goes."

"Well, thanks for coming in, Mr. Grayson," Alan said. "You did the right thing. Where can we reach you?"

"I'm staying with my sister until I get another job. I can give you her address and phone number. Ah...would you...ah tell Dr. Bradford I'm sorry about her husband, and I thank her for what she did for Annie."

*****

The two men stared at each other. "Wow!" Alan exclaimed. "Do you agree we should be looking at Mason for this?"

"Yes, indeed. Mason is our guy. Grayson described him perfectly. I wonder if he's alone in this."

"Our biggest concern now is whether he got someone else to do this or if he did it himself. Someone could be still out there, waiting to finish the job. Did Grayson say what kind of vehicle Mason was driving?"

"He said a black SUV with Connecticut plates. Grayson said he watched the car when Mason sped away. He got the first four numbers of the license. We already have a BOLO in the tri-state area."

"The break we've been looking for. Man, it's about time."

*****

Lauren entered Thad's room. "Good morning, darling." She kissed Thad and pulled a chair close to the bed. "How are you feeling?"

"I'm sore and I have a doozy of a headache. How are you and the children?"

"The children are fine. The twins are asking for you, and I'm concerned about you. Other than that, I'm fine."

"Don't overdo it, Lauren. It's only been three and a half weeks; you need to take it easy."

"Yes, doctor," she said with a sarcastic smirk. "Did Dr. Jordan tell you about your injuries?"

"He did. Seems I got banged up pretty good."

"Thankfully, there's no injury to any vital organs. As it stands now the worst you will have to endure is about six months of recovery at home.

"All you need is another baby to care for." Thad sounded weary. "Has Dan or Alan spoken to you about the accident–about what may have caused it?"

"He said you told them you thought you heard shots before you lost control of the car."

"I'm sure I did, Lauren. I think that's what caused me to lose control. One of the tires must have been hit."

Lauren grasped his hand. "Let's not worry about that now. We need to concentrate on getting you well."

"I know, but it looks like it's going to be a few days before I get out of here, and I'm not going to be much help to you when I do."

"We'll be just fine. Your injuries aren't as severe as they thought. At first, it looked like your shoulder was broken. That cut on your thigh and the gunshot wound are the most severe injuries. If all goes well, I'm sure you'll be home in less than a week."

"I certainly hope so. Even if I can't do anything, I'd feel better if I was home with you and the children."

"I'd feel better too. Gene has been such a comfort."

"Gene is a great brother and a good friend. He's really been here for us throughout this ordeal. What, ah, who else has been there?"

"The same group from the board. Vivian has even sent her housekeeper over to help. I think my family is going to take turns coming. They decided it was best for us to forego the Christmas celebration we'd planned at our house, but you know Michelle and her family are coming, anyway. I couldn't talk her out of it."

Thad gave her a broad smile. "She is your sister, isn't she?"

"And what, dear heart, is that supposed to mean?"

Thad continued to smile, but remained silent on the issue. "Has Dan been by?"

"He came by to tell me about the accident, and then he and Alan brought me here. They also took me home early this morning. I haven't seen or spoken to him since. Why do you ask? Was he supposed to talk to me about something?"

"No. I was just wondering. Who brought you here today?"

"Chuck Bennett. He's one of the new officers. "What is it? Is something bothering you?"

"Lauren." "I'll be okay with you not visiting me every day. You're going to wear yourself out, tying to be here and at home too. Why don't you stay home?"

"You know better than to ask me to do that." She reached for his hand. "You're my husband. I need to be, and want to be here with you."

"The children need you at home. At least one of us should be there. I'm sure Brianna and Brittany are confused about what's happening. I can understand you being away from me, but they don't understand your absence."

"I can't—"

"Do it for me. Please?"

"If that's what you want, but I think there's more to this than you're telling me."

"I just feel you'd be safer at home, and the babies need to get used to your face and your voice. I love you, sweetheart, but the children need you more than I do. I don't want you getting sick running back and forth."

"All right, but you'd better hurry and get out of here."

"Thanks."

"Maybe I'll plan to visit every other day. Did Gene say how long he's planning to stay?"

"He didn't, but he'll probably leave soon, now that I'm out of danger."

"Brad, if I can't be here, I'd feel better if a member of the family was with you at all times. Since Joan is going to be here this afternoon, maybe she and Gene would alternate their visits until Michelle and Ray come."

"Maybe I'll be home by then." He frowned.

"What's the matter? Why are you frowning?"

"I've had a pain in my shoulder all morning. I guess, now that the pain medicine is wearing off I can feel it more. It's pretty intense right now." He winced.

"Did you tell Dr. Jordan?" Lauren asked. She checked his shoulder, and touched his forehead. "You feel pretty warm, and there's some redness and swelling on your shoulder. I'm going to ring for the nurse."

Dr. Jordan entered the room after the nurse summoned him. He examined Thad and ordered a scan. Lauren decided to stay at the hospital until the results came back. "Thad, Lauren." Jordan approached the bed. "The scan shows that there's still a bullet fragment lodged in your shoulder."

"Lauren, we're going to prep Thad for surgery…"

"She can stay until I go into surgery, Stan. Then she's going home. Right Lauren?"

"I'll go home as soon as you come out of recovery."

*****

Dan and Alan strolled into the waiting area. "Hello, Lauren."

"Hi, Dan, Alan. Thad's in surgery. He should be—. Oh God, Dan, what's happening to us? I'm so tired of this. First, me; and then my children, and now my husband. When is it going to stop?"

"Lauren, I'm so sorry about all of this, especially about Thad getting hurt. Please, believe we are doing all we can to find who's behind this." Alan laid a comforting hand against her back.

"I know you are, Alan. I'm just so tired and frightened."

"I can promise you no one is going to get near you, your children, or Thad again. I never thought anyone would go after him."

"I told you as long as he's with me, he's in danger."

Joan and Gene entered the room. "Lauren. How are you? Where is Thad?"

"Oh Joan, am I glad to see you." Lauren cried, throwing her arms around her sister-in-law. "Thad's in surgery. He— he — he was shot," Lauren whispered.

"Lauren, I'm so sorry. Gene told me about the shooting. When is this nightmare going to end? Why is he back in surgery?"

"There's a piece of the bullet still in his shoulder. It was setting up an infection. "

"Darn. What the heck is going on here, Alan?" asked Gene. "What's happening to my family?"

"We've been trying to answer that question for some time now, Gene, and we're not quitting until we find the answer. I'm sorry about Thad."

A nurse interrupted the group, "Excuse me, Agent Coles. Dr. Jordan told me to give you this." She handed him a sample bag containing the bullet fragment that was just removed from Thad's shoulder. "Would you sign here, please? Dr. Jordan will be out to talk with you all shortly."

"Are you okay, Lauren?' Gene touched her shoulder.

"Gene, I don't know if I'm okay or not. I don't know what okay feels like anymore. I'm going to stay until Thad comes out of recovery, and then I'm going to see about my children."

"I can take you home, Lauren," Dan offered.

"Thanks, but I'm not leaving, yet. I really do need to see Thad."

Joan's face pinched with concern. "Lauren, I'm worried about you. You look as if you're about to pass out. You need to rest."

"I need to see my husband, Joan."

Dr. Jordan interrupted, "Thad's in recovery and he's doing very well. There was no serious damage. He's asking for you. You can go in, but remember he's still pretty groggy." Lauren left to visit Thad.

"How are you, darling?" Lauren caressed Thad's brow. He opened his eyes and made a feeble attempt to grasp Lauren's hand "What is it? What are you trying to say?" She took his hand in hers, and peered into his face.

"I'm...fri...n...e, La'ren. Go home...babies," he managed to croak.

"I'll go soon."

"Plesss La'ren," he slurred. "Lo...you." Thad closed his eyes and drifted off to sleep.

"I love you, darling," Lauren whispered in his ear. "I'm going home, now. Gene and Joan are here." Lauren headed for the waiting room.

"Lauren, I'm going to peek in on Thad, and then I'm going home with you. Gene's going to stay here." Joan stood and made her way toward the recovery room.

Dan stayed at the hospital while Alan drove Lauren and Joan to her house.

When they arrived, Joan encouraged her to rest. "Lauren, you really do need to get some sleep. I'll watch over the children with the others."

"Thanks, Joan. I'll take Brianna and Brittany to my room for a while. I feel as if I've neglected them of late." Lauren turned to Captain Wilcox. "Alan, thank you for all that you've done for us, and for chauffeuring me around."

"That's the least I can do. It doesn't seem I can catch who's doing this to you." He ran his fingers through his hair. "If you don't need me for anything else right now, I'm going back to the precinct."

*****

The next day, after her visit with Thad, Lauren passed the nursing station where she spotted Sandy Yates, and overheard her asking for Thad's room number. "Why, hello, Ms. Yates."

"Well, well, well, if it isn't the infamous Dr. Jeffries, the Black Widow." Sandy's voice dripped with sarcasm. "First, your children's father, and now Thad. Men just aren't safe around you, are they?" Sandy turned back to the nurse. "May I have that room number now?"

"You can't have the number, Sandy. My husband isn't receiving visitors."

"You can't stop me from seeing him. I work here."

"We'll see about that." Lauren called out to Alan, who stood near the elevator. "Captain Wilcox, will you please tell Ms. Yates that my husband is not receiving visitors?"

"She's right, Miss. No visitors."

"That's ridiculous!" Sandy lashed out. "Thad and I are friends. We've been friends for years. Much longer than she's been around." She cast Lauren a scathing glare.

"Lauren's his wife; therefore, she calls the shots." Alan told her. "If you have no other business in this area, I suggest you leave."

Sandy glared at Lauren. "It's too bad Thad was driving that car instead of you. One day you'll get what's coming to you." She stormed away. Lauren and Wilcox watched her stomp toward the elevator. Wilcox glanced at Lauren. "What's her story?"

"She was one of the many Bradford wannabes. She was with Brad the day I met him."

"With him as in a couple?"

"No, as in wanting to be with him."

"She might bear investigating. Do you think there's a chance of any jealousy on her part?"

"There was. I don't know about now. I think you need to add more security for Thad. If need be, I'll bear the expense of any extra personnel."

"I don't think that will be necessary. I'm going to talk with Dan to discuss extra security as well as investigating Ms. Yates."

"I need to peek in on Thad, again before I go home."

*****

Lauren arrived home to see Michelle and her family sitting in the kitchen. "Michelle! What are you doing here?"

"Ray was able to take vacation so we decided to come early to help out. And by looking at you, we didn't come a minute too soon."

"Thanks for coming. When did you get here?"

"Wendy said you'd been gone about twenty minutes when we arrived."

"Auntie Lauren, hi," Michelle's eight year old daughter, Amber greeted. "My cousins are pretty. Mommy let me help feed them."

"Thank you, sweetie." Lauren hugged her niece. "It's going to be nice having another babysitter around. She looked to her brother-in-law. "How are you Ray? I can't tell you how much I appreciate you all coming so early."

"That's what families are for." Ray stood from his seat and embraced her. "I wish the circumstances were different, though. How's Thad?"

"He's doing a lot better. There's a possibility he'll be home in two or three days."

"You look worn out, Lauren." Michelle stood. "Why don't you lie down? We're here to take care of you and the children."

"I think I'll do that. I haven't had a good night's sleep in weeks."

CHAPTER FORTY-FIVE

Three days before Christmas, Thad was released from the hospital. Lauren solicited the help of Michelle and Ray to redo the sleeping arrangements so she and Thad could sleep in one of the downstairs bedrooms so he could avoid the stairs.

Michelle and Joan shooed Lauren out of the kitchen when she attempted to help with Christmas dinner preparations.

On Christmas Day, everyone except Thad, Lauren, Wendy and the triplets attended church service. The children were excited to see snow flurries when they exited the church for the trip back to the Bradford's. After a light breakfast, the children were eager to open their presents. Lauren dressed the babies and assisted Thad in his wound care. They now all sat by a cozy, crackling fire in the den.

In addition to the presents the older children received from their relatives, their parents had also brought several of their gifts from home and put them under the tree. The adults watched as they tore into gift after gift with anticipation.

There was the usual fare of CDs, and other electronic gadgets, books, and clothing items. Every family, as well as Mrs. Brown, Wendy, Misti, and Chuck had purchased gifts for the twins and the triplets. Gene and Joan, Michelle and Ray, and Lauren and Thad had all presented Mrs. Brown, Wendy and Misti with generous gifts.

"What a blessed, Christmas." Lauren declared as the group finished opening their presents. "I feel like this is Thanksgiving and Christmas all wrapped in one. God has been so good to us."

"Yes he has, darling, and no one knows it better that I do." Thad gave her a gentle squeeze. "Some of the best presents he's given us are sitting around this fire. We have the best friends ever made. While I don't have all I would like in a family, right now, I'm thankful for what I do have.

Gene, brothers don't come any better than you. Joan, all I can say is thank you for the years of love. Michelle, Ray, thank you for loving Lauren and me.

This time last year, I never dreamed I'd be sitting here today, father to five children, but I wouldn't change it if I could. Mrs. Brown, we're thankful for the love and care you have given all of us. Wendy, Chuck, thanks for putting your lives on the line for us. We're so grateful. Lauren and I know we can never give you a gift that could show you just how grateful we are, so we hope you'll accept this as a small token of our appreciation and love." Lauren gave them each an envelope

Lauren and Mrs. Brown set off to take care of the babies while Joan and Michelle put the final touch on dinner. The children played games and listened to their CDs while Ray and Gene supervised. Thad left to take a nap.

* * * * *

Mrs. Brown's beau paid her a surprise visit, so they encouraged her to take some time off to be with him. Misti, whose family lived in Dalton, received permission to visit with them for the day. Chuck was single with no family in the area, but he would spend time with his girlfriend the next day. Wendy declared she wasn't going to let the Bradfords out of her sight again until after this mess was cleaned up.

* * * * *

Everyone lazed around the fireplace after a sumptuous, traditional, Christmas dinner when the doorbell rang. Wendy unsnapped her gun holster and headed for the door, while Chuck stood poised to back her up. "May I help you?" she asked the young woman standing on the steps.

"Yes, ma'am. My name is Anna Poston. I'm Dr. Thaddeus Bradford's sister. May I speak with him please?"

Wendy left Chuck to stand guard over the woman while she went to informed Thad of her presence.

"Thad." Wendy entered the room. "There's an Anna Poston in the foyer. She says she's your sister."

Thad, Gene, and Joan sat mouths agape in disbelief. They glanced at each other, seeming in shock.

"Is she alone?" Lauren asked.

"Yes she is."

"I'll talk with her." Gene stood and headed out of the room.

Thad reached for Lauren's hand. "Are you all right?" She whispered. Thad nodded in response.

Gene, followed by Wendy and Chuck, led his sister into the den where he made introductions.

"Hello, Thad" Anna greeted.

"Merry Christmas, Anna," Thad replied. "This is Lauren, my wife. I don't think you've ever spoken to her."

"Hello, Lauren." Anna appeared nervous.

"Merry Christmas, Anna. Won't you have a seat? Can we offer you something to eat or drink?" She declined the offer of refreshments.

"You wanted to talk to me, Anna?" Thad asked.

"Excuse us. We are going to leave you and Gene to talk with your sister." Lauren ushered everyone out of the room.

Ray and Michelle joined the children in the game room while Joan and Lauren checked on the triplets. Chuck and Wendy stayed near the den. "What do you make of this, Lauren?" Joan asked as they entered the bedroom.

"You tell me. I don't know Anna. Thad and I have been together almost two and a half years. This is the first time she's ever spoken to me."

"That's so sad. I wonder why she's here–and alone at that."

"I guess we'll find out soon enough. Anyway, it's almost seven o'clock, I'm going to feed the children and get them ready for bed.

After a while, Gene stuck his head in the door. "May I come in for a minute?"

"Sure, come on in."

Gene stepped into the room. Lauren watched as he stuck one hand in his pocket and ran the other over his face. *Something is very wrong. That's exactly what Thad does when he is troubled.* "What is it? I can tell something's troubling you."

Joan touched his arm. "What is it, sweetheart?"

"We just called Alan Wilcox and Dan Coles. We want the two of you as well as Michelle and Ray to join us when they get here."

"Are you alright?" Joan put an arm around his waist.

"I will be." Gene draped an arm around his wife's shoulder. "Anna told us one heck of a story. It's hard to digest."

Dan and Alan arrived together thirty-five minutes later. "Merry Christmas, Dan, Alan." Gene opened the door. "We're sorry to call you away from your families on Christmas Day, but there's something we think you need to hear, and it can't wait until morning." He led the men into the den.

"Agent Coles, Captain Wilcox, this is our sister Anna Poston," Thad said of the young woman sitting in the chair near him. Thad and Gene watched as Dan and Alan shared a surprised glance.

"Anna has a tale to tell, and I think you might want to record it," said Gene.

Dan excused himself to retrieve the recorder and other electronic gear from his vehicle. The ten adults, including the four law enforcement personnel, positioned themselves to hear the tale Anna Poston was about to tell. Lauren pulled a chair close to Thad and reached for his hand. The reassuring pressure he exerted on hers comforted her.

"Mrs. Poston, we are ready when you are. Take as much time as you need," Dan said.

Anna took a deep breath and began. "As I told my brothers, I think our parents are involved in what's been going on with Lauren, and possibly what happened to Thad. They hate Lauren. They hired a private investigating firm to look into her background. They were very upset when they didn't get a negative report. I heard them and the Higgins' discussing how they could get her fired from her job so she'd be forced to leave the area.

They said Thad belonged to Abigail from the day Abigail was born. The same day they planned the merger of the two families. They thought Lauren had gotten the message the day she came to dinner.

Both my family and Elaine's were told to ignore her, which we did. That day, Mother thought Lauren was being obstinate by not answering their questions.

She also thought Thad would see Lauren wasn't welcomed in the family and would stop seeing her, and eventually go back to Abigail. Anna took a sip from the glass of water Joan had placed on the table beside her chair. "Mother," she continued, "told us Lauren attacked her. We had no reason not to believe her. She vowed that Lauren would pay dearly for that." Thad squeezed Lauren's hand.

"Several times when I visited my parents, I heard them talking to Sydney. Sydney said he would take care of her at the hospital. They were frustrated because Lauren wasn't easily frightened. The only time she was frightened was when the targeted her children, so they honed in on them.

For a while, they thought they had scared her away because she was gone for a spell and Thad was still here, but then she returned. Elaine and I were told that if we talked to Lauren we'd both be kicked out of the family just like Thad and Gene. Jerry wasn't happy with this. He was getting tired of Father dictating our lives. He told me I needed to stand up to him. Thad was fast becoming his role model." She turned a faint smile on Thad.

Father was angrier than I'd ever seen him, up to that point, when he returned home one day just before Thad and Lauren were married. He vowed to," Anna turned to Lauren. "Sorry, Lauren, put that harlot in her place once and for all.

Before anything could happen, Thad saved the governor's life. Mother and Father never hid anything from us. I guess they realized we were devoted to them and we wouldn't dare repeat anything that was discussed in the house. Anyway..." She took another sip from the glass. "It was expected that Elaine and I would stop in on our parents several times during the week, and our families had dinner at our parent's house at least once during the week.

On each of these visits, we witnessed their hatred for Lauren. They were so angry her face was splashed across the TV screen and the newspapers along with decent people. This hatred grew when their friends questioned

Thad's marriage. None of them were aware Thad had gotten married before they read about it in the paper. Our parents hoped the marriage would be over before any of their friends found out about it.

"I heard Father telling Sydney to just get it done. You're being well paid to get rid of her. When Mr. Parker died, I heard Father tell Mother, "We need to get rid of that b....for good." He told her that that wench threatened to go to the governor and tell him what had been going on between him and Thad."

Father really went crazy when he found out Lauren was pregnant. I heard him on the phone telling someone that, she is not to have that baby. I didn't know who he was talking to until he said, "Mason, I'm paying you to get the job done, and I expect results. I'm not padding your pockets for nothing. That bastard will never carry the Bradford name." I believe all of what happened to Lauren and Thad is linked to our parents.

I don't know whether or not you all are aware of the fact that Sandra Yates is Dr. Mason's daughter. Yates is her married name, but she's divorced. She had designs on Thad. I think that's why Dr. Mason is so angry with Lauren. There's a woman named Darlene that was supposed to be working for Dr. Mason. I think Father posted bail for her. That's all I know. Elaine might have heard more than I did, but she and Abigail are very close. She wasn't opposed to what our parents were doing to Lauren, and I don't think she would do anything to help her. She feels Lauren should have stayed in her own class. Anna took another sip of water, and then leaned back in the chair.

For several moments after Anna stopped talking, there was total silence in the room. Lauren hugged Thad's neck and kissed the top of his head. Dan and Alan exchanged pointed glances and then looked from Thad and Lauren to Gene and back again. Dan broke the silence by asking, "What made you come here today, Mrs. Poston?"

Anna sighed and leaned forward in the chair again. "Actually, there were two things. When I heard my brother had been shot I realized while I was trying to get up the courage to stand up to my father, I could have lost my brother forever.

I also realized how much I love and miss both of my brothers." She glanced at Thad, and then turned her eyes to Gene. "Even before that, I was getting tired of living under Father's thumb. I wanted to come to you, but I was so ashamed. The other reason was that Jerry told me if I didn't tell you all what was going on, he would. He wasn't aware of everything that transpired before Thad was shot. He told me he'd leave me if I didn't tell you. That threat brought me to my senses. I think that was when I realized I'd really fallen in love with my husband. I didn't want to lose him the way I'd lost my brothers." With hesitation she asked, "Thad, Gene, do you think you could forgive me?" Her eyes held a pleading light. Lauren and Joan glanced at each other and smiled.

*****

Agent Coles and Captain Wilcox grilled Anna for the better part of the next two hours. After they were satisfied she'd given them all the information she could about her parents' involvement in the harassment, they bade the family goodnight.

"I guess I'll be leaving now." Anna turned to Thad. "I'm very sorry for all that has happened. Lauren." She glanced in Lauren's direction. "I'm truly sorry for my part in this. I pray that someday, I'll have the opportunity to get to know you. Please, forgive me."

"We'll talk later, Anna." Thad walked her to the door. "Are you staying in town or are you just here for the day?"

"We're staying at the Royale until tomorrow morning."

"We?" questioned Gene. "Who's with you?"

"Jerry and Jerri Lynn came with me. We thought it would be best if I came to talk to you alone."

"Why don't you and your family stay with us for the rest of the holiday?" Thad invited. "We have a lot of catching up to do."

The families decided Gene and his family would stay in Thad and Lauren's other house with Anna and her family. They would all meet at Thad's for brunch the next day. Anna glanced at Lauren. "Do you mind if I take a peek at the babies before I leave?"

"Of course, I don't. Come this way." Wendy, Michelle, and Joan followed them into the temporary nursery. Anna stood at the foot of the center crib glancing from one baby to the other. A quiet sob escaped her. "Lauren, I'm so sorry. Please, forgive me." Her sobs continued for a few moments before she was able to pull herself together. "I don't know, are they, they're precious. What are their names?"

Lauren stood beside Anna and with a gentle touch to her shoulder, she pointed to the cribs. "This is Ashton, this is Austin, and this is Rachel."

"They're beautiful. I almost missed seeing them." She whispered. "How are the twins?"

"Brittany and Brianna are well. They're sleeping. Why don't you plan to see them tomorrow?"

* * * * *

Thad and Lauren lay in bed after everyone had retired for the night. "How are you feeling, darling?"

Thad sighed. "I'm feeling so much right now. I don't know where to begin. I'm happy, sad, shocked, and angry. I'm happy to see Anna. Give me some time to digest all of this. I don't feel up to talking about it right now. I do want you to know I appreciate the way you handled Anna's request. I love you so much."

"She's your sister, Thad. That makes us family. Anyway, don't you know I would do just about anything to make you happy? I love you, darling. How's your thigh? Do you have any pain?"

"Yes, I have some pain, but it's mostly in my shoulder. We both need to sleep now."

* * * * *

The next day Anna and her family joined Lauren, Thad, and the rest of the family for brunch. Afterwards Michelle and her family excused themselves to allow the Bradfords some privacy.

Jerry was a little awkward at the initial meeting, but Lauren put him at ease, telling him she was happy they desired reconciliation with the brothers.

"I have to admit if you and Anna had come forth sooner with what you know Thad and I would not have suffered through all we did. You have no idea what these past two years have been like for us. If any of this had cost Thad and me our relationship, I would have been hard pressed to forgive you. As it stands, I hold no grudges. I forgive you."

Anna stared at Lauren in amazement. Tears began to form in her eyes. "Thanks Lauren, I don't deserve this, but thank you." She turned to Gene, "What's going to happen to Father when they catch him, Gene?"

"I don't know, Anna. We're not one hundred percent sure; they ordered these attacks on Lauren and Thad. There's the possibility of conspiracy and some other very heavy charges. Mother could be charged, too."

"What about Anna, Gene? Could she be charged with obstruction?" asked Jerry.

"Not unless she's been questioned by law enforcement. Her coming forward on her own is going to weigh heavily in her favor."

Michelle poked her head in the door. "Excuse me Thad, the phone is for you. It's Agent Coles."

Thad answered, "Hey, Dan. What's up?"

"Hey, Thad. I just wanted to let you all know that Darlene was apprehended in New Mexico this morning. She still maintains she doesn't know who hired her to harass Lauren. She was unable to identify Dr. Mason or your dad from their photos."

Dan paused, "and Thad, a man matching your father's description was spotted at the airport in Seattle several days ago, but he was alone.

The Agency is checking to see if anyone matching either of your parent's description boarded a plane. We've been keeping an eye out for Mason at the university too, but he hasn't been spotted. Did you hear that his office had been cleaned of all his personal effects?"

"No, I haven't heard anything except for what you and Alan have told us. Since Sandra Yates is still employed at the hospital, she could have stripped his office for him. Whether or not she would admit it, I don't know. I think she knows where Mason is."

"I'm sure she does. We're going to have another talk with her. I'll keep you posted. It appears that the harassment has stopped for now. Have a good night, Thad. We'll talk tomorrow."

*****

The day before New Year's Eve the Bradford siblings and their families, as well as Michelle and her family, were relaxing in the den after dinner when Dan Coles called to tell Thad to turn on the television. "...and there are several Americans listed among the fatalities. Again, this breaking news." The news reporter on the screen reported. "A Swiss Airliner crashed into a mountainside early this afternoon. All one hundred ninety three passengers and eleven crew members are feared dead. Several Americans are listed among the fatalities, but their names are being withheld until their families can be notified. These are pictures of the ill-fated plane." The camera panned the crash site. "It is reported that pieces of identification belonging to a business man from Boston have been found in the rubble. We're waiting confirmation on this information."

No one in the room moved, or said a word during the broadcast. "Oh, God! Oh, God." cried Anna. "Gene do you think it could be— Oh, God."

Jerry put his arms around Anna. "We don't know anything yet, Anna. Let's not jump to conclusions. There are many businessmen in Boston. Let's wait until we get more information."

"Jerry's right," said Thad. "Let's just wait until there's more news." They spent the rest of the evening in gloomy anticipation. Although the television was on for several hours after the news flash, there was no identification conformation.

Gene, Anna, and their families finally decided they would turn in for the night, but would plan to have an early brunch with Thad and Lauren again in the morning.

"Mommy, Mommy!" Amber shouted, running into the kitchen. "Look! The ground's covered in snow. Do you think we can go out to play? Please, please, Mommy."

"Pipe down, child." Michelle laughed. "You can go out after we eat."

"It sure is pretty," said Lauren. "This is the most snow we've had this year."

"Yes. It is pretty. We haven't had much snow in New Jersey either. It gives everything a pure, serene look."

"For this family's sake I sure hope it stays that way today. We've had enough to contend with this year."

* * * * *

Anna and the men were watching the children in the den while Lauren and the other women cleaned the brunch dishes. Lauren spotted Dan and Alan approaching the door. She hurried to open it before they could ring the bell. "What is it, Dan?" She stared at him for a moment. "Oh, no. The news isn't good is it?"

"I'm sorry, Lauren. It's not good. Not good at all. Both of their parents as well as the Higgins were on that plane."

"Oh, God," cried Joan. "We need to go to them Lauren."

"No, Joan. They should come in here away from the children. Wendy, will you go in with the children?"

"I'll go with her, too. Are you sure you're all going to be okay, Lauren?"

"I'm okay, Sis. It's Thad and his siblings I'm worried about."

Michelle entered the den and told Jerry and the siblings that Lauren needed to see them in the kitchen. Lauren asked Dan and Alan to step out while she gave the siblings the news. She pulled a chair out for Thad and stood near it as Joan put her arms around Gene.

"Darling," Lauren began. "Gene, Anna, I'm so sorry to have to tell you this, but Dan and Alan stopped in to tell us that both of your parents were among the passengers on that plane that went down in Switzerland yesterday. There were no survivors. I'm terribly sorry." Lauren stood behind Thad's chair and let him lean into her while Joan held Gene.

Ray, who had entered the kitchen when he heard Anna's scream, was now trying to help Jerry console her. "No, no, nooo." She wailed. "This can't be. It just can't be. They can't be gone just like that."

Dan and Alan entered the kitchen and offered their condolences. "We have an agent dispatched to the Poconos to tell your sister. No names have been released to the public yet. You...ah...I'm sorry to have to tell you that the Higgins were also on the plane."

"Abigail too?" cried Anna.

"They only said Cecil and Mary Higgins. Is there anything we can do for you?"

Lauren glanced at him. "Thank you, Alan. There's nothing right now. It's going to take some time for all of this to sink in. They have had a lot piled on their plates of late."

"We'll be going then. Thad, Gene, I'm sorry for your loss. Please don't hesitate to call us if you need us."

"Thank you both for all you've done. We appreciate you all so much," Thad said.

"I guess I'm going to have to get back to Massachusetts," Gene declared.

"Me too," sniffed Anna.

"I'm going with you," Ray declared.

"Thanks, but you don't have to do that, Ray."

"I know I don't, Gene." Ray smiled.

CHAPTER FORTY-SIX

The joint memorial service for the elder Bradfords was held in Boston seven days after the plane crash. After consulting Thad's doctor, and learning it was safe for him to attend the services, Lauren encouraged him to go.

"You need to go. You need closure, and you need to forgive your parents. They can't hurt us anymore. Forgive them so you can move on. Anything that hasn't been said or done cannot be done now."

"Come here." He stretched his arms to her. "What have I done to deserve such a smart woman?"

"You really don't know, Mr. Bradford?" She kissed him tenderly on the lips. "You love me. It's a simple as that."

"I do, with all my heart."

*****

Thad and Gene were sitting with their sisters and their spouses after the memorial services for their parents when Gene announced his intent to attend the services for the Higgins the following day. Their sister, Elaine, told them that Abigail didn't want them there. "It's your fault they're dead," she screamed at Thad. "You just had to marry some low-class frump.

Mother and Father would be alive today if they hadn't been trying to save you from a life with that slut and a house full of sniveling brats. Everyone was trying to save you, even the people you worked with. Dr. Mason did everything he could to get rid of her." Elaine, realizing what she had said, quickly covered her mouth with her hand.

"What do you know about all of that, Elaine? Do you know where Mason is?" Gene asked.

"I wouldn't tell you if I did. I wouldn't lift a finger to help that trash."

Anna sighed and glanced at her sister. "Her name is Lauren, Elaine. It's so sad how you and I allowed Mother and Father to make us a party to their hatred of her. In spite of that, I love them, but they're gone now.

They don't have a hold on any of us anymore. We don't have to do their bidding. You know, as well as I, that Abigail is really the slut. Yet, all of us wanted Thad to be tied to her for the rest of his life. Mother and Father knew she aborted a baby, but because Mr. Higgins learned that Father was having an affair with Mrs. Higgins for years, he threatened to tell Mother if Father didn't make Thad marry Abigail. Father had to go along with them." Anna pointed a finger at Elaine. "You know Mother's money was what got Father started in his business, and it sustained the business until it was making a profit. He stood to lose a lot if Mother found out about the affair. Now you want to continue this charade in their name. Abigail doesn't love Thad. She never stopped sleeping around. You would do yourself a great deed if you got to know Lauren. She's the best thing that could have happened to our brother."

The three Bradford siblings stared opened mouth at their younger sister. "How long have you known all of that, Anna?" asked Gene.

"Hump. I've known about Father and Mrs. Higgins since I was a little girl, and I've known about Abigail since high school. I heard her tell Elaine about the abortion."

Thad looked at Elaine. "And you wanted me to marry her anyway, Elaine? You went along with our parents knowing all that? What do you gain by going along with them?"

Elaine sneered. "Now that you and Gene have been written out of their wills, I get half of everything they owned. I am now worth more than twenty million dollars. That's what I gained from all of it, my dear brother."

Alex Varner, Elaine's husband, stared at her in disgust. "I can't believe this. You knew all along that all those things your parents said about Lauren were lies, and you went along with it? I don't believe this." He shook his head. "Thad, I'm so sorry. I wasn't privy to all of the goings on, and I was too much of a coward to say anything about what I did know."

Thad headed for the door. "Gene, I've had enough of this. I'm going back to your house to get Ray so I can get home to sanity- to my family. I feel sorry for you, Elaine."

*****

During the third week into the New Year, there was a semblance of normalcy settling over the Bradford household. Gene, his family, and Michelle and her family had all returned to their homes. There had been no incidents of harassment since Thad's release from the hospital a month before. Except for Wendy, all law enforcement personnel had been dismissed. Although, Thad was recovering well from his ordeal, he decided he would take an indefinite leave of absence from the hospital.

"Would you like some company?" Lauren asked, as she entered the den where Thad sat on the sofa reading a journal.

"I'd love some company. Come sit with me." Thad patted the space beside him. "What's on your mind, love?"

"Nothing in particular," Lauren snuggled against him. "I've been thinking how nice it's been these past weeks. I love having you home all day. I think the children like it too."

"I like it as well, but you do know I plan to return to work at some point in time. Don't you?"

"I know, but I'm really enjoying this. I might even decide to go back myself."

"Are you really, Lauren? You haven't said, but I thought you were planning to stay home at least until the babies started to school."

"Chauvinist. Keep them barefoot and pregnant, huh?"

"Lauren! You know better than that. I'd never do that to you. I just thought that was what you would like to do. I don't want you to think you have to go to work. I can afford—"

Lauren laughed. "I'm only teasing you. I wouldn't dream of going back to work anytime in the near future. Now that the harassment is over, I'm truly enjoying domestic life."

"What am I going to do with you, woman?" He tickled her ribs. Thad stopped the tickling, heaved a deep sigh, and leaned back into the sofa.

"Do you want to talk about it, love?"

"I miss them, Lauren. In spite of all they did to us, I never wanted them to go like that."

"I know you miss them. No one wanted to see that happen. I'll always be here for you when you want to talk, but I think you need to consider talking to a professional. You've had a lot to deal with."

"I think you may be right. I have begun to have nightmares, again." Lauren gave him a faint smile. "You knew didn't you?"

"I love you, Thaddeus Bradford. The only constant in my life for the past three years have been my family--you and our children in particular. I make it my business to know when something is bothering any of you. That's what I signed on for."

"I love you, Lauren Bradford."

CHAPTER FORTY-SEVEN

There wasn't a single incident of harassment during the period between Christmas and Memorial Day. All law enforcement personnel were reassigned, but a police cruiser still passed the Bradford house on a regular basis.

Thad began seeing a therapist in February, and although he was not free of the nightmares he'd been suffering, they were much less frequent. Lauren also noted that he rested better than he had at any time during their marriage. They were also closer than they'd ever been to achieving the peaceful existence they both craved.

Mrs. Brown was still resident nanny, but she would be leaving at the end of the week to marry her Mr. Bill. Dottie King moved in two weeks ago and proved to be an astute student under Ms. Brown's instructions. She was ready to take the reins.

* * * * *

Lauren entered the room and jumped into Thad's lap. "How are you feeling, darling?"

"Ouch!" Thad laughed. "I *was* feeling great" He wrapped his arms around her. "What's gotten into you? I've never seen you like this before."

"I feel so free. Like I'm emerging from a cocoon. This has been a wonderful six months."

"Whatever it is, I like it. I'm sorry you've been subjected to all that mess."

"No. No, my love. We aren't apologizing for anyone else's behavior, anymore. We're just going to be thankful. Okay? By the way, Maureen called while you were out this morning. She wants us to come for a visit next weekend."

"She's a glutton for punishment isn't she?" Thad chuckled.

"Oh, it'll be okay. The triplets are good babies, and the twins are no trouble now that they're potty trained and dressing themselves."

"Excuse me, Dr. Bradford, I think you all might want to turn on the TV, Mrs. King announced from the door." The telephone rang just as Lauren switched on the television.

"Hello," Thad answered. "Yes, we just turned it on." Thad cradled the receiver. "That was Dan Coles. He's on his way over here."

Lauren sat with her eyes fixed on the TV. Thad moved to put his arms around her as they both listened to the news. "*The police have cornered off a seven block area near the home of Drs. Thaddeus and Lauren Bradford. A man matching the description of Dr. Sydney Mason was spotted a few blocks from the Bradford home. As you may recall, Dr. Mason, who was provost at Parkdale Medical where both doctors are employed, was implicated in the attempted murder of Lauren Bradford and the attempted kidnapping of the Bradford triplets six months ago.*"

"Lauren," Thad ordered, "Mrs. King, get the children. Take them into the study. Hurry!" He checked the doors, and joined them. After unlocking a desk drawer, he removed a handgun, and headed for the door.

"Thad, please don't go out there," Lauren cried.

The doorbell chimed. "I have to let Dan in, sweetheart."

Dan greeted Lauren and Mrs. King as he entered the study behind Thad.

Thad frowned. "How did you know he was in the area, Dan?"

"We never stopped looking for him. We knew he'd been in Mexico until three weeks ago. He contacted his daughter yesterday. He made the mistake of driving her car, which he ditched in the shopping mall on Oak Street. That's where we lost him."

Lauren retreated deeper into the study to be closer to her children. "We're going to need some bedding if we are going to be staying in here. It's almost time for the children's lunch, too."

Mrs. King offered to get the bedding, but Lauren said she would get it.

Thad touch Lauren's shoulder. "You stay here with Dan, darling. I'll get it."

*****

Thad had gathered an armful of bedding from the hall linen closet, and headed for the stairs when he thought he saw a shadow behind the drapes in the master bedroom. He dropped the bedding on the floor, and reached for the pistol he'd tucked in the waist of his pants. He inched his way towards the bedroom. As soon as he stepped into the room, a blow to the head knocked him to the floor. Thad was thrown off balance by the blow. Dr. Sydney Mason stood over him with his pistol drawn. "What are you doing?"

"You're in no position to be asking questions, Bradford. Get to your feet."

"What do you want, Mason. How did you get in here?"

"All these months and you haven't figured it out yet, Bradford? We want your precious little slut of a wife."

The muscles jumped in Thad's jaw. "What do you want with Lauren? What has she done to you?"

"Your parents and I did everything we could to run her out of town, but she wouldn't leave. She just had to stay--just had to get her hands on the Bradford fortune."

"What about you Mason? What are you getting out of this? What did Lauren do to you?"

"She had the nerve to treat me like some lowly employee. Me. I'm the provost. She waltzes in here, and everyone acts like she's the second coming, even you. I never wanted her here, anyway. My daughter was falling all over you, but you acted as if she didn't exist. You ignored her, a decent girl, but you were all over Dr. Jeffries, a harlot with two children. Your father even told me he'd rather see you with Sandra than with that slut you were running around with."

"So what are you going to do now? Kill me? You know my parents are both dead don't you?"

"What? Dead?" Mason was visibly shaken. His legs wobbled and his hands fell to his side. At that moment, Agents Coles and Wilcox raced into the room. Dan grabbed Mason's gun, and then cuffed him while Alan trained his gun on him.

Thad stumbled to his feet. "Man! Am I glad to see you guys. How'd you know?"

"Alan came by as soon as you left the study to tell us Mason had been spotted near your neighbor's house. When you didn't return right away, Lauren said if we didn't check on you, she would."

"That's my girl! For once I'm happy that she's as stubborn as she is." Thad smiled weakly. "We'd better get back now before she comes looking for us."

"Are your parents really dead? They owe me seventy-five thousand dollars. Who's going to pay me?"

"Let's go Mason." Alan nudged him. "You're not going to need any money where you're going."

*****

"Is it safe for us to breathe now?" Lauren asked, as she and Thad sat talking with Alan and Dan.

"I think so, Lauren," Dan answered. "All of the major players are in jail. Unfortunately, Thad's parents, who funded the operation, are both dead. The others are harmless now that there is no money for them."

"It's been eight months since Mason was caught. What are you planning to do now? Are you planning to return to work at the hospital?" Alan asked.

"We haven't made any definite plans yet. We've tossed around the idea of relocating, but we have to be here until the trials are over. I might go back to work at the hospital, but Lauren isn't going back any time soon. Right now, we're just going to enjoy being together as a family. I never knew how precious life is until we almost lost ours."

"If there was ever anyone who deserve this quiet time together it's the two of you. By the way, how is Ms. King working out?"

"She's working out well. Mrs. Brown taught her all she needed to know before she left. But, I am certainly going to Miss Dora Lee," Lauren said.

“I can believe that. She was a welcome fixture around here. How are your sisters, Thad? Do you hear from them?”

"We hear from Anna quite frequently. She and her family have visited us a couple of times since Christmas. We're getting close again. As for Elaine, I feel sorry for her. Alex left her. They share joint custody of the children. I guess she has her millions to keep her happy.”

* * * *

The trials began two months after Thad returned to work. Because Lauren and Thad were two of the prosecution’s major witnesses, they were ordered to be at the courthouse during the entire trial.

Lauren begged Alan and Dan to have an officer stay with Mrs. King and the children during the time she and Thad were in the courtroom.

Gene and Joan arrived to support Thad and Lauren during the trials, but Joan, noting the anxiety Lauren was exhibiting relative to leaving the children, decided that she would stay and help Mrs. King with the children instead of going to the courthouse.

Anna and Elaine were subpoenaed to testify for the prosecution. Anna had embraced her family as they met in the courthouse hall, but Elaine ignored her siblings, standing as far away from them as she could.

The trial lasted seven and a half weeks. Anna testified to what she had told Dan and Alan ten months ago, but Elaine, invoking her Fifth Amendment rights, refused to answer any questions.

Lauren and Thad were on the stand a combined total of eleven days. Much to her surprise, Lauren was able to maintain her composure throughout the entire ordeal, but Thad didn't attempt to mask his anger when he was questioned about what his family had endured.

The parade of witnesses included Vivian, Linda, and the other board members to testify to Mason’s treatment of Lauren. The last witness for the prosecution was Lenny Grayson who all but single handedly sealed Mason’s fate.

All totaled, there were six people implicated in the attempted murder of Thad, the attempted kidnapping of the triplets, the attempted murder of Lauren, and terrorist acts against the Bradford family.

Also implicated were the elder Bradfords. When the trial was over Dr. Mason received forty-five years without the possibility of parole in a federal prison. Darlene Tucker plea bargained to fifteen years. It was believed that Mason knew the other players–the woman from the church and the car drivers, but he refused to roll over on them.

The entire story of the trial played out in the local and national newspapers and televisions for weeks.

EPILOGUE

Three years later, Thad and Lauren moved their family into the new house they'd built on the north side of the city. Thad was now Chief of Surgery, permanently. Having given up the idea of returning to work at the university, Lauren began working with several charity organizations in addition to *Women of Substance*. Nevertheless, she enjoyed the life of a stay-at-home-mom, much more. Alex Varner, Thad's brother-in-law, remarried, and won full custody of his son and daughter. Elaine's idea of parenting meant leaving the children in the care of sitters, while she spent her millions jetting from island to island or country to country. She didn't put up much of a fight since she only saw the children six weeks out of the year anyway.

The governor, citing health concerns, decided not to seek another term. Today, the governor and Mrs. Standis, along with Agents Dan Coles, Wendy Greene-Jennson, Captain Alan Wilcox, Vivian Reed, Linda Abrams, Gene and Joan, Michelle and Ray, and Anna and Jerry all brought their children to the Bradford home to celebrate Brittany and Brianna's seventh birthday.

Later that night, Lauren and Thad lay in bed commenting on the day's festivities. Thad stroked his wife's hair. "You know Lauren; in spite of all the unpleasant events we suffered during the first two years, we've had a wonderful existence. I've learned so much about life since I met you, and even more about love." Thad wrapped his arms around her and pulled her closer. "I love you and our children with all my heart and soul."

Lauren elevated her eyes to look into her husband's face. "We're a blessed family. Our children are happy and healthy. We have loving family and friends, and the two of us are healthy. I love you with all my heart. God has blessed us beyond measure."

*****

Twenty-two hundred miles away, Elaine Varner lounged beside the pool in Caracas, Venezuela sipping her sangria. She snapped her fingers to get the attention of the waiter. Remembering how events played out over the past three years, she sneered. *Those stupid cops. They'll never know it was I–not my parents–who orchestrated the harassment of that slut. Their hatred of her played right into my hands. They didn't want to have her killed; they just wanted her to miscarry and to go away. I didn't want her dead either. As long as she lived, Thad would never inherit any of the money. Ah, Mother and Father; it's too bad you had to die in that plane crash.*

Elaine snickered. *Mason was my lap dog, but he became too greedy. He was getting money from me, and my parents. His greed played into my hands, too. Now all of the players are either dead or in jail.* She smiled and turned toward the sound of approaching footsteps. "Hello, darling." Elaine turned her head to receive Abigail's passionate kiss.

"Hello, darling. What a beautiful day." Abigail eased onto the lounger beside her.

"Oh, yes. It is a beautiful day–just the first of many more to come. ...no one to answer to and no one to share our bounty with."

The two multi-millionaires laughed and fell into each other's arms. So absorbed were they that they paid no attention to the statuesque, bikini clad, beauty lounging a few feet away. An FBI badge was clipped inside her wide-brim hat.

~THE END~

About the Author

Beverley Godfrey

Beverley Godfrey, author of *I Am Not Ready to Love You* is a transplanted Virginian, via New Jersey and California. Now, she calls Texas her home. God, family and children's issue head her list of passions.

"I can do all things through Christ which strengthens me."
Philippians 4:13

Coming Soon!
Against My Better Judgment

www.ingramcontent.com/pod-product-compliance
Lightning Source LLC
Chambersburg PA
CBHW030912090426
42737CB00007B/165
* 9 7 8 0 6 1 5 5 8 1 5 9 0 *